'A scholarly and nuanced study on the long-te
British boarding schools: while some people th
too many others the adverse psychological impa(
Benedict Rattigan, _at_   _.. ꞁx-ʋoarder at Eton_

'Boarding is often misunderstood and misrepresented, but this invaluable book provides a wide, and evidence-informed, analysis of the sector. Importantly, the authors allow the voices of the former pupils themselves to speak and in doing so reveal a nuanced and complex series of personal narratives. This is a book that should be read not only by those who work in boarding schools, but by anyone involved in education and child psychology.'
David James, _co-editor of_ The State of Independence

The Psychological Impact of Boarding School

The Psychological Impact of Boarding School is a collection of research-based essays answering a range of questions about boarding school and its long-term impact.

Through a combination of original in-depth first-person narratives as well as larger-scale surveys, this book aims to fill gaps in current boarding school research and present new findings. Topics addressed include gender differences, eating behaviours, loneliness, mental health and relationships, the differences between younger and older boarders, and ex-boarder experiences of therapy. The research results highlight a key role in the age that children start boarding, the way that long-term psychological influences of friendships formed at school, and the larger role that parent and family relationships play in the psychological lives of boarders. Through these findings, the book ultimately challenges the current understanding of 'boarding school syndrome', proposing a move beyond the term and its concept.

The book will appeal to psychologists, psychoanalysts, counsellors, academics, teachers, current and ex-boarders, as well as parents and guardians interested in the impact of boarding schools from either a professional or a personal perspective.

Penny Cavenagh, PhD, is currently a professor of health research and enterprise at the University of Suffolk, visiting professor at the University of Essex and a chartered psychologist. She has published extensively in books and academic journals in the field of medical management, medical education and dysfluency. She boarded for four years at an all-girls school in the early 1970s.

Susan McPherson, PhD, is currently a professor of psychology and sociology at the University of Essex and has been a researcher in the field of mental health for 25 years after studying at the London School of Economics, University College London and Kings College London. She was a full-time boarder from age 8 to 18 during the 1980s and 1990s including three years at a junior boarding school.

Jane Ogden, PhD, is currently a professor of health psychology at the University of Surrey where she has been teaching for the last 18 years. She has written 8 books relating to health psychology, eating behaviour, weight management, parenting and critical thinking and over 230 research papers on many aspects of health psychology.

The Psychological Impact of Boarding School

The Trunk in the Hall

Edited by
Penny Cavenagh, Susan McPherson and
Jane Ogden

 Routledge
Taylor & Francis Group

LONDON AND NEW YORK

Designed cover image: © Getty Images

First published 2024
by Routledge
4 Park Square, Milton Park, Abingdon, Oxon OX14 4RN

and by Routledge
605 Third Avenue, New York, NY 10158

Routledge is an imprint of the Taylor & Francis Group, an informa business

British Library Cataloguing-in-Publication Data
A catalogue record for this book is available from the British Library

Library of Congress Cataloging-in-Publication Data
A catalog record has been requested for this book

ISBN: 978-1-032-24873-8 (hbk)
ISBN: 978-1-032-24872-1 (pbk)
ISBN: 978-1-003-28049-1 (ebk)

DOI: 10.4324/9781003280491

Typeset in Times New Roman
by Taylor & Francis Books

Contents

Tables

Editor biographies

Penny Cavenagh

I am currently a professor of health research and enterprise at the University of Suffolk, visiting professor at the University of Essex and a chartered psychologist. I read psychology at the University of Bristol and did my master's degree in occupational psychology and PhD at Birkbeck College, University of London. I have published extensively in books and academic journals in the field of medical management, medical education and dysfluency. I boarded for four years at an all-girls school in the early 1970s, having previously been a day girl at the same school as my parents moved abroad. My husband went to boarding school and our three sons went to weekly boarding school. It didn't suit one of them, so he transferred to day school. My interest in writing this book emanated from observation of friends, parents, and family who have attended boarding school.

Susan McPherson

I am currently a professor of psychology and sociology at the University of Essex and have been a researcher in the field of mental health for 25 years after studying at the London School of Economics, University College London and Kings College London. I was a full-time boarder in Kent from age 8 to 18 during the 1980s and 1990s, including three years at a junior boarding school. It was a mixed experience and many of the positive and negative experiences described in this book are deeply familiar. I recently completed five years of psychotherapy, which was both life-saving as well as a privilege, but boarding school was not the only issue discussed. I never intended to get into boarding school research, which rather happened by accident but has been illuminating from a professional and personal perspective. I hope we have managed to maintain decent researcher equipoise throughout while also using our personal experiences to enrich our understanding of the data.

Jane Ogden

I completed a degree at Sussex University and a PhD at the University of London and have had academic posts at South Bank and Middlesex Polytechnics as well as Guy's and St Thomas' Medical Schools. For the past 18 years I have been a professor of health psychology at the University of Surrey. I have written eight books relating to health psychology, eating behaviour, weight management, parenting and critical thinking, plus over 230 research papers on many aspects of health psychology. I attended a co-ed state grammar school in north London, which was great fun, mostly due to the presence of boys and the friends I made. When I was 10 my gran became a boys' maid at Eton where she lived in a small flat and looked after the pupils in her house. She loved them and they loved her back. I visited many times and found the posh accents, formal uniforms, sounds of 'boy up', absence of girls and notion of being sent away from home very strange. Many of the boys she looked after are now extremely successful. My interest in this book comes from a sense of sympathy for those who are sent away at an early age, a recognition that some of these seem to thrive and an interest in how what I saw at Eton affects people.

Author biographies

Professor **Frances Blumenfeld** studied at University of Tel Aviv and University of East Anglia. She is currently working as programme director on the University of Essex doctorate in clinical psychology and has more than 30 years' experience working with children and families in the NHS and before then with adults in Israel and the USA. She attended secondary school in Zimbabwe as a day pupil and later a boarding school in Israel.

Dr **Mairi Emerson-Smith** studied at University of Edinburgh, University of London and University of Essex. She is currently working as a clinical psychologist, working with children with neurodevelopmental difficulties in the NHS. She attended a mainstream state school in the 1990s.

Dr **Caroline Floyd** studied at the University of Nottingham, Tecnológico de Monterrey Mexico and the University of Essex. She is currently working as a clinical psychologist with children and families in the NHS. She attended a local comprehensive day school in the 1990s.

Dr **Craig Harris** studied at University of Bangor and University of Leicester. He is a qualified teacher with experience of teaching in mainstream primary schools. He is currently working as a clinical psychologist working with children, young people and families in a paediatric psychology service in the NHS. He attended a mainstream state school in the 1990s and 2000s.

Remy Hayes studied at Brunel University London. He is currently completing a doctorate in clinical psychology at the University of Essex. He attended a non-boarding state school in the 2000s.

Dr **Emma Hopkins** studied at University of Galway, Royal Holloway University of London and University of Essex. She is currently working as a clinical psychologist, with children, teenagers and adults with mental health and neuro-developmental disorders at the Owl Therapy Centre. She attended an Irish Catholic day school in the 1990s.

James Lee studied at University of Roehampton, University College London and is currently completing a doctorate in clinical psychology at the

University of Essex. He attended a non-boarding state school in the 1990s and early 2000s.

Dr **Gareth Morgan** studied at University of Leicester, De Montfort University and the University of Derby. He is currently working as a clinical psychologist and lecturer on the Leicester doctorate in clinical psychology programme. He has 15 years' experience working clinically within adult mental health and intellectual disability services. He attended a non-boarding comprehensive school in the 1980s and 1990s.

Caitlin Phillips studied at University of Oxford, University College London and University of London School of Advanced Study. She is currently working as a clinical lecturer on the University of Essex doctorate in clinical psychology and has 10 years of experience working clinically within adult mental health services. She attended a non-boarding comprehensive state school in the 1980s.

Dr **Alexandra Priestner** studied at University of Plymouth and University of Essex. She is currently working as a clinical psychologist, working with NHS inpatients on a mother and baby unit and an adult acute ward. She attended a state secondary school in the 2000s.

Dr **Daniel Taggart** studied at Queens University, Belfast and University of East Anglia. He worked for two years as the clinical lead and principal psychologist to the truth project on the Independent Inquiry into Child Sexual Abuse; is currently working as a senior lecturer on the University of Essex doctorate in clinical psychology and has 10 years of experience working in adult mental health and parent infant mental health in the NHS. He attended a Catholic grammar school in Belfast in the 1990s.

Jenny Wardman-Browne studied at University of Essex, University of Bath and is currently completing a doctorate in clinical psychology at the University of Essex. She attended a non-boarding state school in the 2000s.

Dr **Alice Welham** studied at Cambridge University, University of Exeter and University of Birmingham. She is currently working as an associate professor on the University of Birmingham doctorate in clinical psychology course.

Acknowledgements

We would like to thank all the individuals who participated in the studies reported in this book through surveys and interviews, as well as those who gave their testimonies to the Truth Project. Without all of these contributions, this book would not have been possible. It was a privilege for us to hear all of these voices and learn about so many individual experiences. We were all deeply moved by the difficulties faced by some of those who took part in the research and the courage it must have taken to share these stories, especially when many have had the experience of being silenced.

Chapter 1

British boarding schools on trial
Making the case for new evidence

*Susan McPherson, Mairi Emerson-Smith and
Penny Cavenagh*

Louis de Bernières, the renowned author of *Captain Corelli's Mandolin*, revealed the extent of his horrific experiences at boarding school in a highly personal and revealing account published in *The Times* in 2021:

> What compensation could there possibly be for the thousands of little boys like me, in prep schools all over the country, who had to go through that hellish abuse when we should have been with our parents at home? [1]

He remarked that he had held off speaking openly about his experiences until his parents had died because they thought they were 'doing their best' for him; and yet he 'never quite managed to forgive them'. De Bernières is not the first nor the last to speak of the horrors of boarding school or the scars it left on his adult self. He may be one of the more well-known. His revelations triggered a barrage of *Times* readers writing to reveal their own similar experiences – a mass outpouring of pent-up emotion. The Great British stiff upper lip was beginning to tremble.

Not for the first time. In *The Making of Them*, psychotherapist Nick Duffell gives an account of his experiences in 1990 when he first started running therapeutic workshops for ex-boarders. He describes how media interest quickly escalated which led to large volumes of letters from ex-boarders revealing their difficult experiences being sent to newspapers as well as directly to Duffell himself [2]. Individual accounts like these can be powerful, especially when penned by a master narrator. Like others before him, De Bernières stirred up repressed memories and unresolved anger among the 'privileged' middle- and upper-class readership of *The Times* who were moved to take up the keyboard and pen their own story, perhaps the start of their own private therapeutic reckoning.

In 2015 an Independent Inquiry into Child Sexual Abuse in England and Wales was established involving a large scale gathering of evidence concerning failures of all types of institutions to protect children in their care. One element of the inquiry was the Truth Project which involved taking witness testimony directly from over 6000 victims between 2016 and 2021, including oral and

DOI: 10.4324/9781003280491-1

written accounts [3]. Of these testimonies, 15% reported abuse taking place in a school setting. Chapter 7 will explore this data in more detail, including the extent of abuse reported to have taken place specifically at boarding schools. The Truth Project testimony discussed in Chapter 7 includes volumes of first-person accounts of rape, inappropriate touching, violations of privacy as well as physical abuse, cruelty and other types of abuse experienced by children like Conall at boarding school:

> He describes the school as 'a place of fear and loneliness' where children were strictly controlled. The abuse began as soon as they arrived at the school. Conall relates that he was beaten, often naked, by the headteacher, who used heavy implements, including a cricket bat. The abuse by the headteacher also included sexual abuse. Conall didn't tell anyone about this for fear of making things worse for himself. He adds that he did not recognise it as abuse at the time, but assumed it was 'a normal form of discipline at a boarding school'.
>
> (Truth Project 'Experiences Shared' extract)

Personal narratives, especially those that lead to a wave of emotive corroborating accounts like that of de Bernières in *The Times*, can be powerful, moving and distressing to hear. But it is worth remembering that not every child that goes to boarding school will experience direct abuse and this book asks whether sending children to boarding school *always* results in psychological distress experienced later in life as some claim; or if there are other factors at play. To begin to answer this question, we think it is important to go beyond personal narratives and witness testimony and to consider other forms of research and evidence too. We must also bear in mind that the culture of boarding schools may have improved significantly in the last 10 to 20 years, particularly British boarding schools, with safeguarding policies and national standards introduced by the Department of Education (also discussed in more detail in Chapter 7) and that testimonies from ex-boarders recounted both publicly in *The Times* and confidentially in the Truth Project are often based on experiences that occurred over 30 to 40 years ago.

Preceding the recent public deluge of monstrous memoirs in *The Times* and the Truth Project, there had been other forms of research and writing emerging about the ways that boarding school can impact on the emotional life of children and their future adult selves. This includes theories put forward by psychotherapists who have worked with adult clients who have connected their current psychological distress to their experiences at boarding school – sometimes but not always as a result of direct physical or sexual abuse. These mainly theoretical accounts are illustrated by case studies from the authors' own experiences and their therapeutic work with ex-boarders, along with examples from fiction (for example, Nick Duffell draws heavily on fictional characters in John le Carré novels). These real and fictional case studies lead the authors to conclude that sending children to boarding school is in essence an abusive practice. We will review these theories later in this chapter.

Another type of evidence is found in published collections of personal memoirs, elicited from adults able to write longer more detailed accounts of their own memories of boarding school and the psychological impacts it had on their adult life. *Men's Accounts of Boarding School: Sent Away* is a published collection of men's own stories while *Finding Our Way Home* is a published collection of women's stories [4],[5]. We will draw on these in our review later in this chapter. These are first person accounts as in *The Times* and the Truth Project, but are generally longer narrative accounts, less focussed on abuse *per se* and more on the overall experience of boarding school and its impact on adulthood. Many of the narrators had been in therapy already and so their stories have the hindsight of having worked through some of their adult crises with an experienced therapist. There is also a small body of formal academic research exploring the psychological impact of boarding school published in academic journals, but these are mainly based on boarding school settings outside the UK. We will attempt to provide an overview of this field of work and explain what this book will add. We will also sketch out the overall aims of the book and discuss the limits of the different ways that writers and researchers try to elicit nuggets of truth in their work and reveal it to their audience. This means that personal anecdotes, therapy case study research and different types of formal research all have limits to what they can reveal. Better understanding can be reached by taking a variety of paths towards knowledge. We will claim that this book attempts to offer a number of additional lenses on the topic and can therefore enrich our understanding of the psychological impacts of boarding school.

1.1 Boarding schools in the UK: Historical context

The British have sent their children away for residential education since at least medieval times when noble houses and monasteries sometimes hosted boys' education. Britain's oldest boarding school, King's School Canterbury, claims that St Augustine 'probably established a school shortly after his arrival in Canterbury, Kent in 597AD' and that King's (formally established in 1541) grew from this foundation [6]. Britain's most renowned boarding school, Eton College, was established in 1440 by Henry VI [7]. In these late middle ages, education was primarily for the purpose of religious training, based on a monastic template involving religious devotion, learning Latin and general preparation for a clerical life. Mathematics was not added to the Eton curriculum until centuries later in 1851 with other subjects following later in the nineteenth century.

While several of Britain's historic boarding schools have survived as a brand in their original locations, modern boarding schools are clearly operating in a very different social, cultural, economic and historical context.

Nowadays, British boarding schools are much less about religious instruction and much more about educating the children of the elite for future high office – those wealthy enough to afford the hefty price tag [8]. According to the Annual Report of the Independent Schools Council [9], the average cost of UK boarding in 2022 was £37,000 a year. There were 441 boarding schools operating in the UK in 2022 with 65,232 children registered as boarders. This figure has been fairly stable for at least the last 20 years barring a slight reduction in 2021 owing to the pandemic. Around 40% of boarders in 2022 were non-British with parents living overseas (the vast majority of these being from Hong Kong or China), meaning that British boarding schools are catering to a significant number of global elite families as well as those in the UK. Junior boarding (below age 11) has also decreased with around 6,000 junior boarders in the year 2000 compared with less than 4,500 in 2022 [9],[10].

There are different types of modern boarding in the UK. Full boarders go home at the end of the academic term and weekly boarders go home at weekends. Flexi-boarding is where children board one to two days a week and on the other days go home after school. Full boarding remains the most popular choice but in recent decades there has been a shift towards weekly or flexible boarding, now at 22.8%. Junior boarding is from age 7. At this age, around 35% are full boarders and around 65% are weekly or flexible boarders. Senior school boarding is from 11 to 16 and is made up of around 75% full boarders and the remainder are either weekly or flexible. From 16 to 18, sixth form boarders include 85% full boarders and the remainder weekly or flexible. In Chapter 2 we will consider the extent to which the age at which children first board might make a difference to the overall psychological impact.

1.2 The case for defence of boarding schools

A growing body of psychotherapy informed research and theory emerging from British authors, which we will review shortly, tends to conclude that boarding should be abolished, at least junior boarding (up to year 6 or age 10). Some authors, as we will explain, even claim that early boarding constitutes child abuse. But let's begin with the case for the defence.

Much of the advertising literature provided by boarding schools about the benefits of boarding for children's wellbeing is not based on formal research. The Boarding Schools Association website currently includes a promotional article claiming that boarding enhances children's wellbeing by helping them find 'balance':

> The extended day allows pupils increased access to learning, enrichment programmes, sport, fun and friendship without the stress and constraints of a commute at the beginning and end of the day. This time also allows us to know pupils well and support not only their academic progress but also their physical and mental wellbeing. At Downe House, as at all good

schools, there is nothing we want more than for pupils to be happy, secure and able to fulfil their true potential.

(www.ukbsa.com/how-boarding-benefits-the-wellbeing-of-pupils)

These ideas may draw on the frameworks of 'positive youth development' and 'extracurricular perspectives' which have informed Australian research on boarding school experiences [11]. The idea is that all children have potential to develop positively when given the right sort of developmental opportunities which can be found in a wide range of extracurricular activities – and that boarding school can provide a diverse extracurricular context enabling children to find their strengths. Building on these theories and frameworks, a small programme of formal research in Australia has examined various impacts of boarding school on quality-of-life and appears to partly support the idea that boarding can be beneficial (or at least not harmful) to children's wellbeing [11, 12, 13].

One key study from this research group focusing specifically on a comparison of psychological wellbeing between day pupils and boarders [11] was funded by the Australian Boarding School Association (ABSA). The study surveyed 5276 children in 12 schools age 11 upwards and with a mean age of fourteen (1477 were boarders and 3799 were day pupils). The survey asked about motivation, personality and various aspects of psychological wellbeing including sense of meaning and purpose, satisfaction with life, emotional instability, relationships and extracurricular activities. The study found that on many measures, boarding school is generally on a par with living at home. The study found some benefits of boarding compared with day school – specifically 'sense of meaning and purpose' and 'life satisfaction' as well as finding that parent-child relationships were more positive for boarders. The study authors speculate that children who board have better relationships with their parents because all the time they spend together is quality time – more joyful because it happens at weekends and in holidays and does not revolve around homework. These findings and claims directly contradict the theories we will come across later – put forward by British psychotherapists – which point to the damaging effect of boarding on parent-child relationships.

Is this study a case of positive spin? The ABSA research was based on one of a number of large-scale surveys directly assessing the psychological wellbeing of boarders compared to day pupils in a way that allows robust statistical analysis. It is always possible that organisations that fund research can influence the findings in some way. The mission statement of the ABSA who funded the research is 'to promote the interests of boarding schools in Australia'. Therefore, the research may have been carried out or reported in such a way as to mask any critical findings. While the overall design of the study and questionnaires used seem appropriate, questionnaires were given out to children by teachers working in their own school. This is problematic because it is likely children would have been concerned about confidentiality and therefore less open about their true feelings. It is also important to note that none of the questionnaires used in the study directly measured children's mental health. Instead, the study used more general and indirect measures of psychological wellbeing such as quality-of-life, potentially avoiding more direct questions about mood and anxiety. The comparisons made between boarders and day pupils were also limited in what they can reveal since finding statistically significant differences between groups of people is more likely the more people you have in your study. Finding a statistically significant difference between two groups of people does not tell us a lot about how meaningful this is in terms of psychological wellbeing. For example, are the statistical differences big enough to tell us if the average score of the boarding group counts as being 'well' and the average score of the day group counts as being 'unwell' in some way? What about individual wellbeing as opposed to group averages? In other words, how many individuals in each group (boarding versus day) had a score considered 'unwell' by normal population standards irrespective of the average score of the group? While studies with large numbers can seem impressive, they can fail to reveal the detail needed to really understand what is happening for all these thousands of children. It therefore seems reasonable to question the ability of these findings to fully inform us about the psychological wellbeing of boarders.

Even if some of the findings noted above have elements of truth, it is important to bear in mind that the idea of 'boarding school syndrome' we will introduce below is that the full force of boarding school trauma does not impact fully until adulthood [14],[15]. The ABSA funded study only attended to the responses of children while they were still children in school and cannot tell us about the longer-term impact of boarding school on adults. There are several similar studies from across the world that have investigated teenagers' mental health and wellbeing while at boarding school, several of which compare boarders with non-boarders and support some of the positive findings seen in this Australian study. There are also a very small number of studies which have investigated psychological impacts for ex-boarders and compared these to non-boarders. These studies were based in the USA and Norway and involved 'indigenous' populations (e.g. Native American, Sami people) and had less positive findings for ex-boarders, pointing to the importance of cultural context in considering research findings. We will review these studies more fully in Chapter 2. We are not aware of any published large-scale surveys directly comparing UK adult ex-boarders with ex-day pupils on measures of psychological wellbeing [16]. Chapter 2 will present data on psychological measures based on a UK sample of adult ex-boarders, although notably it was not possible to recruit enough ex-day pupils to the study to enable comparison, which may in itself tell a story.

We do know something about potential benefits of UK boarding school as told by adult ex-boarders though. Within some of the clinical case studies from the British psychotherapy literature and personal narratives, some benefits (or at least mitigations) of boarding school have been noted. Ex-boarders have indicated that taking part in team sports was good for them, giving a sense of belonging, identity, and for some could compensate against the loss of the familiar home environment [5],[17],[18]. Friendships developed at boarding school were highly valued by some ex-boarders [4],[5]. Some felt that boarding school provided outstanding education and that they learned independence, resilience and determination. Moreover, some ex-boarders felt that boarding school was an escape from a home life that was neglectful, chaotic, or abusive, providing stability and separation away from dysfunctional families [2],[15].

These indications from British psychotherapy research about learning independence is partly corroborated by formal research studies. For example, a survey of 1174 ex-boarders aged from 20 to over 80 from Gordonstoun (in Scotland) elicited generally positive reflections on access to extra-curricula activities at boarding school and their impact on adult life. Follow up focus groups found that ex-Gordonstoun boarders thought they gained 'confidence, self-belief, leadership skills, the ability to remain calm and determination through adversity from these experiences' (although note this research was commissioned by Gordonstoun School) [19].

Outside of the UK, another study collected and analysed personal narratives from 45 adolescents from diverse ethnic backgrounds attending an Australian boarding school [20]. This study found that boarders developed an ability to tolerate and live with peers from diverse backgrounds. Further formal research with 60 Alaskan Native adults who had attended boarding schools in Alaska between 1940 and 1980 found that friendships were very highly valued at school and that the many extracurricular activities had generated significant enjoyment [21]. However, as we will see later on, this study of Alaskan Natives as well as other research on boarding schools for 'indigenous' populations reviewed in Chapter 2 found several negative effects of boarding school too.

It is probably fair to say that at present, there is not enough research available to make a particularly strong case for the defence of British boarding schools when it comes to the short and long-term psychological impacts, beyond possibly developing resilience and independence. This does not mean that the case is closed. We will return to this question in Chapter 9. Nevertheless, we will now review the literature around 'boarding school syndrome' and weigh up the evidence.

1.3 'Boarding school syndrome' and the case against boarding

Attachment theory

The case against boarding school derives mainly from a body of work by British psychotherapists who have observed certain similarities between their therapy patients who had a boarding school background in common. One of the major theories on child development that has informed the way this group of patients has been understood is attachment theory. Attachment theory suggests that the way humans form emotional attachments to other people is a system of behaviour that evolved through natural selection and therefore has features which gives humans survival advantage. Young infants are thought to seek out physical closeness to an attachment figure (a parent or primary caregiver) in order to increase their chances of being protected from genuine threats to their life [22]. During this vulnerable period of a baby's life, parents represent a safe place from which to explore the world [22]. Several classic experiments in psychology have tested this theory and it has stood the test of time across several decades of child development research [23, 24, 25, 26]. The theory goes on to suggest that if a child becomes 'securely attached' early on (feels safe and protected by their parent or caregiver), they will benefit throughout their later childhood in several ways including the healthy development of cognitive, emotional, and social competence, school adaption, peer relationships, and emotion regulation [27, 28, 29].

During childhood and adolescence, children gradually develop more independence from their parents and this can happen at a different pace for different children depending on a whole host of different individual and family situations. While most recognise this increasing independence is a necessary part of child development, the question of boarding school taps into the thorny question of whether separation from parents can happen too soon, too suddenly and for too long. It also raises questions about whether there are other viable substitutes for the parent to provide the necessary sense of security and safety to enable ongoing healthy child development. Attachment theory suggests that at primary school age, children can tolerate a separation of about six hours to attend school [22]. However, the primary school child needs to know it is possible to contact their parent and to reunite if needed, especially after injury, upset, when afraid or when sad. Research shows that at this age, children still prefer parents over peers when they seek comfort [30] suggesting that a substitute parent (as would be the only option at boarding school) may not be adequate.

During adolescence, research shows that parents continue to be important 'attachment figures' [31] and that although peer relationships become increasingly important, most adolescents still seek out parents when in extreme distress [32]. Ideally, families continue to provide a comforting setting during adolescence enabling teenagers to separate gradually without the threat of complete withdrawal of parental support [33]. For children who board, this security is removed and a sharp separation from parents may have consequences for long-term parent-child relationships as well as children's social and emotional development. It is this well-established field of work on child development that underpins much of the research on boarding school syndrome outlined below.

Boarding school syndrome

Nick Duffell devised the term 'boarding school survivor' in the 1990s, aligning the concept with the field of trauma research in which victims are often reframed as trauma survivors [2],[34]. According to Duffell, boarding school survivors are typically high achieving and high functioning but find it difficult to ask for help and are often unaware they are experiencing symptoms linked with having been to boarding school. The term 'survivors' reflects that ex-boarders may be socially able, successful and occupy highly influential positions in professional or social life.

Leading on from this idea, psychotherapist Joy Schaverien coined the term 'boarding school syndrome' in 2004 [35]. She identified a set of symptoms typical of ex-boarder therapy clients [18]. She described clients who were sent to boarding school as young as four years old and experienced ruptures in their attachments to their primary caregivers (usually their parents). Schaverien explains that this repeated loss leads to the shutdown of intimacy. In adulthood, this can lead to suppressing feelings and difficulties with intimate relationships.

Schaverien explains that in her experience, clients with boarding school syndrome have often sought out therapy in adulthood for problems not ostensibly linked to boarding school. These might be relationship difficulties, depression or work-related problems [15]. On deeper exploration in therapy, these difficulties can be linked back to much earlier experiences at boarding school. Symptoms of boarding school syndrome experienced in adulthood include problems with intimacy, self-reliance, denial of pain, a need for control, being an overachiever, discomfort in asking for help, attachment (relationship) issues, depression, anxiety and burnout [18]. Burnout can reduce people's ability to perform at work and often leads to periods of time off work while relationship issues can include marriage breakdown and difficulties bonding with children [18]. While using the words 'syndrome' and 'symptoms', Schaverien sees the syndrome as a group of learned behaviours and emotions and emphasises that it is not intended as a medical diagnosis or way of pathologising individuals [15].

Although a set of symptoms for boarding school syndrome are described, authors in the field tend to focus on the key underlying problem being a difficulty in building and maintaining intimate relationships [4],[5],[8],[35],[36]. Duffell refers to numerous stories from partners of ex-boarders who have described their partners' struggles with intimacy including difficulties expressing love and communicating emotion [2],[8]. Marriage difficulties and parent-child relationship struggles also feature heavily in the personal narrative accounts of women ex-boarders collated by Nikki Simpson in *Finding Our Way Home* [5].

Developing a false self

A theory put forward by the authors working in the field of boarding school syndrome is that while attending boarding school, children develop a 'false self' to protect themselves from any emotional challenges boarding school presents

[4],[5],[8],[18],[37, 38, 39]. This false self is a presentation to the outside world of success, confidence and achievement. Many ex-boarders may claim as adults that it never did them any harm, that it was character building; that they are robust, independent and self-sufficient as a result of having been to boarding school [8]. However, this self-sufficiency is seen as merely exterior dressing to mask the real turmoil underneath [18]. The theory goes that the child boarder creates a protective mask, shield, front, façade or a false self during their boarding school experience to protect against and cope with the unmanageable feelings of being sent away from their parents [4],[5],[8],[18]. As adults, some ex-boarders will admit in therapy that as children they were hiding behind a false persona, hiding their true self through acting and *'learning to feel very little'* [5]. They say that as children they learned to present as successful, happy, and confident when masking desperate distressing feelings below the surface [5].

Emotionally cut-off

Based on their case work with adult ex-boarders, authors in the field submit that boarding schools, parents, guardians, and boarder peers have historically discouraged child boarders from expressing emotions [4],[5],[14],[15],[39],[40]. Their adult clients have relayed how they were expected to build self-reliance and cut themselves off emotionally [4],[5],[41]. Adult ex-boarders talk about having felt a disconnection, shutting down, and dissociation while at boarding school such that they no longer felt anything, they only existed [4],[5]. Adult ex-boarders have spoken to their therapists about how they tried initially to tell their parents about their distress by sending letters or appealing to their parents before going back to school after the holidays. These emotional expressions were shut down and ex-boarders recall being told not to be sad but to be brave and to learn to hide their feelings [5],[40]. This shutting down of emotions led to their emotions being supressed and children learning to get on with it. In these accounts, we hear of strict house mistresses and guardians forbidding crying and discouraging emotional letters home; of children being praised for obedience; and of emotions suppressed to avoid bullying by peers [5],[40].

Being cut-off emotionally is seen as part of a survival strategy adopted by boarders to cope with the extreme cruelty of boarding school [15]. This idea has been extended to the label 'strategic survival personality' [2],[8] reflecting the ways that many ex-boarders appear to have adopted a strategy to survive boarding school that has then stayed with them throughout school and into adulthood, becoming a part of their personality. The strategy includes becoming invisible, not saying anything to expose flaws and only appearing to conform [4],[5].

Effects of abandonment

Going to boarding school precipitates a drastic shift in family life. Existing family ties are abruptly severed and the normal process of child development within a typical family unit is interrupted irrevocably [14]. In attachment theory, this constitutes a serious 'rupture' to normal psychological development and is regarded as a major psychological trauma. This trauma is thought to be the chief instigator of the long-term impact on adult psychological functioning including a diminished ability to form good relationships in adulthood [15],[18]. Because of the severity of the psychological injury that comes from severing a child from its family, both Duffell and Schaverien have claimed that sending young children to boarding school is a form of child abuse and child neglect as we mentioned earlier [14],[35].

Is it fair to equate attending boarding school with child abuse? Child abuse is a type of childhood trauma of which there are different forms: physical, verbal, sexual, or emotional abuse. Child neglect can be physical or emotional. Child abuse is defined as:

> All forms of physical or emotional ill-treatment, sexual abuse, neglect or negligent treatment, or commercial or other exploitation, resulting in actual, or potential, harm to the child's health, survival, development, or dignity, in the context of a relationship of responsibility, trust or power. [42]

Certainly, there are documented examples of specific child abuse that have taken place in boarding schools as we referred to at the start of this chapter and will explore in detail in Chapter 7. These may even be just the tip of the iceberg if many, like de Bernières, are still waiting for their parents to die before they speak out. But does sending a child to boarding school in and of itself constitute child abuse? The clinical case material authors present concerning the effects of abandonment and separation from family does give cause for concern. It appears that the normal gradual separation process that happens in typical child development, when a child is at home with their parents, cannot take place when children are at boarding school [14],[43]. Many of the adult ex-boarders attending therapy have described feeling a sudden and extreme abandonment by their parents [14]. One ex-boarder talked about how his teddy bear had helped to ease the anxiety of separation from his parent, giving a sense of comfort and security. But once at boarding school, even from as young as age four, teddy bears were abandoned, destroyed or ceremonially burned [14]. Extreme abandonment then, followed by a callous disregard for any form of comfort. Whether these result in 'actual or potential harm to the child's health …' is a question this book will ask along the way.

Abandonment of children at boarding school is followed by a chronic absence of parenting [5],[8],[14],[34],[36],[38],[40]. Without a parent, children must survive prolonged periods without 'love, touch, or parental guidance, such as advice, direction, and supervision' [8]. Children experience a 'loss of closeness, love, laughter, and intimacy' [5]. Boarders can have alarmingly persistent anxieties about the emotional and physical distance between them and their parent, such as intense, recurring fears about dying: 'If I die tonight, how long will it take my mother to find me?' [5].

Absence of parenting can reduce a child's ability to negotiate friendships, work through feelings and negotiate the complexity of childhood and teenage friendships [5]. The absence of parents can also leave children feeling unsafe in their new unfamiliar environment, lacking nurture and affection [5],[18]. Ex-boarders report having felt sad and lonely, missing their parents' loving presence, daily hugs, cuddles, kisses goodnight, goodnight stories, and being part of the familiar family unit alongside brothers and sisters.

> Bedtime, lights out! Slowly my heart grows heavy, and I want Mummy to kiss me goodnight, but she is not here. Gradually, a dark, heavy pain of emptiness grows in my chest. [5]

Without a trusted parent close by, children are thought to turn inwards and to build self-reliance [5],[17],[18]. Although modern boarding schools hope that boarding staff can provide a nurturing role *in loco parentis* (in place of the parent) [44], the psychotherapy literature finds that ex-boarders describe boarding as emotionally barren, lacking in closeness and safety. Boarding staff were rarely described as secondary attachment figures able to replace the comforting presence of a parent. While some ex-boarders described the occasional kind or accepting housemistress, staff have mainly been described as strict, fearsome, unapproachable, remote and harsh, and likened to wardens with a sharp tongue who 'never engaged on an emotional level' and were certainly not maternal [5]. Experiencing coldness rather than warmth from those deemed to be *in loco parentis* can lead to emotional detachment and difficulty forming close and trusting relationships, which is thought to cross over into adult life [17],[18]. Ex-boarders are therefore left with a life-long yearning for parenting, someone with whom to share their deepest fears and worries with, someone to acknowledge their pain and tuck it all away somewhere safe each night.

Boarding school as trauma

As we noted earlier, the idea of boarding school survivors directly aligns boarding school with trauma research and frames boarding school as a traumatic experience. There is further evidence from psychotherapy case study literature that supports this idea [14],[18],[36],[45],[46]. People who have experienced various forms of trauma are known to experience a range of ongoing symptoms that have no physical cause such as chronic pain, chronic fatigue and digestive problems. Early childhood trauma, including child abuse and emotional neglect, has been linked to adult psychological disorders including depression, dissociation and post-traumatic stress disorder [47],[48],[49]. Schaverien found that her ex-boarder clients often exhibited signs and symptoms associated with post-traumatic stress disorder – signs that there is a deeper psychological scar lying beneath [15]. She claims that while ex-boarders may appear to lead very successful lives, the full trauma of boarding school can lie dormant underneath and be triggered by an event or memory causing the trauma to come to the surface and resulting in more outward signs of psychological trouble. Later in the book we will talk more about how this idea of boarding school as a trauma has informed the way that therapists have adapted their therapy work with their ex-boarder clients.

1.4 Reconciling contradictory findings

How do we reconcile the alternative views of boarding school presented by these different bodies of research? The Australian research, which found a number of benefits of boarding, involved roughly 1500 boarders. As we will see later in Chapter 2, this is not the only research which has found positive psychological impacts of boarding, but we have introduced it here to illustrate the sorts of contrasting approaches and findings we will come across in the rest of this book in our attempt to explore the field of research and reconcile the different sorts of conclusions that have been drawn.

British psychotherapy case study research is both rich in experience and narrative and is woven in with well-established theories of child development. The latter is also supported by further narrative accounts such as those in *Finding Our Way Home* and *Men's Accounts of Boarding School: Sent Away*, as well as the more recent personal accounts published in national media, and also to an extent by fiction written by ex-boarders like le Carré. The difficulty with this theoretical research is that there is no transparent documentation of the numbers of people it is based on, what other characteristics they had and what weight was given to each individual experience in forming the authors' theories. Moreover, the use of fictional characters to illustrate aspects of the theory might be considered unreliable for the purposes of research. One key question that will arise throughout this book is to what extent we trust scale versus depth: large numbers of survey participants ticking boxes on questionnaires versus a few participants explaining their experience in much more detail. Can both sides of the story be true in some way? Where one type of research gives us a positive story and the other gives us negative stories, could they in fact be telling us two different stories? For example, a story about the experiences of children in modern Australian schools and a different story about the experiences of adults who attended British schools in decades past? Perhaps British schools have changed in recent decades, but what do we do about the chance that we still have a generation of boarders in their middle and older years potentially facing individual and family crises with which they may need support?

What we want to understand is the psychological impact of boarding schools. Yet any approach to answering this question is inevitably flawed in terms of research design, measures used and samples which limit the conclusions that can be drawn. Being able to reconcile different studies involves thinking critically about methodology.

A lot of surveys of boarders and ex-boarders have been based on a 'cross-sectional' research design in which surveys are carried out at one point in time only. While these studies might identify psychological characteristics of the boarders or ex-boarders surveyed, any conclusions about cause and effect are always limited because of two methodological issues. First, while it might look from the data as if going to boarding school causes psychological problems, it may well be the reverse of this. In other words, having psychological problems may 'cause' people to go to boarding school. This problem is called 'reverse causality' and is always an issue when data is collected using a cross-sectional design. Second, while there may be an association between going to boarding school and psychological issues, it is never clear from a cross-sectional design that it was in fact going to boarding school that was the problem. There could be lots of other possible factors that explain this association. This is the 'third factor problem' and describes the possible role of several other confounding factors. For example, people who go to boarding school might have poorer sleep habits which makes their psychological state worse; they might be more exposed to recreational drugs or bullying which are themselves harmful; or they might undertake more exercise or make closer friends which actually improves their wellbeing. With a cross-sectional design, we can never be clear about the actual consequences of going to boarding school.

Other studies use qualitative or case study designs based on narratives (stories) of those who attended boarding school in the past. While generating rich and in-depth data and allowing an insight into individual experiences of going to boarding school, this data is also problematic if we wish to know whether boarding school causes problems in general. In this kind of study, the 'cause' and 'effect' are not separated – we rely on individual story-tellers (ex-boarders being interviewed or receiving therapy) to give their own view on whether there is a link between going to boarding school and their current wellbeing. This provides a novel and exciting insight into personal experiences but at the end of the day this is their individual story, narrative and belief and does not demonstrate with any certainty what causes people to have distress or happiness later in life.

Boarding school research also suffers from problems with how to quantify things we want to measure. Firstly, 'going to boarding school' is more difficult to measure than it might seem as there are many different forms of boarding school (private, state-funded, single sex, co-educational, weekly boarding, full boarding and so on) together with different patterns of boarding (starting at different ages, stopping boarding, re-starting boarding, switching schools and so on). This variation may account for some of the consequences of going to boarding school; yet in research all these differences would be lumped together as boarders versus non-boarders, leading to over-simplification of findings.

Secondly, measuring the consequences of boarding school is problematic because of researcher or responder bias. Researchers try to be objective and may feel that they are neutral in the way they carry out their studies. Yet inevitably what we believe and our own experiences can influence the studies we choose to do, the designs we use, the questions we ask and the way we analyse data. This can help us produce findings that fit in with our pre-conceived ideas. Likewise, study participants can be biased and if they know the aims of the study they may change their answers either to please the researcher (social desirability bias) or a need to emphasise their point and make their experiences seem either worse or better than they actually were.

Finally, there are also problems with the samples used in boarding school research. Research findings are dependent on those people who choose to take part and often these individuals are different to those who choose not to take part. This 'response bias' occurs in all research in all fields. Those who take part in a survey and choose to click on an online link or complete a questionnaire may have different views to those who ignore the advert. Those who talk to a researcher in an in-depth interview and share their experiences with a therapist will be very different to people who keep their experiences to themselves or feel they have nothing to talk about. This is highly relevant to boarding school research, meaning that we may only hear from those who have suffered after boarding school and feel that boarding school was to blame which could amplify a minority voice making it seem more prevalent than it is. We may also only hear from those who feel articulate or confident enough to come forward after boarding school to tell us their experiences; or from those better connected to their boarding school friends and still consider their school days a key part of who they are. These sampling issues limit the conclusions we can draw from research.

So what can be done? There are different ways to address these methodo-logical difficulties. One approach is neither ethical nor feasible: a randomised control trial whereby a random sample of children would be identified, ran-domised to attend either a boarding school or a day school and then followed up 20 years later. A more realistic approach would be to acknowledge the problems with research in any study, be transparent about any biases involved and treat all findings and conclusions with caution. Developing this approach further, we could regard any single study as just part of a bigger integrated picture in that research always has to be incremental with each study adding something extra to the body of knowledge. To take this approach further still, we could look for findings, themes and ideas across different studies and create a narrative which illustrates commonalities and differences, taking into account the limitations of each study as well as the overall body of research.

The aim of this book is to add to existing research studies on the impact of boarding schools while being transparent about methodological limitations, recognising that no study stands alone but can add to the picture being developed from the other studies in the field and to look for commonalities across the different approaches. From this perspective, this book offers a lens through which to integrate different perspectives to understanding the boarding school experience and hopes to illuminate the many consequences of attending boarding school for those who were both fortunate and less fortunate to attend them.

1.5 Enriching the field and the focus of this book

Much has been written about boarding schools and to date there is evidence both for the benefits and harms of this form of education. In this book we hope to shed further light on British boarding school experiences and how they may have impacted on adult psychological wellbeing and relationships. As a collection of formal research studies, the book examines the long-term psychological impacts of attending British boarding school in terms of eating behaviour, loneliness, happiness, experiences of therapy, adult relationships, family relationships and the impact on adult mental health such as depression and anxiety. The book also presents a unique analysis of the recent UK historical institutional abuse inquiry in Chapter 7; what it can tell us about the extent of direct abuse that has been present in British boarding schools historically and what measures can help prevent abuse now and in the future.

To address these topics, we will present a set of research studies, none of which are as large as the Australian survey study but neither are they based on clinical case material alone. All are based on adult reports of their experiences and so able to provide some insight into the longer-term effects of British boarding school. The vast majority of the books and articles that outline the negative psychological impact of attending British boarding schools use case descriptions either from the authors' own life experiences of boarding school, people they have met, or through clinical observations of the authors' own patients in their psychotherapy practice. Case descriptions can provide good exploratory information and give insight into individuals' direct experiences. However, the weaving in of selected case study examples with theoretical insights alongside fiction can be limited in terms of giving a true sense of what proportion of ex-boarders experience these difficulties. We do not know, for example, how the authors selected their examples and how well these examples represent the experiences of other ex-boarders. The examples are already drawn from a highly selected sample: people who have experienced distress and presented themselves for therapy. Moreover the examples are from a narrow group of therapy clients who happened to attend therapy with one of the small number of therapists who specialise in and write about this topic. How do we know if these experiences reflect those of many more ex-boarders who are not having therapy at all or not having therapy with one of these therapists?

The set of studies presented in this volume are not, however, free of bias or other limitations themselves, since no research can be. However, we hope it will provide another lens on the question mark hanging over British boarding schools. The research comprises two survey-based studies which collected questionnaire data from 128 ex-boarders; five interview-based studies involving interviews with 88 ex-boarders altogether (30 drawn from the survey samples); plus a chapter presenting an analysis of 61 accounts of child sexual abuse in residential schools as part of the UK historical institutional abuse inquiry. Our research participants were not selected from therapy caseloads and none of the authors were working as therapists in this field. Instead, participants for the survey and interview studies were found through open recruitment methods seeking out ex-boarders who would chose to put themselves forward to take part in research.

In each chapter we will explain how the ex-boarders involved were identified and how representative they might be of ex-boarders in general. To an extent, this makes the process of selecting examples and illustrations more transparent than in clinical theoretical work based on case studies. None of the work received any funding, which helps to limit any conflicts of interest influencing the way the findings are presented. Some of the authors and editors (including two of the editors) attended boarding school and some did not, detailed further in editor and author biographies. Taking this into account, we have tried to be reflexive throughout the process of doing the research and writing the book – meaning that we have tried to think about how our own experiences and personal biases might be influencing the conclusions we draw and the way we present them.

References

1 de Bernières L.Louis de Bernières: Aged 8, I was sent to hell. *The Times.* 2021. www.thetimes.co.uk/article/louis-de-bernières-aged-8-i-was-sent-to-hell-q9xg63nm6.

2 Duffell N. *The making of them: The British attitude to children and the boarding school system.* London: Lone Arrow Press 2000.

3 Independent Inquiry into Child Sexual Abuse. Truth Project dashboard final 2022. 2022. www.iicsa.org.uk/document/truth-project-dashboard-final-2022.

4 Laughton M, Paech-Ujejski A, Patterson A. *Men's accounts of boarding school: Sent away.* Abingdon: Routledge 2021. doi:10.4324/9781003090168.

5 Simpson N, ed. *Finding our way home.* Abingdon: Routledge 2018. doi:10.4324/9781351065542.

6 King's School Canterbury. The history of King's. www.kings-school.co.uk/about/history/ (accessed 24 Sep 2021).

7 Eton College. Our history. www.etoncollege.com/about-us/our-history/ (accessed 23 Sep 2021).

8 Duffell N. *Wounded leaders: British elitism and the entitlement illusion – a Psychohistory.* London: Lone Arrow Press 2014.

9 Independent Schools Council. *ICS census and annual report 2022.* Independent Schools Council 2022.

10 Independent Schools Council. *ISC census and annual report 2000*. Independent Schools Council 2000.

11 Martin AJ, Papworth B, Ginns P, *et al.* Boarding school, academic motivation and engagement, and psychological well-being: A large-scale investigation. *Am Educ Res J* 2014; 51. doi:10.3102/0002831214532164.

12 Bramston P, Patrick J. Rural adolescents experiencing an urban transition. *Aust J Rural Health* 2007; 15. doi:10.1111/j.1440-1584.2007.00897.x.

13 Papworth B. Attending boarding school: A longitudinal study of its role in students' academic and non-academic outcomes. Thesis, University of Sydney 2014.

14 Duffell N, Basset T. *Trauma, abandonment and privilege: A guide to therapeutic work with boarding school survivors*. Abingdon: Routledge 2016.

15 Schaverien J. *Boarding school syndrome: The psychological trauma of the 'privileged' child*. Abingdon: Routledge 2015. doi:10.4324/9781315716305.

16 Beard R. *Sad little men: Private schools and the ruin of England*. London: Vintage 2022.

17 Lauryn SS. The meaning of adolescent attachment in a male boarding school: an interpretative phenomenological analysis. 2012. https://ethos.bl.uk/OrderDetails.do?uin=uk.bl.ethos.633648.

18 Schaverien J. Boarding school syndrome: Broken attachments a hidden trauma. *Br J Psychother* 2011; 27. doi:10.1111/j.1752-0118.2011.01229.x.

19 Beames S, Mackie C, Scrutton R. Alumni perspectives on a boarding school outdoor education programme. *J Adventure Educ Outdoor Learn* 2020; 20: 123–137. doi:10.1080/14729679.2018.1557059.

20 White M. An Australian co-educational boarding school: A sociological study of Anglo-Australian and overseas students' attitudes from their own memoirs. *Int Educ J* 2004; 5: 65–78.

21 Hirshberg D. 'It was bad or it was good': Alaska natives in past boarding schools. *J Am Indian Educ* 2008; 47: 5–30. www.jstor.org/stable/24398766.

22 Ainsworth MS. Attachments beyond infancy. *Am Psychol* 1989; 44: 709–716. doi:10.1037/0003-066X.44.4.709.

23 De Wolff MS, van Ijzendoorn MH. Sensitivity and attachment: a meta-analysis on parental antecedents of infant attachment. *Child Dev* 1997; 68: 571–591. www.ncbi.nlm.nih.gov/pubmed/9306636.

24 Anderson CW, Nagle RJ, Roberts WA, *et al.* Attachment to substitute caregivers as a function of center quality and caregiver involvement. *Child Dev* 1981; 52: 53. doi:10.2307/1129214.

25 Howes C, Smith EW. Children and their child care caregivers: profiles of relationships. *Soc Dev* 1995; 4: 44–61. doi:10.1111/j.1467-9507.1995.tb00050.x.

26 Howes C, Spieker S. Attachment relationships in the context of multiple caregivers. In: Cassidy J, Shaver P, eds. *Handbook of attachment: Theory, research, and clinical applications*. New York: Guilford Press 2008.

27 Aviezer O, Resnick G, Sagi A, *et al.* School competence in young adolescence: Links to early attachment relationships beyond concurrent self-perceived competence and representations of relationships. *Int J Behav Dev* 2002; 26: 397–409. doi:10.1080/01650250143000328.

28 Kerns K. Attachment in middle childhood. In: Cassidy J, Shaver P, eds. *Handbook of attachment: Theory, research, and clinical applications*. New York: Guilford Press 2008.

29 Thompson R. Early attachment and later development: Familiar questions, new answers. In: Cassidy J, Shaver P, eds. *Handbook of attachment: Theory, research, and clinical applications.* New York: Guilford Press 2008.

30 Kerns KA, Tomich PL, Kim P. Normative trends in children's perceptions of availability and utilization of attachment figures in middle childhood. *Soc Dev* 2006; 15: 1–22. doi:10.1111/j.1467-9507.2006.00327.x.

31 Allen J. The attachment system in adolescence. In: Cassidy J, Shaver P, eds. *Handbook of attachment: Theory, research, and clinical applications.* New York: Guilford Press 2008.

32 Steinberg L. Autonomy, conflict, and harmony in the family relationship. In: Feldman S, Elliott G, eds. *At the threshold: The developing adolescent.* Cambridge, MA: Harvard University Press 1993.

33 Brodey WM. On the dynamics of narcissism. *Psychoanal Study Child* 1965; 20: 165–193. doi:10.1080/00797308.1965.11823230.

34 Duffell N. Boarding school survivors. *Self Soc* 1995; 23. doi:10.1080/03060497. 1995.11085543.

35 Schaverien J. Boarding school: the trauma of the 'privileged' child. *J Anal Psychol* 2004; 49: 683–705. doi:10.1111/j.0021-8774.2004.00495.x.

36 Barclay J. The trauma of boarding at school. *Self Soc* 2011; 38. doi:10.1080/ 03060497.2011.11084168.

37 Bull C, McIntosh A, Clark C. Land, identity, school: exploring women's identity with land in Scotland through the experience of boarding school. *Oral Hist* 2008; 36.

38 Palmer J. Boarding School: a place of privilege or sanctioned persecution? *Self Soc* 2006; 33. doi:10.1080/03060497.2006.11086268.

39 Jack C. *Recovering boarding school trauma narratives: Christopher Robin Milne as a psychological companion on the journey to healing.* Abingdon: Routledge 2020. doi:10.4324/9781003010982.

40 Duffell N. Gender difference and boarding school. *Self Soc* 2000; 28. doi:10.1080/ 03060497.2000.11086040.

41 Duffell N, Basset T. Unmasking survival patterns. In: *Trauma, abandonment and privilege.* Abingdon: Routledge 2018. doi:10.4324/9781315760582-11.

42 Butchart A, Phinney HarveyA. Preventing child maltreatment: a guide to taking action and generating evidence. 2006. https://apps.who.int/iris/bitstream/handle/ 10665/43499/9241594365_eng.pdf?sequence=1&isAllowed=y.

43 Gottlieb M. Working with gay boarding school survivors. *Self Soc* 2005; 33: 16–23. doi:10.1080/03060497.2005.11083883.

44 Hodges J, Sheffield J, Ralph A. Home away from home? Boarding in Australian schools. *Aust J Educ* 2013; 57. doi:10.1177/0004944112472789.

45 Grier F. The hidden traumas of the young boarding school child as seen through the lens of adult couple therapy. In: *Enduring trauma through the life cycle.* Abingdon: Routledge 2018. doi:10.4324/9780429474262-9.

46 Jack CT, Devereux L. Memory objects and boarding school trauma. *Hist Educ Rev* 2019; 48. doi:10.1108/HER-01-2019-0001.

47 Chapman DP, Whitfield CL, Felitti VJ, *et al.* Adverse childhood experiences and the risk of depressive disorders in adulthood. *J Affect Disord* 2004; 82. doi:10.1016/ j.jad.2003.12.013.

48 Dannlowski U, Stuhrmann A, Beutelmann V, *et al.* Limbic scars: Long-term consequences of childhood maltreatment revealed by functional and structural magnetic
resonance imaging. *Biol Psychiatry* 2012; 71. doi:10.1016/j.biopsych.2011.10.021.
49 Spalletta G, Janiri D, Piras F, *et al.*, eds. *Childhood trauma in mental disorders.*
Cham: Springer International Publishing 2020. doi:10.1007/978-3-030-49414-8.

Chapter 2

British boarding schools, mental health and resilience

Survey research

Emma Hopkins, Susan McPherson and Penny Cavenagh

Charles Booth, a nineteenth-century social reformer, is thought of as a pioneer of modern quantitative survey research methods in Britain. He set out to document, in meticulous detail, the social conditions of all people living in London. He documented the features of poverty, wealth, living and working conditions, applying new statistical approaches to understand patterns.

> The comparisons to be made will always be of a general character as between country and country, and more minute as between different places in the same country or different sections of the same town, but in all of them the intensive method of investigation should go hand in hand with the extensive. Without a full comprehension of unexpressed details, general statements are always lifeless, and often misleading.
>
> (Charles Booth 1893 [1])

The quote above reminds us that in order to better understand an issue and avoid unhelpful generalisations, we need to look closely at detailed data from a specific case in point (in his case London) and also to look more broadly, for example comparing different countries. In this chapter we will begin by summarising what survey research from around the world can tell us about the psychological impacts of boarding school. We will then present new data from a survey of ex-boarders specific to the UK and consider what the findings add to our understanding of the topic.

2.1 Psychological surveys of children at boarding school

In Chapter 1, we discussed a survey of children at Australian boarding schools which concluded that boarding was either better than or equal to not boarding in terms of psychological impacts. Similar types of research have investigated psychological impacts on children aged 10 and upwards attending boarding schools in several countries: Australia, Turkey, Germany, Malaysia, China, Russia, US and the UK. Most children surveyed have been over 12 with only a minority of studies including 10- or 11-year-olds. Numbers of children in

DOI: 10.4324/9781003280491-2

these studies range from 124 [2] up to 1477 in the Australian study described in Chapter 1 [3]. Two studies from China have included much larger numbers of children (7,606 and 20,594) but it is not completely clear from the study reports exactly how many of these children were boarders and how many were day pupils [4],[5]. The issues addressed across these studies include homesickness, depression, anxiety, personality difficulties, alcohol use, autonomy, family relationships, loneliness, emotional intelligence, resilience, suicidality and stress. Some studies have surveyed only boarders while others have compared boarders to day pupils, the latter being a good way to know if the findings are pertinent to just boarding or to childhood and education systems more generally.

Depression and anxiety

Several survey studies have measured depression and anxiety in boarding school children. In Malaysia, boarders scored relatively low on a depression scale but were on average quite anxious with 67% scoring in the anxious range [6]. Girls in this study were significantly more depressed and more anxious than boys. A survey study in China found that where depression did occur in boarders, this was often linked with stressful life events and that boys tended to develop 'problematic' smartphone usage as a coping mechanism, exacerbating depression; whereas good peer support could counteract this effect [2].

Neither of these studies had a day pupil comparison group but other surveys have compared boarders with non-boarders. For example, boarders in Australia reported similar levels of depression to day pupils but significantly higher anxiety [7]. The latter study included only 150 boarders, but it used a reliable measure of depression and anxiety unlike the larger Australian study described previously [3].

In China, depression and anxiety were found to be significantly higher in boarders than day pupils, again using reliable measures of depression and anxiety. This study also used a reliable measure of alienation from parents and found that depression and anxiety in boarders were linked to parental alienation [8]. Also from China, a large study of 7606 children found boarders were more anxious than day pupils and that this effect was greater for children from wealthier families [4]. However, using a very large dataset of 20,594 Chinese school children, another research group was able to separate out a specific group of 1,020 children who had only started boarding within the last year and found no differences in anxiety or depression but significantly greater loneliness. When drilling down to boarders classed as 'left behind children' (their parents had left the family home for work), the effect of poorer mental health among boarders emerged [5].

A survey of schoolgirls in Turkey found boarders had no more anxiety or depression than non-boarders; but girls who boarded were much more likely than non-boarders to have symptoms of trauma such as psychoticism and depersonalisation [9].

In summary, there seems to be a fairly common (but not universal) finding of higher anxiety among boarders but less consistency or clarity on depression. In studies which found no differences between boarders and non-boarders in anxiety levels, the boarders had been boarding for no more than a year or were a girls-only group. This may give us a clue that high anxiety among borders may develop over time and more so for boys, whereas secondary school girls may have slightly higher anxiety generally whether boarding or not. The mixed findings on depression could be indicating that while some boarders do get depressed, this may occur in response to specific personal difficulties that arise, combined with a lack of peer support or a feeling of loss of family depending on the family situation.

Family relationships

This leads us into a consideration of survey studies that have looked at family relationships or the child's response to leaving the family home. Homesickness was found to be higher among Russian boarders who had less social support from friends and peers [10]. This chimes with a study of Chinese teenagers which found that support from friends, more so than support from parents, was a critical factor in relation to resilience; yet for boarders, in the absence of support from friends, it was necessary to have high levels of 'emotional intelligence' in order to also display resilience [11].

Homesickness among British boarders seems to reduce over time (potentially within 2 weeks) and was less prominent for those with prior experience of boarding [12],[13]. Relatedly, a survey of 701 adolescents in Germany found that boarders developed more autonomy from their parents than day students yet also tended to feel unsupported by their parents [14]. Family cohesion was also linked with mood among Ethiopian immigrant children attending boarding school in Israel [15].

Taken together, these survey studies suggest that boarders may become more autonomous and resilient out of necessity; that friend and peer support can be an important mitigator of distress but that in the absence of both friend support and (by default) parent support, boarders have to develop a very thick skin to survive, appearing resilient and autonomous.

Alcohol use

Some boarders appear to cope with distress and personal difficulties using alcohol. Survey research in Germany indicates that teenage boarders consume more alcohol more often and from a younger age than non-boarders and that reasons for this are linked to peer pressure and the need to cope with stress as well as greater opportunities to be away from adult supervision [14],[16]. Concerns with alcohol use among boarders have been a prominent issue in research on native American boarding schools. While most research on the effects of these boarding schools has focused on ex-boarders and inter-generational effects (discussed below), a handful of surveys have been under-taken among current boarders in the small number of boarding schools that are now under indigenous control. Alcohol use among teenage native American boarders was found to be higher among those with less family support and with more stressful life events [17]. In a survey published in 1989, alcohol use, depression and poor family support were linked with suicidality with 23% having attempted suicide and 33% having thoughts of suicide [18]. Another survey of native American boarders published in 1994 found over 40% had serious thoughts of suicide and 30% had attempted suicide at least once. Suicidality was strongly associated with alcohol use, drug use and depression [19].

2.2 Psychological surveys of ex-boarders: Indigenous populations and cultural trauma

While understanding the immediate psychological impacts on children while they are at boarding school can give us some indication of potential harms and benefits, the claim in the British psychotherapy literature is that the full effect of boarding school may not appear until ex-boarders reach adulthood. We are not aware of any independent surveys of ex-boarders in the UK that have focused on psychological impacts. There is however a body of research on ex-boarders who attended native American boarding schools as well as similar types of schools for Canadian First Nations people, Eskimo and Sami people (indigenous to Artic regions of Norway, Sweden and Finland). The context of these schools is very different to that of boarding schools in the UK, Australia, China and so on, since in these cases indigenous families were often coerced or compelled by the State to allow their children to attend residential schools with either an implicit or explicit goal of cultural assimilation. Families often had little or no choice and they were not paying school fees, unlike in the UK where fees exclude all but the wealthy from most boarding schools. There is therefore a cultural trauma aspect to this field of work that makes it distinct from research on British boarding. However, it is worth noting some of the main findings given the lack of empirical research of this sort in the British context.

In spite of some positive impacts of boarding mentioned in Chapter 1, studies in this field paint an unhappy picture. A survey of 82 native American and Alaskan ex-boarders found higher rates of alcohol use, drug use, suicidal thoughts and suicide attempts compared to non-boarders [20]. In another study of 60 Alaskan Native adults [21], ex-boarders spoke about loss of culture and language, homesickness and feeling like prisoners in a concentration camp. In some cases there were reports of severe physical and/or sexual abuse. Several participants reported suicide attempts during or after their time at school as well as describing trauma, phobias and alcohol abuse in adulthood directly attributed to their time at boarding school. Some also talked about the negative impact on their relationship with their parents:

All my life I was never able to communicate freely with my mother or my father and-there was no intimacy at all. There wasn't. And then I think that affected my inability to have good relationships, you know, safe relationships or whatever. [21]

A survey of 611 First Nations Canadians who had attended boarding school found that half of those surveyed who had attended a residential school had a history of abuse and a quarter had a history of suicidal thoughts which was then in turn linked to history of abuse [22]. Similar findings of significant depression, addiction and suicidality are documented in a review of 61 studies of Canadian First Nations, Metis and Inuit ex-boarders [23]. Another review of 27 studies of native American ex-boarders also found strong associations between boarding and alcohol use which cannot be accounted for by family background or poor family relationships [24]. This suggests the high levels of alcohol use while at school described earlier, likely continues into adulthood.

In contrast, a large survey of 2,125 Sami ex-boarders found negligible differences between ex-boarders and non-boarders [25]. The researchers propose some factors that may help explain the contrast with North American research. They suggest that the Norwegian policy of cultural assimilation was abandoned earlier than in the US and so the ex-boarders surveyed were older and had more life experiences since boarding. Moreover, Scandinavia is thought to be more egalitarian than the US and has advanced more quickly over the last few decades to ensure better representation of indigenous people in democratic processes and better health and welfare services with additional policies to sustain Sami culture and language within education systems. If correct, the implication is that the various traumas associated with boarding in this context can somehow be ameliorated within a person's lifetime.

2.3 The research study: A UK survey of ex-boarders

To better understand the psychological impact of boarding school in a UK context, we carried out the first independent survey of ex-boarders in the UK. The survey was created using an online survey platform (Qualtrics). Study adverts were circulated widely via social media. No boarding schools were involved in designing the survey or circulating the advert and we did not circulate the advert via therapists or clinics either and so the people who responded might be described as a 'community sample'. The survey included some initial information about the project, followed by an online consent form. The information assured respondents of the voluntary and confidential nature of their responses and the option to withdraw at any time. After reading the information and consenting to take part, survey respondents would go on to complete the main survey online. At the end of the survey, participants had the option to provide their contact details if they wished to take part in a follow-up interview (discussed in Chapter 4). The final screen provided information about sources of support, if required. The project received ethical approval from the University of Essex Faculty of Science and Health.

Given the sorts of psychological issues that seemed to be important in previous survey research, the survey included measures of current depression, anxiety, trauma symptoms, adult relationships and resilience. Reliable questionnaires were used for all of these. The *Hospital Anxiety and Depression Scale* [26] was used to measure depression and anxiety. The *PTSD Checklist for DSM-5* [27] was used to identify trauma symptoms. The *Experience in Close Relationships* questionnaire [28] was used to assess current relationship styles. This assesses two types of romantic attachment: anxious and avoidant. Scoring high on anxious attachment indicates someone who is overly concerned about their worth in the relationship and tends to be fearful of abandonment and rejection. Someone scoring high on avoidant attachment indicates someone who tends to avoid closeness and intimacy and may appear to be independent and not in need of closeness. The *Brief Resilience Scale* [29] was used to measure resilience.

We also wanted to ask people for information about their boarding and early life experiences that may have impacted on their current adult wellbeing and relationships. We therefore collected information about the age they started boarding, any traumatic events or losses they experienced before age 18 and their memories of how they were brought up by their parents. We used a reliable questionnaire for this called *My Memories of Upbringing Questionnaire– Short-Form* [30] which has subscales for different parenting styles: emotional warmth, rejection and overprotection. To capture early life traumas, we used the *Childhood Traumatic Events* scale [31].

In total, 102 ex-boarders responded to the survey in full and Table 2.1 provides descriptive information provided about the respondents.

2.4 Adult mental health and relationships among UK ex-boarders

Average scores on wellbeing scales

In the first instance, we calculated the mean score for each of the adult mental health and relationship scales in order to find out whether, on average, our respondents might be considered as having levels of distress or difficulty on a par with people who seek help for psychological difficulties. The mean scores in Table 2.2 suggest that on average, our sample of ex-boarders do not have psychological distress on a par with people needing psychological treatment. The mean scores for depression, trauma and anxiety are in the normal range. Resilience is medium to high. The scores for anxious and avoidant attachment are both moderate suggesting some degree of difficulty in forming adult relationships.

Although the mean scores do not indicate significant psychological distress in our ex-boarder sample, the range of scores would suggest that a minority of the

Table 2.1 Describing the sample of ex-boarders.

Gender	Male	50%
	Female	50%
Relationship status	Co-habiting	12.7%
	Common law	2.9%
	Divorced	9.8%
	Married	52.9%
	Separated	4.9%
	Single	15.7%
Reasons for boarding	Family tradition	27.5%
	Parent ambition	3.9%
	Parent convenience	4.9%
	Parent in the armed forces	12.7%
	Parent mental illness	2.9%
	Parents living abroad	13.7%
	Quality/availability of local schools	10.8%
	Specific school characteristics*	3.9%
	Unsure/Other	19.6%
Highest level of education	A Levels	7.8%
	Degree	35.3%
	Diploma	9.8%
	Doctorate	8.8%
	GCSE equivalent	4.9%
	Masters	21.6%
	None	2.0%
	Other (e.g. PGCE, MBBS, MPhil)	6.9%
	PG diploma	2.9%
Ethnicity	White	95.1%
	Black/Asian/Mixed	4.8%
Age first boarded	Mean = 10.04, range = 4–16	
Age at time of study	Mean = 53.5, range = 26–75	
Number of natural children	Mean = 1.6, range = 0–5	

*e.g. sport, drama, religion, school for blind

people in our sample are experiencing levels of distress that would be on a par with people needing psychological support. We therefore examined the data in more detail to find out what factors might be linked to worse mental health or worse relationship styles.

Table 2.2 Average scores on mental health and relationship scales.

Adult well-being and relationship styles	Number	Mini-mum	Max-imum	Mean	Stan-dard devia-tion	Scale category for mean score
Depression	102	0	17.0	4.7	3.9	No depression
Anxiety	102	0	20.0	8.9	4.7	Normal
Trauma symptoms	86	0	71.0	29.4	18.9	Below diagnosis level
Resilience	84	2.2	3.8	3.0	0.3	Medium-high
Anxious attachment	94	1.0	6.8	3.7	1.6	Moderate
Avoidant attachment	94	1.0	6.7	3.5	1.5	Moderate

Effects of early boarding

First we ask the question whether the age at which children first boarded is linked to adult wellbeing. Do people who boarded from a younger age experience more distress as adults? Table 2.3 shows the results of this analysis.

What these results suggest is that the younger children were when they first start boarding, the more anxiously attached they are in adult relationships. Also, the younger children were when they first boarded, the more trauma symptoms they have as an adult. These associations (the Pearson's r number) are fairly modest, meaning that there are probably factors other than age at first boarding which also impact on whether adult ex-boarders experience trauma and anxious attachments. The age at which our respondents first boarded is not associated with depression, anxiety, resilience or an avoidant attachment style.

We see a similar pattern when we split our respondents into two groups: those who first boarded up to the age of 11 ($\leq$11) and those who first boarded above the age of 11 (>11). We carried out a test to compare these two groups

Table 2.3 Relationship between age at first boarding and adult wellbeing.

	Pearson's r	Significance (2-tailed)	Number
Anxiety	−0.191	0.068	92
Depression	−0.105	0.320	92
Trauma symptoms	−0.277[*]	0.014	79
Resilience	−0.182	0.111	78
Anxious attachment	−0.262[*]	0.015	85
Avoidant attachment	−0.158	0.150	85

* Correlation is significant at the 0.05 level (2-tailed)

Table 2.4 Adult wellbeing comparisons of early boarders (≤11) versus older boarders (>11).

	Age first boarded	Number	Mean	Standard deviation	t	Significance (2- tailed)
Resilience	≤11	39	3.1	0.3	1.2	0.22
	>11	40	3.0	0.3		
Anxious attachment	≤11	45	4.1	1.5	2.7**	0.01
	>11	41	3.3	1.5		
Avoidant attachment	≤11	45	3.7	1.6	1.1	0.27
	>11	41	3.3	1.5		
PTSD Checklist	≤11	39	36.0	16.7	3.2**	0.00
	>11	41	23.7	18.1		
Depression	≤11	47	5.3	3.7	1.3	0.19
	>11	46	4.2	3.8		
Anxiety	≤11	47	10.1	4.4	2.6**	0.01
	>11	46	7.7	4.7		

**Significant $p < 0.01$

on our adult wellbeing measures (see Table 2.4). This shows that early boarders have more of an anxious attachment style (fearful of rejection) and significantly more trauma symptoms (in line with our finding above). In addition, we find that early boarders score significantly higher on anxiety symptoms with the early boarder average score for anxiety falling into the borderline category for clinical anxiety.

Effects of parenting and early trauma

Next, we ask the question whether parental upbringing style or early life traumas are linked to adult wellbeing. To answer this question, we divided our respondents into categories according to whether they score above or below the 'clinical' range, known as the clinical cut-off score. Each of the measures we used has a given score which is considered to indicate the point at which the respondent falls into a 'clinical' category – someone who might need psychological support to help them with their distress. We labelled these as 'cases' and those falling below this cut-off were labelled as 'non-cases'. Tables 2.5–2.7 show us the results of comparing cases with non-cases on early life factors for anxiety, depression and trauma.

The findings in Tables 2.5–2.7 suggest that clinically anxious ex-boarders boarded *slightly* younger, had more early life traumas, felt more rejected by parents as children, experienced less parental warmth and felt more overprotected. Clinically depressed ex-boarders felt more rejected by parents and less parental warmth in their early life. Ex-boarders experiencing trauma

Table 2.5 Comparison of anxiety cases and non-cases on early life factors.

		Number	Mean	Standard deviation	t	Significance
Age first boarded	Case	33	9.2	2.4	−2.5**	0.016
	Non-case	59	10.5	2.5		
Number of early life traumas	Case	31	2.6	1.3	3.1**	0.002
	Non-case	58	1.7	1.2		
Parental rejection	Case	33	15.9	4.9	4.7**	0.000
	Non-case	57	11.2	4.3		
Parental warmth	Case	33	12.7	3.8	−2.7**	0.009
	Non-case	57	15.2	4.5		
Parental over-protection	Case	33	22.2	6.2	3.2**	0.002
	Non-case	57	18.4	5.0		

**Significant $p < 0.01$

Table 2.6 Comparison of depression cases and non-cases on early life factors.

		Number	Mean	Standard deviation	Mann–Whitney†
Age first boarded	Case	8	9.5	1.8	NA
	Non-case	84	10.1	2.6	
Number of early life traumas	Case	8	2.9	1.5	NA
	Non-case	81	1.9	1.2	
Parental rejection	Case	8	15.8	3.9	0.38*
	Non-case	82	12.6	5.1	
Parental warmth	Case	8	11.3	3.3	0.37*
	Non-case	82	14.5	4.4	
Parental overprotection	Case	8	22.4	5.2	0.17
	Non-case	82	19.5	5.7	

*Significant $p < 0.05$

† Depression cases are very few ($n = 8$) so a non-parametric test was used.

symptoms on par with people with PTSD had significantly more early life traumas, boarded slightly younger, felt more rejected by parents, experienced less warmth and more overprotection from parents. Taken together, these findings indicate that while early boarding is a factor in the development of adult psychological distress, other early life traumas along with problematic parenting styles also seem to be relevant.

Table 2.7 Comparison of trauma cases and non-cases on early life factors.

		Number	Mean	Standard deviation	t	Significance
Age first boarded	Case	35	9.4	2.5	–2.1*	0.040
	Non-case	44	10.6	2.6		
Number of early life traumas	Case	36	2.5	1.3	2.9**	0.005
	Non-case	48	1.7	1.2		
Parental rejection	Case	35	15.8	5.2	4.7**	0.000
	Non-case	49	11.1	4.1		
Parental warmth	Case	35	12.1	4.1	–4.1**	0.000
	Non-case	49	15.9	4.1		
Parental overprotection	Case	35	22.2	5.4	3.6**	0.000
	Non-case	49	17.9	5.3		

*Significant $p < 0.05$

**Significant $p < 0.01$

Resilience

Finally, we wanted to examine resilience among our sample of ex-boarders as to whether any early life factors (including age of first boarding, early traumas and parenting styles) had any association with levels of resilience. Resilience was not statistically associated with any of these factors. There was also no difference between early boarders (≤11) and older boarders (>11). There were no statistical differences between males and females. This suggests that while resilience is moderate in a general ex-boarding population, resilience is not associated with any specific early life factors including age of first boarding.

2.5 Discussion

Our survey findings are limited by the lack of a comparison group of non-boarders and a relatively small sample size, which prevents more complex analysis which could model the relative contribution of different factors to adult psychological distress. However, using scales of depression, anxiety and trauma which have been used widely in different populations, we are able to draw some conclusions about how our respondents compare to people seen in clinical settings providing psychological support.

Our findings from this UK survey of ex-boarders suggests that on average, ex-boarders are not experiencing significant psychological distress at levels requiring psychological treatment. Nevertheless, there are sub-groups within our sample who are experiencing significant psychological distress, particularly in terms of trauma and anxiety, less so with depression. This corresponds with the survey research presented earlier about children while they were still at boarding school which also suggested that levels of anxiety were elevated but depression was less often a problem.

Not many previous survey studies have specifically measured trauma symptoms in boarders or ex-boarders, with the exception of the Turkish study which found elevated levels of trauma symptoms including dissociation in adolescent girls at boarding school [9]. Our survey is the first we know of to measure trauma symptoms in adult ex-boarders and findings suggest that while the experience of trauma is not universal, over 40% of respondents were experiencing clinical levels of trauma symptoms, which is considerably higher than we would expect in a general community sample. Higher levels of trauma symptoms were associated with having boarded younger, problematic parenting styles and number of other early life traumas which could include the death of a friend or loved one, sexual assault, serious injury or illness, violence or major upheavals. Unfortunately our data cannot tell us whether many of these early traumas happened at or as a result of being at boarding school and how many might have happened anyway. Nevertheless, they account for some of the ongoing distress experienced by our adult ex-boarder sample.

In Chapter 1, we discussed the British psychotherapy research which implies that early boarding is inhumane and should be abolished. Our findings suggest that early boarding may be having some impact on adult psychological distress (specifically trauma, anxiety and having an anxious style of adult attachment). However, it is not universally detrimental and parenting style appears to have a significant contributory role, specifically when perceived as rejecting or lacking warmth. This fits with previous survey research on child boarders examining the role of family which found lack of parental support to compound emotional difficulties experienced by boarders.

It is also important to consider the cultural context of British boarding and the extent to which the sentiment described by Nick Duffell in *The Making of Them* may exacerbate the detrimental role of families in the British context. In other words, is there (or was there) a particularly British attitude to sending children to boarding school that encourages parents to suppress their parental instinct and adopt a seemingly uncaring approach prior to and at the point of abandoning their children at school in the belief this will stimulate resilience and be 'the making of them'? It is important to remember that early boarding has become much less common in recent times and perhaps this is accompanied by a change in parent attitudes to sending children away so young. However, where early boarding does persist and if some parents maintain this kind of attitude towards toughening up their children at an early age, we might want to ask if early boarding can be rehabilitated by a change in attitude among pastoral staff in schools towards homesickness and autonomy and developing more ways that parents can recognise the importance of and continue to be involved in their children's emotional lives while they are at boarding school.

In summary, this UK survey suggests that while the majority of ex-boarders in our sample were not experiencing psychological distress at levels requiring psychological treatment, sub-groups within our sample reported significant psychological distress, particularly anxiety, anxious and avoidant attachment. Further, over 40% of respondents reported experiencing clinical levels of trauma symptoms, which was associated with having boarded younger, problematic parenting styles and other early life traumas such as the death of a friend or loved one, sexual assault, serious injury or illness, violence or major upheavals. There therefore remains a significant minority of ex-boarders who are now adults experiencing significant levels of anxiety and trauma and who are likely to have strained relationships with their parents (where their parents are still alive). These adults are also likely to be having difficulties in their relationships with spouses, partners and perhaps also their own children. To an extent this fits with some of the claims made by British psychotherapists about the sorts of distress they have observed among their therapy clients, but it also suggests a more complex picture in that boarding school is clearly not leaving a permanent legacy of distress for the majority of adult ex-boarders.

References

1 Booth, C. Life and labour of the people in London: First results of an inquiry based on the 1891 census. Opening address of Charles Booth, Esq., president of the Royal Statistical Society. Session 1893–94. *J R Stat Soc* 1893; 56(4): 557–593. doi:10.2307/2979431.

2 Xie J-Q, Zimmerman MA, Rost DH, *et al.* Stressful life events and problematic smartphone usage among Chinese boarding-school adolescents: a moderated mediation model of peer support and depressive symptoms. *Addict Res Theory* 2020; 28: 493–500. doi:10.1080/16066359.2019.1692824.

3 Martin AJ, Papworth B, Ginns P, *et al.* Boarding school, academic motivation and engagement, and psychological well-being: A large-scale investigation. *Am Educ Res J* 2014; 51. doi:10.3102/0002831214532164.

4 Chen Q, Chen Y, Zhao Q. Impacts of boarding on primary school students' mental health outcomes: Instrumental-variable evidence from rural northwestern China. *Econ Hum Biol* 2020; 39: 100920. doi:10.1016/j.ehb.2020.100920.

5 Tang B, Wang Y, Gao Y, *et al.* The effect of boarding on the mental health of primary school students in western rural China. *Int J Environ Res Public Health* 2020; 17. doi:10.3390/ijerph17218200.

6 Wahab S, Rahman FNA, Wan Hasan WMH, *et al.* Stressors in secondary boarding school students: association with stress, anxiety and depressive symptoms. *Asia Pac Psychiatry* 2013; 5 Suppl 1: 82–89. doi:10.1111/appy.12067.

7 Mander DJ, Lester L. A longitudinal study into indicators of mental health, strengths and difficulties reported by boarding students as they transition from primary school to secondary boarding schools in Perth, Western Australia. *J Psychol Couns Sch* 2017; 27: 139–152. doi:10.1017/jgc.2017.1.

8 Xing J, Leng L, Ho RTH. Boarding school attendance and mental health among Chinese adolescents: The potential role of alienation from parents. *Child Youth Serv Rev* 2021; 127. doi:10.1016/j.childyouth.2021.106074.

9 Mutluer T, Fatih P, Tayakısı E, *et al.* Psychopathology and dissociation among boarding school students in eastern Turkey. *J Child Adolesc Trauma* 2021; 14: 201–207. doi:10.1007/s40653-021-00351-3.

10 Zulkarnain Z, Daulay DA, Yusuf EA, *et al.* Homesickness, locus of control and social support among first-year boarding-school students. *Psychol Russ State Art* 2020; 12: 134–145. doi:10.11621/pir.2019.0210.

11 Chen S. Chinese adolescents' emotional intelligence, perceived social support, and resilience: The impact of school type selection. *Front Psychol* 2019; 10. doi:10.3389/fpsyg.2019.01299.

12 Fisher S, Frazer N, Murray K. The transition from home to boarding school: A diary-style analysis of the problems and worries of boarding school pupils. *J Environ Psychol* 1984; 4: 211–221. https://search.ebscohost.com/login.aspx?direct=true&db=psyh&AN=1986-07659-001&site=ehost-live&authtype=sso&custid=s9814295.

13 Fisher S, Frazer N, Murray K. Homesickness and health in boarding school children. *J Environ Psychol* 1986; 6: 35–47. doi:10.1016/S0272-4944(86)80033-0.

14 Pfeiffer JP, Pinquart M, Krick K. Social relationships, prosocial behaviour, and perceived social support in students from boarding schools. *Can J Sch Psychol* 2016; 31: 279–289. doi:10.1177/0829573516630303.

15 Ben-David A, Erez-Darvish T. The effect of the family on the emotional life of Ethiopian immigrant adolescents in boarding schools in Israel. *Resid Treat Child Youth* 1997; 15: 39–50. doi:10.1300/J007v15n02_04.

16 Pfeiffer JP, Pinquart M. Alcohol use among students from boarding schools in comparison to students from day schools. *Int J Child Adolesc health* 2017; 10: 315–323. https://search.ebscohost.com/login.aspx?direct=true&db=psyh&AN=2018-08780-007&site=ehost-live&authtype=sso&custid=s9814295.

17 Dick RW, Manson SM, Beals J. Alcohol use among male and female Native American adolescents: Patterns and correlates of student drinking in a boarding school. *J Stud Alcohol* 1993; 54: 172–177. doi:10.15288/jsa.1993.54.172.

18 Manson SM, Beals J, Dick RW, *et al.* Risk factors for suicide among Indian adolescents at a boarding school. *Public Health Rep* 1989; 104: 609–614. https://search.ebscohost.com/login.aspx?direct=true&db=mnh&AN=2511594&site=ehost-live&authtype=sso&custid=s9814295.

19 Dinges NG, Duong-Tran Q. Suicide ideation and suicide attempt among American Indian and Alaska Native boarding school adolescents. *Am Indian Alaska Nativ Ment Heal Res* 1994; 4: 167–188. doi:10.5820/aian.mono04.1994.167.

20 Evans-Campbell T, Walters KL, Pearson CR, *et al.* Indian boarding school experience, substance use, and mental health among urban two-spirit American Indian/Alaska natives. *Am J Drug Alcohol Abuse* 2012; 38: 421–427. doi:10.3109/00952990.2012.701358.

21 Hirshberg D. 'It was bad or it was good': Alaska Natives in past boarding schools. *J Am Indian Educ* 2008; 47: 5–30. www.jstor.org/stable/24398766.

22 Elias B, Mignone J, Hall M, *et al.* Trauma and suicide behaviour histories among a Canadian indigenous population: An empirical exploration of the potential role of Canada's residential school system. *Soc Sci Med* 2012; 74: 1560–1569. doi:10.1016/j.socscimed.2012.01.026.

23 Wilk P, Maltby A, Cooke M. Residential schools and the effects on Indigenous health and well-being in Canada-a scoping review. *Public Health Rev* 2017; 38: 8. doi:10.1186/s40985-017-0055-6.

24 Zephier OlsonMD, DombrowskiK. A systematic review of Indian boarding schools and attachment in the context of substance use studies of Native Americans. *J racial Ethn Heal disparities* 2020; 7: 62–71. doi:10.1007/s40615-019-00634-4.

25 Friborg O, Sørlie T, Schei B, *et al.* Do childhood boarding school experiences predict health, well-being and disability pension in adults? A SAMINOR study. *J Cross Cult Psychol* 2020; 51: 848–875. doi:10.1177/0022022120962571.

26 Zigmond AS, Snaith RP. The hospital anxiety and depression scale. *Acta Psychiatr Scand* 1983; 67: 361–370. doi:10.1111/j.1600-0447.1983.tb09716.x.

27 Blevins CA, Weathers FW, Davis MT, *et al.* The posttraumatic stress disorder checklist for DSM-5 (PCL-5): Development and initial psychometric evaluation. *J Trauma Stress* 2015; 28: 489–498. doi:10.1002/jts.22059.

28 Brennan KA, Clark CL, Shaver PR. Self-report measurement of adult attachment: An integrative overview. In: Simpson JA, Rholes WS, eds. *Attachment theory and close relationships.* New York: Guilford Press 1998. 46–76.

29 Smith BW, Dalen J, Wiggins K, et al. The brief resilience scale: Assessing the ability to bounce back. *Int J Behav Med* 2008; 15: 194–200. doi:10.1080/10705500802222972.

30 Arrindell WA, Sanavio E, Aguilar G, *et al.* The development of a short form of the EMBU: Its appraisal with students in Greece, Guatemala, Hungary and Italy. *Pers Individ Dif* 1999; 27: 613–628. doi:10.1016/S0191-8869(98)00192-5.

31 Pennebaker JW, Susman JR. Disclosure of traumas and psychosomatic processes. *Soc Sci Med* 1988; 26: 327–332. doi:10.1016/0277-9536(88)90397-8.

Chapter 3

The impact of boarding school on adult relationships

Men's accounts

Craig Harris, Gareth Morgan and Alice Welham

While direct research evidence is scarce, there are indications from a number of sources that experiences of boarding may have long lasting impacts on adult relationships as illustrated by Roald Dahl's memoirs:

> None of these things is important, but each of them made such a tremendous impression on me that I have never been able to get them out of my mind. Each of them, even after a lapse of fifty and sometimes sixty years, has remained seared on my memory. I didn't have to search for any of them. All I had to do was skim them off the top of my consciousness and write them down. Some are funny. Some are painful. Some are unpleasant. I suppose that is why I have always remembered them so vividly. All are true.
>
> (Roald Dahl [1])

Schaverien's case studies of individuals engaged in psychotherapeutic work suggested a common cluster of behaviours centred around problems with intimacy [2]. The ex-boarders she described were reported to find intimacy dangerous or threatening; were unable to talk about or share feelings; and oscillated between a desperate need for love and rejection or abandonment of their partners [3]. Similarly, Duffell sought to describe the traumatic early experience of boarding and how it may later shape boarders' relationships and identity [4]. While Duffell recognises that many boarders recall happy experiences of school, he describes how many also develop 'strategic survival personalities' as a means of protecting themselves. He also suggests that cultural and societal narratives around privilege have significant roles in shaping how boarding experiences impact boarders' identity and relationships.

Several areas of psychological research highlight potential mechanisms through which boarding may exert such effects. For example, evidence suggests that separation from caregivers can affect attachment [5], which may then be related to adult relationship patterns and early experiences more generally are known to affect adult relationships [6],[7]. Separation from caregivers can be experienced as a type of trauma [8], which is also linked with changes in the ways children relate to other people in their lives and

DOI: 10.4324/9781003280491-3

their experiences in adulthood [9],[10]. Events such as bullying, which may of course affect any child (boarding or not), have been found to have more significant effects when children are unable to share what happened with their parents or caregivers to help them make sense of their experiences and cope with distress [11]. While other factors may be at play here, an interesting example of these effects is that wartime evacuees appear to have significantly different patterns of marriage and having children than children who had not been evacuated [12].

Historically, most boarders (in the UK, at least) have been male, with many of the major UK boarding schools (Rugby, Eton, Harrow and so on) having started out as single sex institutions for boys. While some former boys' schools have turned co-educational over the years, and while several single sex girls' boarding schools also have a long and continuing history, it seems likely that males may have a distinct experience of the boarding school system [13]. Even when boarding schools are mixed-sex, pupils may be segregated for much of their lives, with separate female and male boarding houses, sports facilities and so on. The boarding environments of boys and girls and relatedly, the experiences of male and female individuals in boarding schools, are likely to differ.

Both the boarding environment itself and the specific impacts of these environments on individuals, at cognitive, social, emotional, and neurological levels, may depend in complex ways on sex and gender-related variables (including hormonal, neurodevelopmental and social/cultural factors). We know from other areas of psychological research that parents' and caregivers' communication with boys about emotional responses may differ from communication with girls [14]. As adults, it has been suggested that men have a greater tendency to 'hold in' emotions [15],[16]; these are differences which may develop owing to a complex interplay of factors over the course of childhood [17]. This highlights the possibility that if boarding schools tend to encourage suppression of emotional expression, there may be specific manifestations and implications for males. Given the key role of emotional expression in interpersonal relationships, this may represent one set of mechanisms via which boarding can impact later social and emotional functioning, with sex, and/or gender-specific elements.

If boarding does impact how people relate to each other, the fact that a significant portion of the British ruling class have experienced boarding could have broader socio-political implications, as considered by Nick Duffell in *Wounded Leaders* [18]. Again, this may arguably apply especially to men who are over-represented in both positions of political and socio-economic power and among the group of UK ex-boarders.

While there is reason to believe boarding may have an impact on adult relationships, it is difficult to access information from boarding schools on this topic, as they act to ensure their privacy and reputations [2],[3],[19]. The existence of support organisations for ex-boarders, alongside accounts provided by psychotherapist authors working in the field [2],[3],[20], suggest that some ex-boarders consider themselves and their adult relationships to have been affected by their previous experiences of boarding. The research we report in this chapter offers the opportunity to explore in detail the experiences and sense-making of a group of eleven ex-boarder men in the UK, who consider boarding to have affected them and their adult relationships.

3.1 The research study

We carried out eleven semi-structured interviews with male participants who had previous experience of boarding. We asked them questions about their time at boarding school; the culture of the school; their home life around this time and how they felt it related to their experiences of school; how they felt their experiences at school affected them as boys and young men; their current relationships and whether they imagined things may be different had they not been to boarding school.

We recruited men mainly through advertisements distributed by directors of boarding school support organisations or through an advert shared on social media. In order to be eligible for the study our participants had to be male, aged 30–70 and have experience of attending boarding school. We also collected information relating to each participant's age at interview, at initial transition to boarding school, type of institution attended and length of attendance. These are presented in Table 3.1.

The interviews were transcribed and analysed using thematic analysis – a way of producing a set of themes that best reflect the key features across the interviews [21]. Our analysis resulted in three key themes: 'Disempowered

Table 3.1 Characteristics of participants.

Pseudonym	Age at interview	Type of institution	Length of attendance
Theo	35	Co-ed boarding	10 Years
Alan	45	All-boys boarding	10 Years
John	36	Co-ed boarding	7 Years
Daniel	36	Co-ed boarding	7 Years
Lucas	68	All-boys boarding	7 Years
Michael	64	All-boys boarding	10 Years
David	37	Co-ed boarding	3 Years
Andy	45	All-boys boarding	6 Years
Steven	36	All-boys boarding	11 Years
Martin	57	All-boys boarding	5 Years
Nathan	37	All-boys boarding	10 years

boys: men's relationships to power and control', 'Fearing and craving intimacy: boys' and men's relationships', and 'Anger and acceptance: different ways of living in the present'. These are illustrated below with exemplar quotes from the interviews.

3.2 Theme 1: Disempowered boys: Men's relationships to power and control

We found that all our male ex-boarders shared experiences from their early childhood, at school and at home, where they felt powerless to influence decisions or events in their life. They felt disempowered by those with more power and talked of feeling controlled; unable to articulate distress or feel heard; growing up in a masculine dominated environment; and how this impacted their later relationships. They experienced their childhood selves as having little to no ability to impact on the decision to go to boarding school.

> I mean as a fait accompli my parents put my name down pretty much when I was born. So, over the years I was in the stream. I went to prep school, so for five years old. You know you are in the stream and you know where this is heading.
>
> (Martin)

> There was no way whether I had any choice whether I went to boarding school or not as an eight-year-old.
>
> (Nathan)

The men described an environment where they were fearful of staff; where violent or threatening behaviour of staff and peers was normalised; and how this often felt unsafe.

> Punishment was still used in a very aggressive way ... You don't have to hit someone to make people feel scared or worried ... We had teachers who would shout to the point where you believed that they might do something to you.
>
> (Theo)

> And I remember sort of when I was ... just gone into senior school. A few of us got beaten [by peers] until we fell asleep effectively. And just thinking back on it, it's just like, it's just like it's so brutal.
>
> (Steven)

As a response to feeling controlled and constrained in the environment, many of our ex-boarders talked of 'mini rebellions', how they fought back against the system in small but meaningful ways.

When I ran away from home at the end of that half term, I was trying to communicate some anger. But ... it's actually fucking annoying because I wish I had been more angry [laughter] because I wouldn't be having this feeling now. But I was eight what else could I do?

(Nathan)

Although everyone talked of limited freedom while boarding, several also spoke of how greater freedom was afforded them as they moved their way through school, and how much they enjoyed this.

We were still managed from hour to hour, but we had a little more freedom, especially as we got older.

(Theo)

In my top year, my dad bought me a car and I used to drive back and forth, which was a great freedom.

(Alan)

The men describe a controlling and hierarchical culture where boys were expected to become leaders and powerful men, where there was limited space for vulnerability and masculine traits were celebrated:

... it was dominated by all masculine teachers and masculine energy ... So it was just a whole culture of the place in my situation. It was competitive ... we were sort of pitching against each other to some extent to perform. And they were there to prepare young men going into military situations and defending their country, leading other men into battle and running the Empire and all that stuff. ... There wasn't room for any softness.

(Michael)

Boys were often placed in roles of leadership in lieu of adult supervision, and the culture of the school was maintained by peers in hierarchical positions of power:

It's about making sure the school runs; it's about making sure people do what they are supposed to. I was a prefect, and I became a part of the establishment.

(Theo)

Growing up in a predominantly masculine environment provided the boys with limited experience and understanding of women through childhood and adolescence, often only seeing women in stereotypically female roles and as weak, emotional and mysterious creatures.

Matron ... she provided a very small amount of femininity in the environment, but not much really. She wasn't really there. But I can remember her, probably just because she was the only woman in the place.

(Lucas)

The men described the ways that these early experiences of being powerless or controlled have led to difficulties in their later relationships. They noted how the experience of having such little agency may have led to a desire to take firm control over their lives, realising how patterns of control had emerged in relationships with partners and children.

I hate losing control, I hate someone driving me. I hate not knowing where I'm going. I have to be in control ... And that's probably why I just go to the complete other extreme of being probably quite selfish and hurting people because I just do what I like.

(John)

Maybe I'm just a controlling person anyway but somehow the defences I'd put in place to survive boarding school, somehow made me defended against my daughter when she was a teenager ... something was going on that made me get very angry with her when she was a defiant teenager.

(Lucas)

They also described how following these experiences, they went through life fearful of authority and people in power, unsure of how to relate to them or manage them in work environments.

I naturally have an anxiety of people who are in power. I struggle with people in power, especially people who use their personality traits as a way of getting power. And by that, I mean there are people in the work-place who use their reputation to manage people ... I struggle with people like that.

(Theo)

There was also a sense that others would be unwilling to listen or unable to understand their experiences of distress or continued to be sensitive to feeling 'not listened to' in future relationships.

[sharing my experience with others was difficult because] they would have probably belonged to the category many people would belong to, which was … your parents sent you … that you were privileged to go so don't complain.

(David)

When we have an argument, she just maintains her calmness … And I'm just there about to explode and she … I'm wanting a reaction … clearly linking back to boarding school again where you try and get a reaction out of your parents. You're getting dropped off, you're crying your eyes out. 'Come on, why aren't you listening to me?', and off they go.

(Daniel)

3.3 Theme 2: Fearing and craving intimacy: Boys' and men's relationships

'*I had to survive*', explained one of our ex-boarders. This encapsulates how they felt they needed to create a 'masked self' in order to survive the boarding school environment. This meant altering their behaviour and suppressing or hiding emotion and parts of their identity. There was a sense that if boys expressed emotion, this meant they were vulnerable, weak and perfect targets for bullying.

You don't show your feelings, you can't show your vulnerability because other boys will project their own fears onto you and then you will get picked on for it, as the weak one.

(Michael)

I can remember really clearly that, that's what it took for me to shut down. So, realising very quickly that actually I had to change, I had to do whatever I needed to do to survive … for the next five years I kept my head down and did what I needed to do to get through.

(Martin)

Many of our ex-boarders felt unable to speak openly with parents about their experiences for fear they would be blamed, criticised or seen as failing.

[boarders] never tell their parents … hardly ever. And that's the mysterious thing because it seems obvious that that's what they should be doing, but they don't. And I didn't. And it's to do with lack of agency in a young person or agency on a deep psychological level to process and articulate stuff like that and to make statements and to explain to people, the lack of ability to explain what's going on in your inner world. And some kind of sense that some people say … well it must be your fault if you're not coping.

(Lucas)

So, I didn't communicate it no, I just cried. I said I missed home you know, and they [parents] would go I know you do, but don't worry there's no need to cry.

(Nathan)

Needing others but fearing intimacy describes our ex-boarders' experiences of moving away from their family and missing the nurture, care and safety derived from being at home. They still needed to be with, connected to, or close to others in order to feel safe but for many this was a double-bind, as close relationships often evoked feelings of vulnerability. Some talked about how the experience of being dropped off triggered painful emotions.

Like something had been taken from me ... ripped out of me like a real kind of loss.

(Theo)

It was a constant feeling of anger and feeling I guess abandoned I think.

(Daniel)

Participants often felt distant and disconnected from the safety and nurture of their family, especially their mothers.

[I was] out of reach of the love and support and safety of my family home and particularly my mother.

(Michael)

I just missed them; I wasn't really angry at them... I remember wanting Mum to just like appear, you know?

(Nathan)

Relationships with peers offered some sense of protection and closeness; these relationships were deemed necessary for getting by. However close relationships felt dangerous and there was an inherent risk in forming bonds with peers.

I think there was a lot of camaraderie ... and alliances between friends and things like that, which probably meant so much more than anything that was explicitly shared, but can be felt, subtly felt.

(Michael)

I couldn't trust anyone; I didn't know what their motives were being friendly with me. And I was in this double bind, that I wanted to hide so that I wouldn't attract this unwanted attention, and at the same time I was so starved of positive attention, of being appreciated.

(Michael)

Although most of our ex-boarders talked of constantly wanting to be at home with family, some also shared that this didn't always offer the contrasting warm, safe and loving environment they craved.

> In my family there were … very few sort of soft moments or vulnerabilities or hugs … no 'I love you', or no sensitivities … When I was at school I wanted to be at home, and when I was at home I wanted to be at school, which is just an awful situation to be in.
>
> (Alan)

> There were times where I was home and didn't feel relaxed, it didn't feel like I was home.
>
> (Daniel)

The men talked about on-going difficulties with emotion and identity and how their adult relationships were often still shaped by behaviours that were learned and employed to maintain a sense of safety. They spoke of how their boarding experiences led to a confused sense of identity masking their true self as described earlier.

> I think that's another key theme … something that I feel very strongly about is this confusion of, like, 'Who am I?' If I am not this person that has been imprinted so strongly.
>
> (Steven)

> [I'm] trying to step out from behind this false self that still jumps in, to protect, to get me to withdraw, to find safety. Which doesn't help [laughter] in a relationship.
>
> (Michael)

They described how they (or their partner) had noticed a constant or desperate need for love, attention, and nurture from their intimate relationships.

> I feel the need for constant attention … and constant comfort as well. Like … most people would need a hug once a day from the person they love. I need to be hugged 15–20 times a day. It sounds a really odd thing, but I need to be constantly hugged and I need to be told constantly that she loves me.
>
> (Theo)

> So one thing I was struck by with my experience as well is that there is this sort of desperate … need for connection and the need for loving.
>
> (Steven)

Others spoke of a pattern of repeatedly ending relationships at the point of feeling close and how closeness in relationships prompted feelings of vulnerability and led to barriers.

> We'll have a great time and then as things get too close, personal, then the contact is pretty much broken. And that's a pattern which in retrospect has happened throughout my life.
>
> (John)

> I can feel overwhelmed by the other in an intimate relationship quite easily. The intimacy is too much … I can't bear it. And I can't respond with it either. But equally I can feel abandonment very easily as well.
>
> (Michael)

In contrast, some spoke of how learned strategies held some value for them and could be employed in situations or relationships as a protective strategy.

> Whatever trauma you go through and whatever sort of survival mechanism, there are some benefits to these processes because everything that doesn't kill you makes you stronger in a way. Or opens up to new areas of your personality or something. So there are some benefits to all this stuff.
>
> (Lucas)

> I can still hook into it now, you know workaholism, or stretch myself, or not getting involved in emotional type situations … I can still call upon it now … it's a very successful technique because it gets you through, it protects you.
>
> (Martin)

3.4 Theme 3: Anger and acceptance: Different ways of living in the present

Men interviewed in this study clearly felt profound impacts of boarding school on their current adult lives, particularly in the context of intimate relationships and other important ways of relating to others such as colleagues, friends and so on. Attributing these life-long difficulties to experiences at boarding school left these men needing to find some way to reconcile with the past. Some were left with considerable anger towards parents or teachers or towards things that happened that they deemed to be unfair, neglectful or wrong; some spoke of having made some sort of peace with what had been done to them; either way the processing the past has taken time and is ongoing for many.

> It's been my modus operandi pretty much. It hasn't been career or money or prestige, it's been how am I going to continue to emotionally recover

from, you know, this, you know, these institutions, this situation that just
sapped my whole spirit.

(Alan)

It's not gone away now, it's, as I kind of alluded to, it's part of who I
am. I'm pissed off I was sent away as an eight-year-old; I'm pissed off
that everyone thought it was kind of normal and yeah ... That they
don't just sort of fucking shut down the system or make it illegal to
do that.

(Nathan)

Theo described how finding peace was necessary, as it would be too painful to
acknowledge that his parents did not have his best interests in mind when sending him to school.

I think your parents fundamentally is where you learn how to love, how
to relate, how to care, and if you're basing that on the fact that your
parents made decisions that were not based on that, then ... that completely blows wide open how you relate to others. And I think I have to
think about it like that, and I genuinely believe that whatever may have
happened, whatever happened, whatever he may not have done, fundamentally he made a decision based on care. It was a loving decision even
if it was the wrong decision.

(Theo)

Feeling listened to and understood by partners, therapists and support
groups, and the discovery that others shared their experience helped them to
make significant positive changes.

I consider myself very lucky to have a partner who is very understanding ... She is fully abreast of all the impacts that can result for
me.

(Steven)

Having talked to other people who had been to boarding school, and actually been a bit more open with my wife ... it's kind of flipped it all on its
head almost.

(Theo)

The influence of boarding school on my life is profound. Knowing and
recognising that that is the case has helped me understand myself better,
has allowed me to forgive myself a bit better because, the guilt that you
feel ...

(Andy)

3.5 Discussion

This chapter explored the experiences of eleven ex-boarding males and the difficulties they faced in later relationships which they attribute to their time at boarding school. Before drawing any conclusions, we should recap what we know about the men we interviewed in order to understand how common their experiences may be. The men were aged between 35 and 68 at the time of interview and therefore would have been at boarding school in the UK between the 1960s and 1990s. They were recruited through ex-boarder support organisations and are not therefore representative of the wider population of UK boarders. We don't know if they had had psychotherapy but none had required specialist mental healthcare. We don't know if any of them experienced child sexual abuse while at school (although none mentioned it) and we don't have a full history of their adult relationships and jobs.

It is important therefore to be cautious about what we conclude but it does seem as though the accounts of these men overlap with some of the ideas put forward by British psychotherapists, particularly the idea of 'strategic survival personality' and the 'false self'. Joy Schaverien, through her work with ex-boarders as a psychotherapist, has described how the experience of boarding school, and child–parent separation may cause significant trauma and long-term repercussions in adult relationships. Similarly, Nick Duffell described how boarding schools replaced the character of boarders 'with a coat of armour filled with fear, loneliness and alienation' [4] and in response to this they develop strategic survival personalities that allow them to navigate life through boarding school, but introduce ongoing and repeating difficulties in later relationships. These are psychotherapeutic theories derived from case studies of clients in which clients' direct spoken words were not captured and analysed systematically like they are in recorded interviews. Perhaps because a non-therapeutic interview takes a more open and non-theoretical approach to exploring men's experiences, our data offer some potentially interesting new or additional angles on concepts like 'strategic survival personality'.

The first theme, 'Disempowered boys: men's relationships to power and control', illustrated boys' feelings of powerlessness when at home and at school. Our participants described feeling disempowered and controlled by others in a male dominated environment. This later impacted on how they related (as men) to power and control both in intimate relationships as well as at work and with friends. Some specifically discussed finding it unbearable to feel out of control in relationships, and how this often provoked a controlling response – needing to be independent and take control of their lives. In contrast, some described how they continued to go through life fearful of authority and people in power, unsure of how to relate to them or manage them in work environments. There were therefore varied ways that men manifested issues with power and control but overall, our data provide some clues as to how some of these connections between boys' and men's experiences may occur.

The brutal disempowering of boys at school (reinforced by parents' apparent complicity) emphasised to boys the need to display exaggerated masculine traits at a time when they still very much craved feminised forms of care from their mother. Lack of power permeated every aspect of boys' experiences, from the absence of influence in the decision to board, to control over aspects of their lives such as who they spent time with and when they could see their attachment figures (their parents). The men interviewed indicate that as boys they were exposed to fiercely stereotypical ideas about masculinity, for example that they should not display emotion, that vulnerability portrays weakness, that boys don't cry. These culturally specific ideas about boyhood may have prevented them from making sense of their experiences in a way that did not locate their problems (distress, fear, tearfulness) within themselves.

This fits with an idea put forward by sociologists Connell and Messerschmidt referred to as 'hegemonic masculinity' [22] and refers to cultural expectations that pressure boys and men to be a particular way, maintaining male oppression of women in society. As boys, the men interviewed in this study seem to have experienced themselves as incompetent or failures when experiencing distress or thoughts that did not fit with the ideals of competitive masculinity that engulfed them. The way they made sense of this as boys may have been constrained by their relative powerlessness in relation to their parents as well as teachers and older boys in the school. Attachment theorists have suggested that, when experiencing rejection from caregivers, it can be more adaptive for a child to experience them self as the source of the problem. This idea can be easier for a child to cope with short term because it implies they have the capacity to change their behaviour in some way to obtain the nurture they crave [23].

Boarding schools sometimes claim to offer a nurturing environment which can be a 'home from home' for boarders. Australian research supports this idea suggesting that primary bonds can be formed with both family and boarding house [24]. However, this research was based on accounts of boarders while still at school in Australia in the 2000s who were not yet adults and therefore not representative of adults who attended British boarding schools in earlier decades. The men interviewed in the present study may have experienced a number of threats to core needs while they were boys at school, and in response, developed ways to cope. Having limited or no access to home and not being within safe proximity of primary caregivers, boys were deprived of the love and physical contact of their family. Some specifically mentioned craving their mother in particular. This need for physical contact and nurture could not be adequately met by staff. Boys were therefore left feeling unsafe and lacking the secure base required for the healthy development of confidence, competence, and resilience [25]. It seems important to emphasise that the overall sense of disempowerment combined with lack of nurture was felt not only at school but also in the family context, suggesting that any long-lasting impact on men's ways of responding to or relating to power in relationships could be attributed to a combination of home and school environments, not just the environment at school. This may tell us something about cultural norms in families who send their boys to boarding school in the UK.

The second theme, 'Fearing and craving intimacy: boys' and men's relationships' showed the ways in which survival strategies developed in response to the boarding school environment and how this led to difficulties in adult intimate relationships. As men, our participants describe both craving and fearing intimacy. Our data give some clues as to how this may have developed. It seems these boys found themselves in a double bind. While they were desperate for connection, relationships with peers were intrinsically risky. They had to be distrusting, hypervigilant to the motives of others, and keep parts of themselves hidden. This kind of behaviour is similar to what attachment theorists refer to as 'disorganised attachment' [26]. This refers to children oscillating between seeking out nurture (expressing the need for love) and self-protective behaviours. This type of attachment behaviour is thought to come about when a child has been harmed by their adult caregiver (usually a parent) [27]. In the case of the men interviewed in this study, this oscillation between distrust of others and feeling desperate for connection may have come about from being harmed prior to going to school in some way by a caregiver; but may equally have come about because of the high threat environment experienced at school without adequate availability of nurturing care and protection from staff *in loco parentis.*

While living in the boarding environment, the behaviours developed by boys to mitigate the relational, emotional, social and environmental threats seemed to work well enough for most, but these may have become second nature, or internalised in boys' understanding of how to relate to themselves, to others and the world around them. The men reported that they continued to employ previously learned strategies in situations where the threat was no longer present, and in some cases this introduced difficulties or further barriers to them having their emotional needs met.

The experience of getting close to partners, before feeling vulnerable and pulling back, was described by many as a repeating pattern that emerged in romantic relationships soon after leaving school and into adulthood. Avoidant or dismissive patterns of attachment in adults is often characterised by the avoidance of intimacy (due to a fear of rejection), an over-focus on one's own needs, difficulty disclosing thoughts and feelings to partners and a vulnerability to slights and rejections [28]. These were common patterns reported by the men interviewed and also fits with psychotherapeutic models of boarding school trauma. For some of the men, these difficulties were felt to be the barrier to experiencing close, intimate relationships, while others found enough resource through experience of a healthy relationship to overcome these challenges. This highlights that adult difficulties in relationships may take very different forms even for men united by the experience of boarding school. Not all men who have boarded become the stereotypical 'wounded leader' exhibiting extreme controlling behaviour as described by Nick Duffell. There are clearly different manifestations of boarding school trauma among adults and this may vary according to different family environments as well as what sorts of partners and jobs men find themselves in early on in adulthood when there may still be room for identity development.

The final theme, 'Anger and acceptance: different ways of living in the present', illustrates very different ways in which men have tried to come to terms with the long-term impacts that boarding school has had on their adult lives. Of course, at the time of interview each of the men may have been at a different stage of coming to terms with this and may well feel differently (more angry or more accepting) in the future. Although seemingly impacted by these early experiences, most of the men were in work, had partners, children and had avoided the need for contact with specialist mental health services. This too may relate to the degree to which they were somewhat privileged: they were all white men, had access to paid education, job opportunities and personal wealth. These factors are known to be associated with reduced distress [29] and may act as protective factors against early and ongoing threats to core needs.

In summary, our interviews with eleven male ex-boarders provide insights into their experiences with their narratives illustrating the ways in which their time at boarding school created a sense of powerlessness, challenged their ability to form intimate relationships and had a longer lasting impact on their lives into the present time. Overall, therefore, for these men, boarding school seems to have had a fundamental impact upon their sense of self and fundamentally their notion of masculinity. Therefore while the privileged outcomes of boarding school may have an 'opportunity cost' in terms of emotional health for some boarders, we must pose the question for those affected whether it is a price worth paying.

References

1 Dahl R. *More about boy: Tales of childhood.* New York: Puffin 2009.
2 Schaverien J. Boarding school syndrome: Broken attachments a hidden trauma. *Br J Psychother* 2011; 27. doi:10.1111/j.1752-0118.2011.01229.x.
3 Schaverien J. Boarding school: the trauma of the 'privileged' child. *J Anal Psychol* 2004; 49: 683–705. doi:10.1111/j.0021-8774.2004.00495.x.
4 Duffell N. *The making of them: The British attitude to children and the boarding school system.* London: Lone Arrow Press 2000. p31.
5 Ainsworth MS, Bowlby J. An ethological approach to personality development. *Am Psychol* 1991; 46: 333.
6 Daniel SIF. Adult attachment patterns and individual psychotherapy: A review. *Clin Psychol Rev* 2006; 26: 968–984.
7 Feeney JA, Noller P. Attachment style as a predictor of adult romantic relationships. *J Pers Soc Psychol* 1990; 58: 281.

8 Chapman DP, Whitfield CL, Felitti VJ, *et al.* Adverse childhood experiences and the risk of depressive disorders in adulthood. *J Affect Disord* 2004; 82. doi:10.1016/j.jad.2003.12.013.

9 Busby DM, Walker EC, Holman TB. The association of childhood trauma with perceptions of self and the partner in adult romantic relationships. *Pers Relatsh* 2011; 18: 547–561.

10 Purnell C. Childhood trauma and adult attachment. *Healthc Couns Psychother J* 2010; 10: 1–7.

11 Bryant RA, Creamer M, O'donnell M, *et al.* Separation from parents during childhood trauma predicts adult attachment security and post-traumatic stress disorder. *Psychol Med* 2017; 47: 2028–2035.

12 Pesonen A, Räikkönen K, Heinonen K, *et al.* Reproductive traits following a parent–child separation trauma during childhood: a natural experiment during World War II. *Am J Hum Biol Off J Hum Biol Assoc* 2008; 20: 345–351.

13 Duffell N, Basset T. *Trauma, abandonment and privilege: A guide to therapeutic work with boarding school survivors.* Abingdon: Routledge 2016.

14 van der Pol LD, Groeneveld MG, van Berkel SR, *et al.* Fathers' and mothers' emotion talk with their girls and boys from toddlerhood to preschool age. *Emotion* 2015; 15: 854.

15 Buck R. Nonverbal behavior and the theory of emotion: The facial feedback hypothesis. *J Pers Soc Psychol* 1980; 38: 811–824. doi:10.1037/0022-3514.38.5.811.

16 Levenson RW, Carstensen LL, Gottman JM. Influence of age and gender on affect, physiology, and their interrelations: A study of long-term marriages. *J Pers Soc Psychol* 1994; 67: 56.

17 Chaplin TM. Gender and emotion expression: A developmental contextual perspective. *Emot Rev* 2015; 7: 14–21.

18 Duffell N. *Wounded leaders: British elitism and the entitlement illusion – a psychohistory.* London: Lone Arrow Press 2014.

19 Poynting S, Donaldson M. Snakes and leaders: Hegemonic masculinity in ruling-class boys' boarding schools. *Men Masc* 2005; 7: 325–346. doi:10.1177/1097184X03260968.

20 Duffell N. 'Boarding school syndrome: Broken attachments a hidden trauma': Reply. *Br J Psychother* 2012; 28: 126–128. doi:10.1111/j.1752-0118.2012.01278.x.

21 Braun V, Clarke V. Using thematic analysis in psychology. *Qual Res Psychol* 2006; 3: 77–101. doi:10.1191/1478088706qp063oa.

22 Connell RW, Messerschmidt JW. Hegemonic masculinity. *Gend Soc* 2005; 19: 829–859. doi:10.1177/0891243205278639.

23 Golding K. *Nurturing attachments: Supporting children who are fostered or adopted.* London: Jessica Kingsley 2008.

24 White M. An Australian co-educational boarding school: A sociological study of Anglo-Australian and overseas students' attitudes from their own memoirs. *Int Educ J*; 5: 65–78.

25 van der Kolk BA. Developmental trauma disorder: Toward a rational diagnosis for children with complex trauma histories. *Psychiatr Ann* 2005; 35: 401–408. doi:10.3928/00485713-20050501-06.

26 Main M, Solomon J. Procedures for identifying infants as disorganized/disoriented during the Ainsworth Strange Situation. In: *Attachment in the preschool years: Theory, research, and intervention.* Chicago, IL: The University of Chicago Press 1990. 121–160.

27 Bacon H, Richardson S. Attachment theory and child abuse: an overview of the literature for practitioners. *Child Abus Rev* 2001; 10: 377–397. doi:10.1002/car.718.

28 Fraley RC, Brumbaugh CC, Marks MJ. The evolution and function of adult attachment: A comparative and phylogenetic analysis. *J Pers Soc Psychol* 2005; 89: 731–746. doi:10.1037/0022-3514.89.5.751.

29 Pickett K, Wilkinson R. The spirit level: A case study of the public dissemination of health inequalities research. In: *Health inequalities*. Oxford: Oxford University Press 2015. 282–296. doi:10.1093/acprof:oso/9780198703358.003.0020.

Chapter 4

It's not all down to boarding

Early family and peer relationships among boarders

James Lee, Jenny Wardman-Browne, Emma Hopkins, Susan McPherson and Penny Cavenagh

The importance of the role of caregivers in the early life of children has been clearly established. The way children are cared for in their early years is understood to play a key role in their long-term mental wellbeing and adult relationships [1]. Research on attachment has tended to focus on the negative outcomes of caregiver absence or maltreatment. It has explored the consequences arising from various contexts in which caregiving may be lacking and when biological parents are replaced by institutional forms of caregiving such as hospital settings [2], orphanages, foster homes and community child rearing cultures [3]. Research in these settings tends to find children displaying varying forms of disrupted attachment and negative long-term impacts. In these contexts, the age at which the parent-child attachment is broken varies, although a lot of attachment research has been based on examples where this occurs in early infancy, for example fostering and adoption in cases of maltreatment.

Boarding school similarly represents a form of institutionalised upbringing away from home and some of the knowledge learned from attachment research may be applicable or transferable to understanding the impact of boarding school. But it is also important to be aware of differences which might limit any comparisons. For example, children tend to begin boarding later on in childhood (age seven for junior boarders and 11 for senior boarders). There is also a significant difference between children being removed from families because of safeguarding concerns versus parents choosing to send their children to a residential school because of the perceived social and educational advantages it represents. Having said this, as discussed at length in previous chapters, British psychotherapy theories concerning boarding school imply that much of this context is immaterial since the core wound inflicted on a child sent to boarding school is the separation from home and parents.

Taken at face value, this perspective is in line with current UK law. According to the UK Children Act 1989, children are 'best looked after by their family unless an intervention … is essential' [4]. Later legislation places a duty on local authorities and independent schools to act to protect a child they suspect is or is likely to suffer harm, specifically stating that authorities can act if the child is not being cared for in a way that it would be reasonable to expect a parent to provide

DOI: 10.4324/9781003280491-4

[4]. Given that attachment theories, attachment research and research concerning other forms of institutional child rearing all point towards the potential for long-lasting harm of growing up away from families of origin, it could be argued that boarding schools might be an inherent safeguarding risk. Although there is a growing lobby calling for boarding schools to be closed down as an inherent safeguarding threat, there is relatively little momentum behind this lobby perhaps owing to a socio-economic narrative concerning abuse and neglect that focuses attention around safeguarding on low socio-economic status families [5] and because child protection is located in social work practice which is primarily concerned with disadvantaged communities [6].

Although it is difficult to totally eradicate safeguarding risks in all schools and particularly in boarding schools, there have been a number of developments in the last couple of decades to minimise risks. The Department for Education has introduced safeguarding policies and minimum national standards which are reviewed at regular intervals. Independent schools are inspected regularly and boarding schools more so by the Independent Schools Inspectorate. These policies are discussed in more detail in Chapter 7. These developments support claims by boarding school associations that boarding schools are not inherently a safeguarding risk; that boarding schools can not only provide a nurturing environment for children away from the family home, but can even enhance positive parental relationships by removing conflicts and distractions [7]. It has also been suggested that boarding can provide a shelter from dysfunctional families at home [8],[9]. We previously discussed the limitations of some of these studies and noted, for example, that studies showing positive impacts of boarding school are either based outside the UK and/or have been funded by organisations with conflicts of interest. Nevertheless, there is a body of attachment research, unrelated to boarding school, that points towards the possibility of children forming positive relationships with adults and peers other than those in their immediate family and that healthy adult attachment is not solely reliant on primary attachment figures' regular physical presence [10].

For example, research with young children removed from their family of origin and placed in foster care has indicated that after about two months in foster care, children previously neglected show signs of forming secure attachments with caregiving adults [11]. A review of studies with adopted children and adoptive families indicates that children who were abused or neglected early on are still able to form positive attachments with adoptive parents, although there still appear to be long-term impacts of early adversity on adult relationship styles in general [12]. This points to two possibilities. One, that it is theoretically possible (within attachment theory and research) that attending a residential school and being distant from parents for extended periods of time may not in and of itself prevent children developing secure attachments with alternative adult caregivers in addition to maintaining positive bonds with their parents. Second, if the family of origin of boarders is in any way neglectful, there is also potential for children sent to boarding school to develop secure attachments with alternative adults which may support the development of healthier adult attachment styles.

These possibilities would clearly depend on staff at boarding school being adequately nurturing, since the research referred to above primarily concerned foster and adoptive parents with an explicit intent to care for children likely to have been maltreated. There is plenty of literature to indicate that the availability of nurturing staff at British boarding schools cannot be taken for granted. However, these possibilities in turn raise further questions about what sorts of familial relationships exist in families who send their children to boarding school. Other research in this book, such as in Chapter 3, alludes to the important role of culture and attitudes within families in determining future adult wellbeing and healthy relationships, for example in relation to male stereotypes around expressing emotion and responding to power. Children who go to boarding school have not been permanently removed from their families like children in adoptive care have been and can (according to each family) continue to have contact through school holidays, *exeat* weekends and parental visits. Taking attachment theory as a broad body of knowledge extending beyond just early mother-infant relationships, it seems important to take into consideration that family, peers and boarding school staff all play some kind of role in the way that boarder identities form and relationship styles develop throughout childhood. It therefore seems important to ask what role relationships with family members and peers have in the development of ex-boarder adult wellbeing and relationships.

The current interview study aimed to explore the possibility that ex-boarder adult relationship difficulties may not be exclusively linked to separation from family caregivers in and of itself but rather could result from an interaction between various factors, including the nature of family and peer relationships prior to and during children's time at boarding school.

4.1 The research study

Participants for this study were drawn from the larger survey of ex-boarders described in Chapter 2. As described previously, participants were recruited via social media and through community networks rather than via therapists or survivor organisations. Those people who had completed the survey and indicated they would like to take part in an interview were contacted to provide further consent and to arrange a time for the interview. Interviews were recorded with consent and covered topics including early family life; relationships with parents in the context of school life; the impact of these on current relationships. Interviews were then transcribed verbatim and analysed following thematic analysis [13], as described in the previous chapter.

Sixteen people were interviewed for this study – eight men and eight women. At the time of interview, they were aged between 37 and 71 and so would have boarded from the 1950s to the 1990s. The youngest age any of them started boarding was four years old; less than half were 11 or older when they started boarding. Eleven had experienced some traumatic event in childhood such as death of a close friend or family member, parents' divorce, being extremely ill or having a traumatic sexual experience such as rape or molestation. Three of these traumatic experiences were sexual and these were all reported by men in the group. A third of participants were divorced or separated at the time of interview. All participants were White though described this in different ways when asked about their ethnicity (see Table 4.1). Twelve of the participants said that either one or both of their parents had attended boarding

Table 4.1 Participant characteristics.

Pseudonym	Gender	Age	Marital status	Children	Age started boarding	Highest qualification	Ethnicity
Tom	Male	37	Co-habiting	0	8	Masters	White British
Fiona	Female	47	Divorced	3	12	GCSE	White
Helen	Female	48	Married	2	13	Degree	European
David	Male	48	Married	2	12	Degree	White
Nick	Male	57	Married	2	12	Masters	White
Paul	Male	57	Divorced	2	7	Diploma	White British
Rose	Female	58	Married	2	4	Diploma	Caucasian
Piers	Male	58	Divorced	1	8	A Levels	White British
Duncan	Male	61	Married	3	Unknown	Diploma	Caucasian
Cara	Female	62	Married	4	6	Other	White British
Charlotte	Female	65	Single	0	10	Degree	White British
Bonnie	Female	66	Married	1	11	PhD	Caucasian
Mia	Female	68	Divorced	4	8	Degree	White British
Simon	Male	68	Separated	3	7	Degree	Caucasian
Emily	Female	69	Married	2	13	Masters	White
Jay	Male	71	Married	3	8	Degree	White British

school. Academic achievements were extremely varied ranging from GCSE up to PhD. Nevertheless, most were or had been in some form of work and at least seven were employed in professions relating to mental health such as psychology, counselling, psychotherapy or addiction support. This figure may be higher as some reported their occupation as retired without stating their previous occupation.

Following analysis of data, two main themes were identified that describe the experience of forming attachments prior to and while attending boarding school and how they relate to each other. The two themes are 'Institutionalised families and emotionally unavailable parents' and 'Peer relationships: the next best thing for emotional security'.

4.2 Theme 1: Institutionalised families and emotionally unavailable parents

This theme illustrates the ways in which some ex-boarders talked about their parents having been raised in institutional settings that encouraged conformity and discouraged vulnerability and emotional expression. These parents were perceived as distant, cold, emotionally illiterate, often coping with their own difficulties and emotionally unavailable to their children. Unreliable attachments with such parents seem to have been further undermined when parents unilaterally decided to send them to boarding school without discussion or concern about their emotional responses.

Participants described being raised in home environments in which there was a multi-generational experience of attending boarding schools. Attendance at boarding school was treated as a natural, normal part of upbringing, a family tradition.

> It was the family tradition both my parents had been, and my grandparents, at least two aunts... to the same school. I think I was the 13th member of my family to go to that boarding school.
>
> (Emily)

Yet this family tradition had fostered 'a never spoken about' repression of emotional communication among adults in the family. Parents would deny they had been harmed in any way by their experience and insisted that their time as boarders was wholly positive. According to one participant, their parents had both gone to boarding school and described it as 'the best thing that ever happened to them' (David).

Below, Simon seems to suggest that tradition and the paramount value placed on education had such a strong hold on the family that even when there are signs or hints in the family of negative effects (one uncle speaking out against it, a brother becoming 'subdued'), these are ignored and the child is sent away anyway.

If you wanted a good education you went to a private school and you made sacrifices to do it and my parents certainly did that. I know that my uncle … who also went to boarding school was adamantly opposed to boarding school, hated it, and wasn't going to send his kids there … And there is all sorts of stuff I can see in the family, but anyway, the decision to go there was essentially tradition if you will plus a desire to get an education. … I remember by mother saying that my older brother David went away a bright cheerful little kid and came back sort of much more subdued and so on. So, she somewhat recognised the impact the boarding school was having on him, but then I went off as well age seven.

(Simon)

Despite the benefits of boarding school exalted by parents, ex-boarders believed that boarding school was to blame for their parents being emotionally cut-off. As one participant explained:

I can look at my mum, my father, and understand their limitations on intimacy and emotion from boarding school.

(David)

Other participants also talked about their parents being limited in how they could communicate about emotions and how their parents avoided showing any vulnerability. Consequently, the decision to send the child to boarding school was not discussed openly with participants who claim that their feelings were never considered.

I remember being fairly shocked by the whole idea and buying a uniform and so on I found very shocking at the time … that the decision was made and there was no point in even … I would surely have said, 'I don't want to go', but there was no discussion about that, it was just 'well, that's what's going to happen'.

(Jay)

Well, by that time I was older obviously and I basically saw this letter from another school saying 'yes, we'd be pleased to interview [Charlotte]' or 'say hello to [Charlotte]' or whatever and I said, 'what's all this about?' and they'd deliberately left the letter on the table for me to find because they didn't know how to tell me.

(Charlotte)

This experience ranged from some reporting being talked to about boarding school but not feeling free to object, to others being surprised with an admissions letter and no further discussions. This was especially difficult to process when other siblings had not gone to boarding school – usually female siblings held back due to gendered expectations around education. This reasoning was not disclosed to the child at the time but only emerged later in adulthood.

The lack of discussion or consultation before a decision was made was sometimes followed by feelings of sadness and impotent rage over being ignored or rejected.

> I remember my dad saying this to me at one point... I remember being upset about something and him saying to me: 'you're not hurt, what are you even crying for, you're not hurt?' ... But that was just so typical of my dad. And so that's him having to shut things down from such an early age and then not allowing anyone else to have feelings or emotion that would come up.
>
> (Helen)

Strained emotional communication between parents and children appears to have followed these ex-boarders into adulthood. Mia describes writing a letter to her father before he died:

> I remember sending a letter to my dad before he died. I knew he was dying. I was told. He had 6 months to live and [I was] writing him a sloppy letter, and he was a very ... I think he was a bit autistic, my father actually. I knew he loved me, but he was unable to show emotion at all. And writing him a letter and saying you were a great dad and that I loved him, and he rang me up and he says, 'Hmm, thank you [Mia] for your letter and I am pleased that all of you like and admire each other so much.'
>
> (Mia)

Several participants seemed to be still looking for explanations or excuses for their parents' seeming lack of affection or their decision to send them away. In the quote above, Mia puts it down to her father being 'a bit autistic' and clearly craved the love that she believes was underneath his lack of emotional expression. Others describe their parents as lacking an ability to form secure attachments struggling with their own mental health difficulties including depression, substance misuse, gambling addictions and trauma, some of which had required hospitalisation. Some attributed their parents' emotional difficulties directly to their also having been to boarding school:

> My mother didn't know how to build an attachment ... So, at any opportunity, she was quite happy to dispense with being responsible for me.
>
> (Cara)

Another participant, Rose, implied her mother was uninterested rather than unable to form an attachment as she had other priorities and this seems to have left her anger about this abandonment still unresolved:

My mother was a single parent – my father died when I was very young so my mother was a single-parent and in her life she had always travelled around a lot and I think she wanted to carry on with that sort of life. ... So I think she did it because I think she wanted to work full-time, I don't think that's a reason to send someone to boarding school, and I think she did this because she wanted to carry on with her sort of life. It sounds harsh but I probably have quite a lot of residual anger around that, so it's probably quite difficult for me to be completely clear about why she did that. But that was the choice that she made.

(Rose)

Similarly, Charlotte felt her parents prioritised themselves over her and this likewise seems an unresolved resentment:

I think instinctively I knew that they actually wanted me to be a boarder. Because I think their marriage worked better without children.

(Charlotte)

This meant that prior to attending boarding school some participants felt they lacked strong emotional bonds with their parents. They described a lack of physical intimacy at times as well as emotional invalidation.

[My father] was emotionally retarded for his whole life, poor old boy. He just really couldn't sort of communicate proper emotion ... I think he only ever shook my hand once in all the years ... And he had great difficulty communicating, his sort of his general feeling to his daughters particularly ... Both his parents were doctors, it was very early days of medicine, I just don't think they had any time for him ... And then he and his brother were left to be brought up by the cook, the housekeeper and private education.

(Duncan)

Some participants felt that the problems their parents faced, and the subsequent lack of parent-child bond made boarding school a refuge in some ways. One participant commented:

I thought [boarding school] is the lesser of the evils because my mother was fairly depressive, as it was called in those days, and the implacable father ... It also, it felt like it got me, conveniently, it's a dreadful thought, but out of the way. And he believed, or certainly he told me on at least one occasion that he thought that my coming home made my mother ill [depression].

(Jay)

However another participant indicates that having been brought up by parents lacking affection or emotional expression meant that she was unable to cope with the way this left her unbearably alone in her own mind when sent away to boarding school:

> Oh, it was terrible. First of all you weren't allowed to cry. I was brought up [by] parents who are like that as well … so the fact that I would wake up really early in the morning, I will go down to the bathroom and I will sit and cry on my own. I basically lived in the private world on my own.
>
> (Fiona)

Despite their often overwhelming unhappiness, girls in particular felt the need to shield their parents from their suffering. They took responsibility to protect their parents rather than expecting their parents to protect them. Fiona explains how she received messages not to worry or upset her parents:

> Although that wasn't a spoken rule and you were never told you not allowed to cry, I remember the first time I spoke to my parents I could barely speak because all I wanted to do was cry and I remember the matron saying to me, 'Don't, because you'll just upset your parents'. And that was it, I realised then I better not cry because I'd upset them.
>
> (Fiona)

Mia explains how she desperately wanted her parents to know how she felt and for them to carry her home but also wanted to protect them so they would not be upset:

> I can remember getting out in my night dress and throwing notes to my parents in the wind to tell them how unhappy I was hoping that they would be carried home. I must have been quite little to think that would happen but also I must've been really unhappy but I never told my parents … I never would have dreamt of telling them I was unhappy … I wouldn't want to upset them.
>
> (Mia)

4.3 Theme 2: Peer relationships: The next best thing for emotional security

This theme illustrates how, once at boarding school, participants encountered adults who were emotionally neglectful and actively disdainful of any expressions of sadness or vulnerability, especially homesickness. Ex-boarders talked about how they sought out peers instead for emotional support, soothing and a form of secure base. However, prior experiences with adults in their family and adults in the school had taught them that too much vulnerability is risky and may lead to rejection. In addition to this, because of the turnover of students and lack of control in determining who they would spend time with, participants described a hesitancy to form strong relationships which they may lose without warning. Consequently, boarders learned to either assimilate with the needs of the cohort or face bullying and isolation from peers.

The vast majority of the ex-boarder accounts of their transition into boarding school stress that staff offered little to nothing in the form of pastoral care and emotional support. Instead, a virtue was made of moving on from difficult feelings to focus on the day-to-day activities and requirements of the institution.

> There was no support whatsoever. Basically, stiff upper lip, you know. Stop crying, no, you don't need your mother. Just man up and do it.
>
> (Simon)

In these environments, adults were at best absent and at worst potential sources of further distress. Many interviews depicted staff in student liaison roles (such as matrons and teaching staff) as being aloof, unapproachable, and at times actively hostile. Some participants even described adults as a potential threat with rumours of potential sexual exploitation; some such rumours were reportedly substantiated in due course.

Unsure of how to process difficult emotions and actively discouraged from doing so, participants described repressing their feelings. These feelings, especially homesickness, were perceived as particularly dangerous to talk about. Even among peers, it was difficult for participants to discuss these feelings as the shared coping mechanism was not to acknowledge difficult feelings.

> You wanted to fit in, so you learned very rapidly not to be emotional, not to talk about parents or anything like that, because it was too risky.
>
> (Simon)

Many ex-boarders experienced relationships as either unreliable or hostile. Unreliable owing to the ease with which caregivers severed the parent-child bond as well as the impermanence of fellow boarders. Hostile owing to the perceived aloofness or brutality of adult staff at boarding school. This seemed to promote a sense of isolation masked as independence.

> You couldn't, as a little kid, you couldn't trust anyone there. The only person you could rely on was yourself.
>
> (Simon)

Distrust of relationships in general was therefore a common response among participants. Having had family relationships severed, adult support absent or

actively hostile, boarders described an often indifferent boarding school admin-
istration that would make forging reliable peer relationships difficult.

> Friendships were potentially quite dangerous in a way. You could be so
> dependent on them and things could change. You want to go back to
> school after term and the first thing that would determine how your year
> went was who you would be sharing a dorm with ... I don't know who
> decided that. It certainly wasn't us.
>
> (Rose)

As highlighted above, friendships were risky and could be 'dangerous',
although the term 'bullying' was not normally used by participants. Nevertheless, it is clear that within the boarding school environment, a child is unable
to escape or find a safe place as they live in the same physical space as those they
may find intimidating. Rose highlights here how peers could pick on each other:

> They fold your bottom sheet up so when you get into bed you can't put
> your feet down ... it was a nasty thing to do to someone, when you get
> into bed and your bottom sheet has been folded up and you can't put
> your feet down.
>
> (Rose)

While the security of relationships was put into doubt, many participant
accounts describe having to ingratiate themselves with a social group as a
matter of survival. These relationships helped to protect them from bullying
and also provided important emotional connections. There were also indications
of an unarticulated sense of camaraderie in the boarding school experience and
of missing home and family.

> I think that was very hidden and yet there is a sense which you are all in the
> same boat, all in the same school and there is a ... camaraderie of sorts.
>
> (Paul)

> I remember surviving. I remember that the deal was to survive, to make
> sure you had the right friends to be in the right place in the play-
> ground ... I don't remember anything academically at all.
>
> (Cara)

When peer relationships are formed for survival, many take on the form of
surrogate family members, providing emotional soothing and something resem-
bling a secure base to return to, albeit not the real deal of an adult caregiver.

> But you're all just children and you're trying to play adult roles. You're
> trying to advise each other and help each other and it's pretty crazy when

you think about it. And how you're trying to manage all these emotions and you're desperate for a mother and you have no mother and so you're relying on other girls to be your mother and your friends and everything else.

(Helen)

Participants described how members of a social group would develop a keen sense of which peers required support. This, along with the dual threat that relationships represented, led to a shared sense of emotional hypervigilance among peers. These relationships were sometimes seen as reparative not only for the overall experience of boarding but for prior dysfunctional family dynamics.

Having very intense friendships with people is something that's normal at boarding school, because it replaces relationships you're not having at home for some people who have very bad relationships at home, but friendships have become as important if not more important than their family relationships.

(Mia)

Some participants described a difficulty in connecting with their peers however – partly a consequence of not being able to successfully compartmentalise difficult feelings of separation and leaving home.

I actually went out of my way not to make friends to be honest because I kept thinking in my head when I see my mum and dad they'll understand, take me out, I won't be here for longer anyway. That was my sort of mentality at the time that's how I thought according to how I felt.

(Fiona)

Being unable to conform to the social needs of their peers, some of those interviewed described themselves as loners who would withdraw into solitary activities (such as reading in the library). This isolation, combined with the absence of adult support, left them vulnerable to bullying, further deepening a distrust of relationships.

Participants often looked back on their life and reflected on difficulties they had with trust. One common reflection that participants spoke about was difficulties they had in their adult relationships as a partner, friend, child and parent. Cara highlights her mistrust and fear of being let down by others and so relies only on herself:

I'm really cautious around my friendships. I don't rely on my friends I could never go to my friends for help really. I've always been adamant as I look out for myself really.

(Cara)

4.4 Discussion

Ex-boarders in this study were sixteen males and females who had been at British boarding schools between the 1950s and 1990s. We know a little about them in terms of work history, marriage, children and family background. We also know from the survey data that three of the men interviewed had a traumatic sexual experience during their childhood but we do not know if this occurred at school or elsewhere. Given the nature of the findings, it is particularly interesting that a significant proportion of participants worked professionally in psychology related fields and are likely to have been aware of the concept of 'boarding school syndrome' prior to the interview. Some described having undergone personal therapy specific to boarding school syndrome, having researched the topic, or having attended survivors' group meetings. This should be taken into account when considering the ways in which some participants described their parents in particular ways, referring to terms such as being 'emotionally cut off' and presenting a 'false self'. This may bias the results to an extent since some participants may have retrospectively created an understanding of their parents' characters and their relationships with them through the lens of boarding school syndrome. This does not negate participants' experiences however, since they may argue that these concepts, when they discovered them, simply provided a very good fit for what they remember about their childhood. Nevertheless, future investigations may benefit from participants naïve to the concept of boarding school syndrome to explore how reliable these findings are.

Some helpful findings have emerged from this study which provide a slightly different angle on the psychological impacts of boarding school. Specifically, the first theme, 'Institutionalised families and emotionally unavailable parents', highlights the importance of considering family and home environments as at least equally important as boarding school in helping to shape the future adult. This finding also emerged from the study presented in Chapter 3, but the present study provides a much stronger emphasis on this perhaps because the interviews specifically aimed to explore the topic of early family life. Specifically, the theme demonstrates how early relationships for most of these boarders were already impaired prior to attending boarding school, often by a family tradition of boarding. This meant that some families were in a sense institutionalised into the emotionally hostile culture of boarding school. In many instances participants described their parents having traits that prevented the necessary process of forming secure bonds between parents and children. These traits, such as projecting a false self, being emotionally cut-off, and dismissive of others' emotional states clearly fit with the descriptions of 'boarding school syndrome' but as mentioned above, were also probably primed to an extent by participants' knowledge of these theories [14],[15].

These findings challenge some of the core assumptions of British psychotherapy literature on boarding school which claim that the boarding school experience, in and of itself, represents a primary trauma and directly leads to poor attachment styles and poor mental wellbeing in adulthood. As previously discussed, attachment research has shown poor early attachment to caregivers can have a detrimental effect on later adult relationships [16],[17]. Our findings are in line with this and may indicate that emotional issues in boarders may have taken root prior to boarding school. However, attachment research also indicates that early poor attachment can either be repaired or the consequences mitigated by the availability of alternative nurturing adults such as adoptive parents. The narratives presented by participants in this study and in other studies in this book indicate that boarding schools have not traditionally provided those sorts of alternative adult relationships and have instead sometimes offered the opposite of nurturing staff. Accounts of this are however historic and cannot be assumed to be the case in current boarding schools.

Early family experiences left these ex-boarders ill equipped to cope with the demands of boarding school, with many stating that discussing feelings was frowned upon and self-reliance was praised over vulnerability. This in turn was entirely reinforced by the boarding school environment. Participants consistently described an environment in which open expression of vulner-ability was at best socially ostracising and at worse an invitation to abuse.

The second theme, 'Peer relationships: the next best thing for emotional security', illustrates how peer relationships were forged out of necessity as the only available alternative to safe relationships with adults. Participants recall desperate efforts to adhere to the socially accepted behaviours of not directly discussing difficult feelings of being abandoned by parents. They formed peer friendships to fulfil their need for surrogate family roles and to relieve homesickness.

This theme is consistent with research that shows children and adolescents in particular naturally orient towards peers as they get older [18]. However, where this theme may depart from the understanding of this seemingly common and natural development is that many participants describe these peer relationships in survivalist terms and state that they only exist within the boarding environment. Moreover, they are not in addition to positive rela-tionships with adults, they are instead of adult relationships – formed out of a lack rather than enabled by the presence of an early secure bond with parents.

Earlier we referred to the UK Children Act 1989 which states that children are 'best looked after by their family unless an intervention … is essential' [4]. We also referred to legislation which requires independent schools to act to protect a child they suspect is or is likely to suffer harm [4]. The lack of pas-toral care experienced by ex-boarders in this study could (if it had occurred in more recent times after this legislation was in place) constitute a failure to provide the care that 'would be reasonable to expect a parent to give them' [4]. However, what our findings suggest is that there is no guarantee things would have been better for these participants if looked after at home. The long-standing institutionalisation of some families seems to have created a complicated intergenerational pattern which would unlikely be solved immediately if boarding schools were abolished as some authors have called for.

We cannot conclude from the research presented so far whether the peer relationships as 'the next best thing' are not in any case the better option under the circumstances as one participant alluded to. It should also be acknowledged that the participants in this study attended boarding school over 30 years ago and there have been many changes in the culture of contemporary boarding schools since this time, as well as the range of support services now available to ex-boarders. Indeed, the recognition of supportive practices to promote and sustain psychological wellbeing for those attending boarding school have also been embedded into good practice guidance and policies [19],[20]. Ofsted standards for boarding seek to ensure best practice and boarders are now encouraged to be in regular communication with their parents [21].

In summary, this study has described complex interactions between boarders, their relationship to parents pre-boarding, their relationship to their peers while boarding, and the institutions of boarding schools themselves. While early family life appears to have instilled relational habits, such as presenting a false self and being emotionally cut-off, boarding school then reinforced and promoted this by removing what parental security there was and often offering little in the way of pastoral care. What this study adds to the existing literature is the notion that intergenerational experiences of boarding may already set the stage for poor attachment styles to early caregivers, with parents characterised as emotionally withdrawn. This leads to later difficulties in establishing secure relationships with peers in and out of boarding school settings.

References

1 Bowlby J. Attachment and loss: Retrospect and prospect. *Am J Orthopsych* 1982; 52: 664–678. doi:10.1111/j.1939-0025.1982.tb01456.x.
2 Ainsworth MS, Bowlby J. An ethological approach to personality development. *Am Psychol* 1991; 46: 333–341. doi:10.1037/0003-066X.46.4.333.
3 Weiss Y, Shilkret R. The importance of the peer group in the Israeli kibbutz for adult attachment style. *Smith Coll Stud Soc Work* 2010; 80: 2–19. doi:10.1080/00377310903504841.
4 Foster D. An overview of child protection legislation in England. *House Commons Libr Brief Pap* 2020; 6787. https://researchbriefings.files.parliament.uk/documents/SN06787/SN06787.pdf.
5 Featherstone B, Firmin C, Gupta A, *et al.* The social model and contextual safeguarding: Key messages for practice. 2020. www.csnetwork.org.uk/en/publications/the-social-model-and-contextual-safeguarding-key-messages-for-practice.
6 Parton N. Social work, child protection and politics: Some critical and constructive reflections. *Br J Soc Work* 2014; 44: 2042–2056. doi:10.1093/bjsw/bcu091.

7 Martin AJ, Papworth B, Ginns P, *et al.* Boarding school, academic motivation and engagement, and psychological well-being: A large-scale investigation. *Am Educ Res J* 2014; 51. doi:10.3102/0002831214532164.

8 Duffell N. *The making of them: The British attitude to children and the boarding school system.* London: Lone Arrow Press 2000.

9 Schaverien J. *Boarding school syndrome: The psychological trauma of the 'privileged' child.* Abingdon: Routledge 2015. doi:10.4324/9781315716305.

10 Howes C, Spieker S. Attachment relationships in the context of multiple caregivers. In: Cassidy J, Shaver P, eds. *Handbook of attachment: Theory, research, and clinical applications.* New York: Guilford Press 2008.

11 Howes C, Segal J. Children's relationships with alternative caregivers: The special case of maltreated children removed from their homes. *J Appl Dev Psychol* 1993; 14: 71–81. doi:10.1016/0193-3973(93)90024-P.

12 Raby KL, Dozier M. Attachment across the lifespan: insights from adoptive families. *Curr Opin Psychol* 2019; 25: 81–85. doi:10.1016/j.copsyc.2018.03.011.

13 Braun V, Clarke V. Using thematic analysis in psychology. *Qual Res Psychol* 2006; 3: 77–101. doi:10.1191/1478088706qp063oa.

14 Schaverien J. Boarding school syndrome: Broken attachments a hidden trauma. *Br J Psychother* 2011; 27. doi:10.1111/j.1752-0118.2011.01229.x.

15 Duffell N. 'Boarding school syndrome: Broken attachments a hidden trauma': Reply. *Br J Psychother* 2012; 28: 126–128. doi:10.1111/j.1752-0118.2012.01278.x.

16 McCarthy G, Maughan B. Negative childhood experiences and adult love relationships: The role of internal working models of attachment. *Attach Hum Dev* 2010; 12: 445–461. doi:10.1080/14616734.2010.501968.

17 Girme YU, Jones RE, Fleck C, *et al.* Infants' attachment insecurity predicts attachment-relevant emotion regulation strategies in adulthood. *Emotion* 2021; 21: 260–272. doi:10.1037/emo0000721.

18 Guassi Moreira JF, Tashjian SM, Galván A, *et al.* Parents versus peers: Assessing the impact of social agents on decision making in young adults. *Psychol Sci* 2018; 29: 1526–1539. doi:10.1177/0956797618778497.

19 Anderson E. *Residential and boarding education and care for young people.* Abingdon: Routledge 2004. doi:10.4324/9780203694534.

20 Department for Education. Boarding schools: National minimum standards. 2012. www.gov.uk/government/publications/boarding-schools-national-minimum-standards.

21 Greene H, Greene M. *The Greenes' guide to boarding schools.* 1st edition. Lawrenceville, NJ: Petersons.

Chapter 5

The impact of boarding school on adult eating behaviour

Alexandra Priestner, Jane Ogden, Penny Cavenagh and Susan McPherson

Eating problems referred to as disordered eating behaviours include weight fluctuations; specific and rigid rules surrounding food and exercise; significant guilt or shame around food consumption; compensatory behaviours in relation to consuming food or over exercising; and a preoccupation with food [1]. Eating disorders are more pronounced forms of disordered eating behaviour, characterised by 'abnormal' eating behaviours and negative self-image. The two most prominent eating disorders are anorexia nervosa and bulimia nervosa, which are formal psychiatric diagnoses [2]. Disordered eating and eating disorders have been increasing recently, as has the prevalence of obesity in both adults and children [3]. Disordered eating tended to emerge in childhood or adolescence and there are many possible drivers including psychological factors, family, broader society and school.

Known psychological drivers include perfectionism, compliancy and impaired autonomy [4] as well obsessive personality traits [5]. Low self-esteem and body consciousness can also play a role as teenagers may try to alter their appearance through diet [6]. Attachment styles are linked with eating behaviour, for example, insecure attachment styles are associated with anorexia nervosa, bulimia nervosa and binge eating disorder [7],[8], probably because people turn to food rather than relationships to manage difficult emotions.

Parents' eating behaviours are known to strongly influence their children's eating behaviour [9] probably through parental control over food, modelling behaviour, formation of food habits and preferences in the family and transmission of food attitudes [10, 11, 12, 13, 14]. Social attitudes also play a role in eating behaviours. The ideal of a 'perfect' body shape infers subliminal messages that achievement and success are gained through being thin, resulting in a pressure to conform [15],[16] and a 'fear of fatness' [17]. Women and girls are more likely to have body dissatisfaction and to engage in disordered eating [18, 19, 20] although men and boys are more likely to engage in exercise behaviours to compensate their diet [21]. Anorexia Nervosa and Bulimia Nervosa are more common in upper-class and middle-class girls from developed countries [22] although we are now seeing increases among other socioeconomic groups [23].

DOI: 10.4324/9781003280491-5

In terms of the school environment, socialisation with peers and the pressure and focus on achievement can influence eating behaviours [24, 25, 26]. Many of the factors associated with the development of disordered eating may be exacerbated by attending boarding school. As discussed in previous chapters, children who attend boarding school may have disrupted attachments leading to an insecure attachment style [27]; and this may result in the use of food for emotional regulation. We have also seen that boarders can experience extreme stress, homesickness, academic pressure, fear of bullying and a lack of parental support which could all be expressed in a problematic relationship with food [28]. Historically, food had been tightly regulated for boarders with strict daily routines centred around mealtimes with limited choice or control. There is evidence of fairly high prevalence of eating disorders in boarding schools, especially in all-girls' schools [29] but little is known about the long-term impact of boarding school on eating behaviour. In this chapter we present findings of a study exploring the food-related experiences of women who attended boarding school and their thoughts about how their current relationship with food has been influenced by boarding school experiences.

5.1 The research study

We carried out interviews with 17 adult women who had attended boarding school for at least one year during their childhood. Although five were recruited via psychotherapy contacts, the majority were recruited through general social media advertising. Topics discussed in interviews covered women's eating experiences at different time periods along with the impact and influence of boarding schooling. Women taking part all felt that they currently or previously had some sort of difficulty in their relationship with food. Difficulties varied in impact, complexity and duration. Thirteen said they struggled with 'disordered eating behaviours' either relating to restriction and/or bingeing. Most reported their difficulties to be lifelong and debilitating. Only two had managed to find relief from these as they progressed through life. Two women had been treated for diagnosed eating disorders. Two did not have 'disordered eating behaviours' but felt that they were 'controlled' in relation to eating and felt anxious around obtaining food. Participants were excluded if they had current severe mental health difficulties or were currently receiving psychiatric care.

The 17 women were aged between 19 and 73 years old and had boarded between 2 and 10 years, having started boarding between 6 and 16 years old. All but one had attended and all-girls boarding school. See Table 5.1.

The interviews were transcribed and analysed using thematic analysis as described in previous chapters. We constructed four key themes to present our analysis. These were 'The comfort of tuck in response to abandonment'; 'Body image mandates: friends and family scripts'; 'Boarding as a full-time competition'; and 'Food as a self-defeating rebellion'.

Table 5.1 Characteristics of participants.

Pseudonym	Age at interview	Age started boarding	Length of attendance
Sophie	73	Aged 7	10 years
Emily	46	Aged 16	2 years
Isabelle	63	Aged 6	10 years
Evelyn	49	Aged 11	7 years
Charlotte	42	Aged 12	7 years
Alice	43	Aged 12	7 years
Violet	43	Aged 11	8 years
Imogen	26	Aged 11	5 years
Christina	25	Aged 9	7 years
Harriet	19	Aged 16	2 years
Rose	52	Aged 16	2 years
Mabel	19	Aged 6	9 years
Anna	60	Aged 12	5 years
Gracie	70	Aged 9	10 years
Ruby	66	Aged 8	8 years
Amelia	46	Aged 7	9 years
Maisie	38	Aged 7	4 years

5.2 Theme 1: The comfort of tuck in response to abandonment

Similar to ex-boarders' experiences presented in earlier chapters, several of the women discussed challenging family dynamics in their childhood such as feeling unwanted or uncared for by their parents, sometimes because they had been to boarding school themselves. They talked about parents' lack of emotional support and suppression of emotions within the family home as well as in the boarding school environment. However, more specifically, these women seemed to make a number of links between the painful aspects of being sent to boarding school and the use of food as a substitute for comfort – specifically tuck, sweets and treats. Initially this manifested as seeing the provision of tuck by parents as some sort of sign that their parents still cared for them in spite of the abandonment.

> Yeah … even if you sent your child off to school with a tuck box and a pair of [inaudible], I know it sounds tripe but it kind of suggests somebody gives a shit. When you don't have that you kind of thing, mmm, does that mean they don't?
> (Isabelle)

Women described accessing the warmth they desired through puddings with custard, or comfort through calorie dense foods such as cakes, chocolate, and sweets. Comfort food then became an important part of the boarding experience overall as it provided something they felt boarding school was lacking – warmth, comfort, and love.

> There was a real deficit for pleasure and love … so I started to reach out for stuff which could provide me with some … elements of love, you know, when somebody gives you food that's usually love, so I think that it deprived me of … love basically … and to a large extent care.
>
> (Sophie)

Some women explained how, while at school, restrictions on treats were gradually lifted as they progressed through the years, highlighting the way that access to sugary food was associated with increasing hierarchy within the school system.

> It sort of fell into two camps, because we were sort of denied food … when we got older we were allowed toast, finally when we were 16, and that was a big thing, then I got really fat as I ate like 16 pieces of toast a day with sugar on.
>
> (Violet)

The pleasure of tuck and treats was in stark contrast to the main meals provided by school which were felt to be distinctly lacking in love or warmth in content and delivery.

> Boarding school was quite a cold British place… the teachers, the house, the woman who was in charge of the house had not a shot of warmth in her body, no warmth whatsoever, she was just there to make sure we went to meals and she was a very unemotional woman.
>
> (Emily)

Through the association of certain types of food (sweets and treats) with comfort and happiness, some of the women reflected on how this association resulted in difficulties in later life, including alcohol dependence or weight problems.

> I think it was purely comfort. There was no reward about it, it was something that I knew, it was instant pleasure and instant, a bit of instant happiness was what it was, I think in many ways it paved the way for the alcoholism later, like 'just eat this marshmallow and you'll feel better'.
>
> (Sophie)

5.3 Theme 2: Body image mandates: Friends and family scripts

Potentially incompatible with the craving for comfort food with high sugar content, were the ideas about appropriate body shape and weight imposed on the women we interviewed. Beliefs about weight, body shape and diet tended to be formed initially within the family home but seemed to be compounded by being at boarding school. Beliefs held within the family pertaining to body image and appearance were projected onto them from an early age, altering their eating behaviours. These dynamics were often directed at the participants by their mothers, but in a few cases, fathers also held strong appearance related beliefs.

> I think she was aspiring to this, this image, that was partly her, partly the family that she wanted ... something in her head, I don't know quite what it was, but she wanted, it was just, we didn't go that many places or anything, but she had this idea of what she wanted her family to be and somehow felt that I spoiled that.
>
> (Anna)

> My father was weight-conscious ... he's lean and strong, very fit ... he's quite proud to say he weighs the same as he did on his wedding day, so he's got a strong physique. He's sort of controlled, and I think he equates being ... overweight with being unattractive, but also with being slightly weak.
>
> (Emily)

Some received very strong messages around the social repercussions of being overweight.

> Like if someone's fat then they would say 'you don't want to end up like that' or laugh at them, or even watching TV you would point out who is the fattest person and say 'oh gosh, I would kill myself if I looked like that'.
>
> (Christina)

Some of the women were directly criticised by their parents about their weight which had a detrimental impact on their self-esteem or thoughts about their bodies throughout their lives.

> ...then my dad, he was visiting me and we went for a run one day and he was really big on me getting a lot of physical activity because I was 'fat' and he was like 'oh my gosh, you are really fat, you need to lose weight ASAP', and he was like mad at me, as I was wearing shorts and he could see the fat.
>
> (Harriet)

While these scripts about acceptable body size tended to be received prior to boarding, the messages were reinforced by peers and experiences at boarding school. This was not immediate since, food was initially seen as a desirable, comforting thing and could enable popularity; but eventually there was a radical shift towards food as something that must be avoided in order to maintain an acceptable weight.

> Then food became something to be resisted, it became cool not to eat, it became kind of, it became very cool to be thin.
>
> (Charlotte)

Some spoke about comparing each other's bodies and judging appearance and weight.

> ...we used to like lie down and see if anything like flopped, like if any skin like moved or whatever, so I went from this like, gentle place to this like, competitive, like 'how does your body look?'.
>
> (Amelia)

Many of the women spoke about the danger of being overweight, or that individuals who did not conform to the ideal would be bullied.

> ...if you weren't sporty and you ate quite a lot of food, you were bullied, people really teased you, and I remember the, the first year and people were going on the apple diet, people were just eating apples, we were like 12 or 13 really, really young, then food became this battle ground.
>
> (Amelia)

For most, these scripts learned early on before and during school have stuck with them into their adult lives.

> You think after all these years, you know 50 years later, it wouldn't still influence, but it's almost like an indoctrination isn't it.
>
> (Ruby)

5.4 Theme 3: Boarding as full-time competition

Worrying about weight and appearance may be a fairly common trend among teenage girls but the boarding school environment may have made these concerns more intense. In particular, those interviewed described how being surrounded by others all day at school meant they had no privacy and were being constantly observed and judged in relation to their body, appearance and eating. This impacted on their eating behaviour, attitude to sports, romantic relationships, friendships and self-esteem.

> ... you would be watched to see how you were eating your food ... there was this manners system and you either went up or down the grades ... I

think the bottom was something like a piglet, and then the top was a royal guest.

(Amelia)

This judgemental atmosphere felt amplified due to the lack of privacy and lack of opportunity to be alone. Girls were required to change clothing in front of other people resulting in more frequent exposure to body related judgements.

Your teachers would watch you get changed ... I used to try and get changed behind the curtains and people would be like 'oh come on, come on out', and it was really intrusive, there's no privacy whatsoever.

(Christina)

Food was a central part of the competitive school environment either in relation to being rewarded with food or, in contrast, competition around ability to restrict food, creating a paradox. On the one hand there was a fear of not being liked and being rewarded or manipulated with food which had stuck with women into adulthood.

You then have got the prefect who, at any house, whoever it is, who is allocating the food on the basis of, who they like, or who they think has behaved well, on top of 'oh you have been a really good girl today so here we go, I'll give you another dollop of this' ... it's a very ... manipulative way of ... dealing with people.... [As an adult] there is something inside of me that needs to be ... thought of as being an okay person, so I can't normally withstand it if, people thinking that somehow ... I am not doing an okay job, that I am lesser than, it is dependent, I won't get as good slice of the cake.

(Anna)

Food was used by other boarders as a tool for gaining popularity, asserting status and to control others. Thus, a strong symbolic link was formed at boarding school between status, popularity and the giving and receiving of food.

Everyone knew this, it was like common ground ... four people got corners, so maybe another 10 or 15 people got edge, then everyone else got middle, which was shit. So, it was this huge thing you know, who gets the corners of the birthday girl's cake ... it was a big deal for everyone, not just me, like everyone was quite interested in that, like it was a symbol, it wasn't just about the cake being nice, it was a statement, a public statement about who I prefer, like who are my favourite three or four people.

(Charlotte)

On the other hand, there was also a drive to compete with other girls in their dieting and weight loss practices. The women shared memories where food was used as a tool for popularity, such as being invited for toast, midnight feasts or comparisons around what was in one's tuck box. They shared the incongruence of these concepts as they felt pressure to be thin to fit in, but then also wanted to attend and overindulge when invited to social events involving food.

> I think by starting to diet because I was trying to fit in with other people, was probably my biggest fall down, and my sister was the same, and both of us have yo-yoed all of our lives, from then.
>
> (Ruby)

Having said this, not all aspects of food consumption at boarding school were competitive. One woman enjoyed the social aspect of mealtimes at boarding school and the camaraderie associated with making toast with friends.

> I guess it's also the times when you are in classes and things it's not so sociable but mealtimes is when you socialise so again you fit in, make friends, you are all making toast... food was always like an exciting chaotic environment, everyone is there, there is so much going so I guess, you get a lot of social feedback from eating like if you weren't eating the only ways you would be able to do that would be to go and hide in the loo and then obviously you would miss out on so much social interaction, so I guess social.
>
> (Imogen)

Nevertheless, positive experiences relating to food were relatively rare across the set of interviews.

5.5 Theme 4: Food as a self-defeating rebellion

Among this complex dynamic of high sugar food as comfort versus a threat to weight along with the intensity of competition sited in food practices, food seemed to manifest for many women as a focus of rebellion in different forms. Because food was controlled and restricted either by parents or at boarding school, it became more desirable inspiring ways of navigating rules in order to obtain food illicitly. This rebellion eventually, however, led to lifelong habits such as secretive eating, hoarding or over-eating – even when as adults there were no longer any threats or controls making these food practices unnecessary and potentially harmful.

Women recalled not being allowed certain treats or sweets, which in turn made them seek these out as soon as they did become available.

I think food became a bit forbidden ... naughty ... illicit rebellion ... I remember being at countless little kids' parties and no parents around, or not my parents and other peoples' parents didn't give a shit about how many crisps I had eaten so it was like the opportunity was there, the gloves are off.

(Charlotte)

The concept of tuck and treats at boarding school being restricted or against the rules increased their desirability and value to the extent that at times nothing else seemed more important.

I have got a really horrible story ... but it's very shaming, which was the tuck shop where we got this tiny bit of sweetness was so important to me, that I was in the queue one day and there was this fire door and it shut on my friend's thumb, and it severed her thumb, pretty much, and I stayed in the queue as it was more important to me to get the sweets.

(Evelyn)

For some, explicitly disordered eating became a conscious form of rebellion against school as well as the rest of the world.

The bulimic behaviour itself was a kind of anarchic, two fingers up at the world type of behaviour, everyone can fuck off at the point in time.

(Emily)

The eating and the times I've been overweight ... in my life, that in a sense has been a kind of rebellion, but it's more comfort eating.

(Charlotte)

As a corollary to over-eating as a rebellion, some of the women explained how food aversions in adult life also developed as a reaction to excessive control imposed on them at boarding school in that being forced to finish their plates, including foods they disliked, meant as an adult they could now rebel by avoiding those foods they were forced to eat.

A lot of it was, you just had to eat it all, whether you liked it or not, I have a lot of food aversions, as I was forced to eat things that were quite nasty or badly cooked.

(Maisie)

Some women talked about how it was difficult to learn how to self-regulate as new choices became available and adult autonomy emerged. For example, because tuck sometimes 'disappeared' or was taken away, this left a fear that any food they had would disappear and thus the instinct to eat food straight away.

I couldn't really rationalise why I did that, but it was in case they dis-appeared, it goes back to, when you have them you eat them, otherwise you will lose them. It's that logical part of your brain that goes 'you are an adult now you don't need to do that, it's not going to disappear if you put them in the cupboard'.

(Maisie)

Similarly, some talked about how hoarding food or secretive eating devel-oped from a childhood instinct to find ways of getting around the rules and restrictions imposed at boarding school.

I went to uni and I became quite a secret eater, I used to like hoard food and ... literally go to a shop and buy loads of food that I had never been allowed up until that point.

(Amelia)

For most, these minor or major rebellions, ways of circumventing rules, restrictions and limited autonomy led to the formation of unhealthy eating behaviours in adulthood. For some, this led to very serious weight issues in adulthood requiring physical intervention.

I have now had a gastric sleeve operation and I've lost 10 stone, but the mental food issues haven't gone away ... I can no longer have massive meals and that's that, but do you know what I would rather do, I would rather miss that meal and have the snacks, because it hasn't sorted out my brain, my brain has the same issues it has always had, eating in secret, eating the sweet things, hiding things, it's still got that.

(Maisie)

5.6 Discussion

Our interviews with these 17 women help us begin to build a picture of how disordered eating behaviours might develop among female boarders. It seems a combination of factors may put some girls at particular risk. Negative family scripts about appearance and the need to control weight tend to have been embedded before girls start boarding. This mandate to be slim is then confounded by cravings for calorie dense foods which develop in response to intense feelings of abandonment when sent away to school. Certain features of the boarding environment such as lack of warmth, food restrictions and the exposure to constant competition with peers over body shape, diet and popularity then create a constant tension between craving comfort food versus wanting to restrict food and lose weight. Alongside this, as teenagers, girls are developing a growing need for autonomy which is often impeded in relation to food practices at boarding school. This provokes rebellions against food related rules and restrictions which can turn into unhelpful food habits later in life. Given the women we interviewed specifically responded to a call for former boarders who felt they had a problematic relationship with food, this picture is specific to these women and we would not want to suggest that all girls who go to boarding school are likely to develop eating difficulties. Yet our findings suggest that for some girls, where there may be a certain combination of factors, modern boarding schools may need to consider additional ways they can help prevent the development of disordered eating.

Turning to calorie-dense foods for comfort in response to stress has been observed in various animal species including primates [30] and also in human studies [31] indicating that comfort eating is not in itself pathological. Indeed, consuming calorie dense foods at times of crisis may even have an adaptive function outside the context of contemporary high-income countries where there is no overall shortage of food to support the population and no major threats to food supply such as war or drought. Eating high calorie foods occurs for many reasons other than stress, however, including boredom and simple availability which can trigger mindless eating [32]. Children may also crave high calorie foods which have been conceptualised as 'forbidden' due to parenting scripts and covert forms of parental control which paradoxically make some foods seem more attractive [10, 11, 12, 13, 14]. This was a strong feature of our interviews with many of the women describing how the restriction of these foods by both families and school, made them seem more desirable. While there remains some discussion as to whether messaging about ideal weight and control over treats is a response to weight gain or a cause, some experimental research indicates that increasing control does indeed increase a child's preoccupation with food [33]. Furthermore, longitudinal research indicates that when a parent overtly controls a forbidden food, two years later, the child is more likely to have a preference for that food [14].

What does appear to be particularly relevant is that since emerging autonomy is a core aspect of adolescence, the dynamic between restriction and craving may become more marked as adolescents negotiate autonomy and boundaries with parents and authority figures at school, hence the various forms of rebellion we have observed above. Supporting a child with cravings for sweets and treats through adolescence may ordinarily require a delicate balance of guidance and negotiation versus restrictions. This may be impossible to get right if the adolescent is in a boarding environment with a considerably less personalised approach and where stress levels are increased through the initial sense of abandonment and then intense competition with other girls. Indeed some of the women specifically noted the focus on the collective, rather than the individual, was yet another aspect of stress as they felt no-one was there to care for them or to make them feel special. This lack of individualised attention could potentially make eating behaviours yet more problematic with some saying that they would restrict their eating to gain staff attention. Some even said they stopped eating altogether for a period to feel noticed by staff and/or parents.

Our findings may help us identify ways in which schools may be able to develop more supportive and protective strategies. Although in the minority, some women noted that the ability to choose food items helped them to develop self-regulatory practices in relation to food consumption. These women thought about eating as a relaxed and less stressful experience which reduced its desirability. In keeping with this field of research, UK policy over the last 20 years has seen increasing emphasis on schools delivering a range of health and wellbeing initiatives. The Healthy Schools Programme, which began in 1998, encouraged schools to develop programmes around personal, social and health education (PHSE), healthy eating, physical activity and emotional wellbeing. This has been coupled with related government policies to tackle obesity such as *Healthy Weight, Healthy Lives* (2008) which included strategies for schools to increase physical activity, introduce healthy food policies, educate children and parents on making healthy choices. These approaches to food, health and diet, which are often mirrored or alluded to in boarding school marketing material, appear to be informed by the concept of encouraging healthy choices rather than restriction. The 2008 *Healthy Weight Healthy Lives* policy, for example, noted government's role to be 'not in hectoring or lecturing but in expanding the opportunities people have to make the right choices for themselves and their families' [34].

We are not able to be certain the extent to which boarding schools have adapted food and healthy eating practices in recent years and we do not have figures on how many follow the national Healthy Schools Programme. However, in 2012, the government issued national minimum standards for boarding schools which included standards for food which emphasised choice and quality:

> 8.1 All boarders, including those with special dietary, medical or religious needs, are provided with meals which are adequate in nutrition, quantity, quality, choice and variety.
> 8.2 Suitable accommodation is provided for the hygienic preparation, serving and consumption of boarders' main meals. This may be situated in the main school provided it is adjacent to or reasonably accessible from the boarding accommodation.
> 8.3 In addition to main meals, boarders have access to drinking water and to food or the means of hygienically preparing food at reasonable times. [35]

The standards were updated in 2022 to require *good* food (rather than *adequate*) and *good* facilities (rather than *suitable*) although these terms are likely to be open to interpretation [36]. Younger participants in our study did not appear to share the experience of having to finish their plate of food and reported more choices at mealtimes, suggesting the standards in place since 2012 may have had some positive impacts, while adults now in their 30s and older may have experienced harsher regimes. Nevertheless, these policies tend to focus on the nutritional and health aspects of food and do not directly address the avoidance of disordered eating behaviours. There are separate standards which address strategies for promoting emotional wellbeing of boarders but there is no explicit connection between emotional wellbeing and food nor any explicit acknowledgement of the psychological link between these areas of adolescent development. It may therefore be necessary for boarding schools, especially girls' schools, to go further still and consider developing more focused strategies to prevent disordered eating given the added risks adolescent boarders appear to face. In other countries, Canada for example, eating disorder prevention programmes have been developed for school age children including programmes which target high risk groups and others which are based on the idea of universal prevention across an entire school population. Programmes include workshops for teachers, peer support groups, school wide activities (e.g. drama activities) promoting healthy body image plus multiple forms of messaging around the school about positive body image. These sorts of programmes have been found to have positive effects including reducing the internalisation of body ideals and reducing disordered eating [37].

As with the Healthy Schools Programme, it is also important that strategies for encouraging healthy eating and positive body image are in the context of wider health and personal development across the curriculum and embedded in the school culture since our findings indicate the complexity of interacting aspects of social and academic life at boarding school. It seems important that boarding schools adopt the wider package of strategies recommended for state schools but that these need to be adapted to acknowledge the additional emotional challenges of boarding and the unique environment such as the way that boarders are exposed to competitive dynamics 24/7 and have limited personalised care. A holistic approach to health and emotional wellbeing would ensure that girls who were experiencing any emotional difficulties feel able to approach staff and seek out personalised support and care which may encompass a range of issues including food, weight and body image. Staff designated for pastoral or emotional support should be knowledgeable about a range of emotional difficulties and be able to identify the emergence of disordered eating so that they can support or signpost girls to more personalised targeted support.

It is particularly important for boarding schools to review and address their policies and practices in these domains now given that incidence of mental health difficulties among school aged children increased dramatically following the COVID-19 pandemic, eating disorders especially [38]. The numbers of children with possible eating problems have increased since 2017 from 6.7% to 13% in 11- to 16-year-olds and from 44.6% to 58.2% in 17- to 19-year-olds [38], indicating an extremely high level of eating difficulties within the teenage and school-age population generally. The potential for these difficulties to be located in boarding schools is considerable and the findings of the current study highlight the lifelong and debilitating impact of this.

In summary, while pre-existing issues such as negative family body-related scripts and the need for weight control may set the scene, our interviews with 17 women illustrate the ways in which disordered eating behaviours might develop among female boarders. In particular, intense feelings of abandonment when sent away to school could compound the drive to use food as a form of comfort; body image criticism could be exacerbated by constant scrutiny and always being watched by friends at school; the competitive nature of boarding school could make achieving the perfect body a goal while paradoxically making food a means through which to gain status and popularity; and the rules, rigidity and control imposed upon food by the school structure could make food the ideal forum for rebellion which seem to backfire as the girls grew older. These findings therefore illustrate that while not the only cause of disordered eating, boarding school certainly seems to play a key contributory role. It is therefore critically important that boarding schools consider how to play a part in early detection and treatment of disordered eating to prevent lifelong harm.

References

1 Panão I, Carraça EV. Effects of exercise motivations on body image and eating habits/behaviours: A systematic review. *Nutr Diet* 2020; 77: 41–59. doi:10.1111/1747-0080.12575.
2 Berkman ND, Lohr KN, Bulik CM. Outcomes of eating disorders: A systematic review of the literature. *Int J Eat Disord* 2007; 40: 293–309. doi:10.1002/eat.20369.
3 de Zwaan M. Binge eating disorder and obesity. *Int J Obes* 2001; 25: S51–55. doi:10.1038/sj.ijo.0801699.
4 Rothenberg A. Eating disorder as a modern obsessive-compulsive syndrome. *Psychiatry* 1986; 49: 45–53. doi:10.1080/00332747.1986.11024306.
5 Goodwin H, Haycraft E, Taranis L, *et al.* Psychometric evaluation of the compulsive exercise test (CET) in an adolescent population: Links with eating psychopathology. *Eur Eat Disord Rev* 2011; 19: 269–279. doi:10.1002/erv.1109.
6 Brechan I, Kvalem IL. Relationship between body dissatisfaction and disordered eating: mediating role of self-esteem and depression. *Eat Behav* 2015; 17: 49–58. doi:10.1016/j.eatbeh.2014.12.008.
7 Ward A, Ramsay R, Treasure J. Attachment research in eating disorders. *Br J Med Psychol* 2000; 73: 35–51. doi:10.1348/000711200160282.
8 Zachrisson HD, Skårderud F. Feelings of insecurity: Review of attachment and eating disorders. *Eur Eat Disord Rev* 2010; 18: 97–106. doi:10.1002/erv.999.
9 Scaglioni S, Salvioni M, Galimberti C. Influence of parental attitudes in the development of children eating behaviour. *Br J Nutr* 2008; 99: S22–25. doi:10.1017/S0007114508892471.
10 Brown R, Ogden J. Children's eating attitudes and behaviour: a study of the modelling and control theories of parental influence. *Health Educ Res* 2004; 19: 261–271. doi:10.1093/her/cyg040.

11 Wardle J. Parental influences on children's diets. *Proc Nutr Soc* 1995; 54: 747–758. doi:10.1079/PNS19950074.

12 Ogden J, Reynolds R, Smith A. Expanding the concept of parental control: A role for overt and covert control in children's snacking behaviour? *Appetite* 2006; 47: 100–106. doi:10.1016/j.appet.2006.03.330.

13 Brown KA, Ogden J, Vögele C, *et al.* The role of parental control practices in explaining children's diet and BMI. *Appetite* 2008; 50: 252–259. doi:10.1016/j.appet.2007.07.010.

14 Jarman M, Ogden J, Inskip H, *et al.* How do mothers manage their preschool children's eating habits and does this change as children grow older? A longitudinal analysis. *Appetite* 2015; 95: 466–474. doi:10.1016/j.appet.2015.08.008.

15 Bedford JL, Johnson CS. Societal influences on body image dissatisfaction in younger and older women. *J Women Aging* 2006; 18: 41–55. doi:10.1300/J074v18n01_04.

16 Kirk G, Singh K, Getz H. Risk of eating disorders among female college athletes and nonathletes. *J Coll Couns* 2001; 4: 122–132. doi:10.1002/j.2161-1882.2001.tb00192.x.

17 Katzman MA, Lee S. Beyond body image: The integration of feminist and trans-cultural theories in the understanding of self starvation. *Int J Eat Disord* 1997; 22: 385–394. doi:10.1002/(SICI)1098-108X(199712)22:4-385:AID-EAT3-3.0.CO;2-I.

18 Jones JM, Bennett S, Olmsted MP, *et al.* Disordered eating attitudes and beha-viours in teenaged girls: a school-based study. *Can Med Assoc J* 2001; 165: 547–552. http://www.ncbi.nlm.nih.gov/pubmed/11563206.

19 Furnham A, Tan T, McManus C. Waist-to-hip ratio and preferences for body shape: A replication and extension. *Pers Individ Dif* 1997; 22: 539–549. doi:10.1016/S0191-8869(96)00241-3.

20 Bartholdy S, Allen K, Hodsoll J, *et al.* Identifying disordered eating behaviours in adolescents: how do parent and adolescent reports differ by sex and age? *Eur Child Adolesc Psychiatry* 2017; 26: 691–701. doi:10.1007/s00787-016-0935-1.

21 Stanford JN, McCabe MP. Sociocultural influences on adolescent boys' body image and body change strategies. *Body Image* 2005; 2: 105–113. doi:10.1016/j.bodyim.2005.03.002.

22 Rolls BJ, Fedoroff IC, Guthrie JF. Gender differences in eating behavior and body weight regulation. *Heal Psychol* 1991; 10: 133–142. doi:10.1037/0278-6133.10.2.133.

23 Steiner H, Lock J. Anorexia nervosa and bulimia nervosa in children and adoles-cents: A review of the past 10 years. *J Am Acad Child Adolesc Psychiatry* 1998; 37: 352–359. doi:10.1097/00004583-199804000-00011.

24 Kinderman T. Peer group influences on students' academic motivation. In: Wentzel K, Ramani G, eds. *Handbook of social influences in school contexts: Social-emotional, motivation, and cognitive outcomes.* New York: Routledge 2016.

25 Polivy J. Psychological consequences of food restriction. *J Am Diet Assoc* 1996; 96: 589–592. doi:10.1016/S0002-8223(96)00161-7.

26 Evans J, Rich E, Holroyd R. Disordered eating and disordered schooling: what schools do to middle class girls. *Br J Sociol Educ* 2004; 25: 123–142. doi:10.1080/0142569042000205154.

27 Troisi A, Di Lorenzo G, Alcini S, *et al.* Body dissatisfaction in women with eating disorders: Relationship to early separation anxiety and insecure attachment. *Psychosom Med* 2006; 68: 449–453. doi:10.1097/01.psy.0000204923.09390.5b.

28 Fisher S, Frazer N, Murray K. Homesickness and health in boarding school children. *J Environ Psychol* 1986; 6: 35–47. doi:10.1016/S0272-4944(86)80033-0.

29 Stewart M, Troop N, Todd G, *et al.* Eating disorders in boarding schools: A survey of school matrons. *Eur Eat Disord Rev* 1994; 2: 106–113. doi:10.1002/erv.2400020206.

30 Harlow HF, Zimmermann RR. The development of affectional responses in infant monkeys. *Proc Am Philos Soc* 1958; 102: 501–509.

31 Tomiyama AJ, Dallman MF, Epel ES. Comfort food is comforting to those most stressed: Evidence of the chronic stress response network in high stress women. *Psychoneuroendocrinology* 2011; 36: 1513–1519. doi:10.1016/j.psyneuen.2011.04.005.

32 Wansink B. Environmental factors that increase the food intake and consumption volume of unknowing consumers. *Annu Rev Nutr* 2004; 24: 455–479. doi:10.1146/annurev.nutr.24.012003.132140.

33 Ogden J, Cordey P, Cutler L, *et al.* Parental restriction and children's diets. The chocolate coin and Easter egg experiments. *Appetite* 2013; 61: 36–44. doi:10.1016/j.appet.2012.10.021.

34 Cross Government Obesity Unit. *Healthy weight, Healthy lives: a cross-government strategy for England.* London: Department of Health and Department of Children Schools and Families 2008. https://webarchive.nationalarchives.gov.uk/ukgwa/20100407220245/http://www.dh.gov.uk/en/Publicationsandstatistics/Publications/PublicationsPolicyAndGuidance/DH_082378.

35 Department for Education. Boarding schools: national minimum standards. 2012. https://www.gov.uk/government/publications/boarding-schools-national-minimum-standards.

36 Department for Education. Boarding schools: national minimum standards. 2022. https://assets.publishing.service.gov.uk/government/uploads/system/uploads/attachment_data/file/1102344/National_minimum_standards_for_boarding_schools.pdf.

37 McVey G, Tweed S, Blackmore E. Healthy schools-healthy kids: A controlled evaluation of a comprehensive universal eating disorder prevention program. *Body Image* 2007; 4: 115–136. doi:10.1016/j.bodyim.2007.01.004.

38 NHS Digital. Mental health of children and young people in England 2021 – wave 2 follow up to the 2017 survey. 2021. https://digital.nhs.uk/data-and-information/publications/statistical/mental-health-of-children-and-young-people-in-england/2021-follow-up-to-the-2017-survey.

Chapter 6

How does boarding school influence feelings of loneliness?

Caroline Floyd, Susan McPherson and Penny Cavenagh

According to figures from the Campaign to End Loneliness [1], more than 9 million adults in the UK feel lonely 'always' or 'often'. Under-25s and over-65s are more likely to feel lonely [2] with loneliness peaking at age 19 [3]. Loneliness can be felt as intermittent or ongoing for an extended period of time with most people who report feeling lonely saying that they have experienced loneliness at previous times in their life too [4]. Because childhood and adolescence are important periods in our life for developing interpersonal skills, the school environment could play a pivotal role in shaping early and later experiences of loneliness. In particular, a sense of belonging-ness at school – 'the extent to which students feel personally accepted, respected, included and supported by others in the school social environment' [5] – has been shown to predict wellbeing outcomes including loneliness [6].

Loneliness is an important area of study, not least because it is understood to be associated with several related difficulties such as bullying, homesickness, attachment issues and mental health difficulties both in children and adults. In turn, these are difficulties boarders may be more exposed to, making them more at risk of loneliness either at school, as adults or both. Loneliness in adults, for example, is more common among those who have been involved in childhood bullying [7],[8] and research indicates that boarders are significantly more likely to be both perpetrators and victims of bullying [9],[10]. It is very difficult for boarders to escape bullies and retreat to the family environment for reassurance and support. Similarly, as discussed in earlier chapters, boarders are at risk of attachment difficulties as a result of early separation from their parents. This in turn may place them at further risk of loneliness, since research has found that poor parent attachment can lead to loneliness [11] as well as to low self-esteem which then leads to loneliness [12]. Homesickness – 'a feeling of longing for one's home during a period of absence' [13] – is common among boarders in their first years [14] and is associated with anxiety, loneliness, social isolation and depression [15] as well as insomnia, memory problems, digestive issues, immune deficiency and diabetes [16].

In addition to these risks boarders are exposed to, they are also particularly vulnerable to experiencing loneliness because they need to rapidly adapt from

DOI: 10.4324/9781003280491-6

daily to intermittent, limited contact with family and fit in among a new group of peers. Boarding is therefore a unique socialisation environment where children and adolescents live during key developmental years. Large scale survey research with Chinese school children has shown that children report increased loneliness after one year of boarding compared to children of the same age who did not start boarding [17]. It is therefore possible that if boarders are more likely to develop loneliness while at school, this may become a feature of their adulthood too, whether ongoing or intermittently. The study of Chinese boarders is fairly unique since loneliness is usually not examined in research concerned with emotional wellbeing of current or ex-boarders. In this chapter we explore experiences of loneliness among adults who attended boarding school in the UK and their retrospective accounts of their life to date. These retrospective accounts help us to identify key time periods of loneliness and how they may be connected, if at all, to experiences at boarding school.

6.1 The research study

We invited people who had been to boarding school and had experienced loneliness at some point in their life to take part in our study. Initially we contacted individuals we knew had attended boarding school and asked if they wanted to participate. Then snowball sampling was used, where participants referred people who they knew into the study. We interviewed 18 adults aged 22–31 who had previously been to boarding school for between two and 11 years, starting from age five upwards. They were asked about experiences of loneliness before, during and after boarding school. They were also asked what loneliness means to them and how it feels inside their body. Half (nine) had been full boarders and the rest had been flexi, weekly boarders or a mixture. We interviewed six men and 12 women. Most had been to mixed schools but one of the men went to an all-boys school and four of the women had been to all-girls' schools. Everyone we interviewed was White British. None had any children, although one person was pregnant at the time of interview. Most were employed except one of the men was self-employed and one of the women was a full-time student. One of the men and five of the women had received either cognitive behavioural therapy or counselling before but none had received any long-term therapy. Other characteristics of the people interviewed are described in Table 6.1.

Interviews were transcribed and analysed as described in previous chapters using Thematic Analysis – a way of producing a set of themes that best reflect the key features across the interviews. Our analysis resulted in five key themes: 'Identifying loneliness: feeling sad, anxious and isolated'; 'I just have to crack on'; 'Going into the 'big world''; 'Keeping busy: avoidance and resilience'; and 'Family closeness and remoteness'.

Table 6.1 Characteristics of participants.

Pseudonym	Age at interview	Age started boarding	Gender	Current relationship status	Currently lives with
Greg	31	9	Male	Married	Wife
Simon	31	7	Male	Single	Alone
Hugh	29	13	Male	Engaged	Fiancé
Sam	22	13	Male	Single	Brother
Craig	31	7	Male	Single	Friend
Ben	27	11	Male	Single	Friends
Scarlet	29	11	Female	Married	Husband
Summer	28	11	Female	Single	Friend
Lily	29	14	Female	In a relationship	Siblings
Cara	29	13	Female	Engaged	Fiancé
Ruby	27	13	Female	In a relationship	Friends
Poppy	28	5	Female	Engaged	Fiancé
Alexis	29	14	Female	In a relationship	Boyfriend
Claire	29	9	Female	Single	Alone
Louise	28	16	Female	Engaged	Fiancé
Jenny	27	12	Female	Engaged	Fiancé/ lodger
Rebecca	31	11	Female	Single	Alone
Rachel	28	7	Female	In a relationship	Family

6.2 Theme 1: Identifying loneliness: feeling sad, anxious and isolated

There was no uniform definition of loneliness among those we interviewed although there was a common distinction in terms of being alone versus feeling alone. Some only felt lonely when they lacked the physical presence of others:

> I think I only feel loneliness if I'm not actually physically with another person, like I don't tend to feel lonely if I've got other people around me.
>
> (Poppy)

Those who thought of loneliness like this connected it explicitly to constantly being around people at boarding school:

> I would say that boarding school is the reason why I probably feel loneliness as being a physical presence, because you're never on your own at boarding school so when I am on my own, I'm like, 'Erm, what?'!
>
> (Lily)

However, most said that for them, loneliness consists of more than just lacking the physical presence of others and linked feeling lonely to lacking an emotional connection to other people.

> I can still feel lonely if I'm around loads of people; it's not always about the bodily contact, it's feeling the emotional connection.
>
> (Ruby)

This was also linked to always being around people at boarding school but in a different way in terms of not necessarily feeling any emotional connection to those around them or not finding the presence of others supportive:

> … feeling lonely but, even when I'm surrounded by loads of people – maybe that's from boarding school because you're always around people so even if you do feel lonely there's still going to be people there. I don't think being around loads of people in boarding school eliminates loneliness from your life if you know what I mean. So maybe I still have that in social situations.
>
> (Ruby)

> …not necessarily a physical experience, more of an internal experience … so you can be around a lot of people and feel lonely. There's that component … so that feeling of disconnect maybe from other people and that feeling of self … you really have yourself to rely on. You don't have an external support system.
>
> (Poppy)

Most acknowledged that loneliness is complex and experienced differently by different people. Some seemed to find it hard to explain what loneliness means to them, taking their time to respond when asked and often acknowledging it is a difficult experience to describe. There was considerable variation in how loneliness was described, although '*sad*' and '*anxious*' were the most common terms used. Some were able to offer a felt sense of loneliness very quickly, with little hesitation. Others seemed to find it more difficult to access descriptive words to explain the experience. Some, but not all, linked feeling lonely to a particular part of their body, often their stomach.

> I would say in my tummy and things … feels a bit like your stomach is churning. I don't know, sometimes it feels cold like you want to wrap up in a duvet just feel a bit down, and low and your tummy feels a bit shaky.
>
> (Summer)

One thing everyone agreed on was that feeling lonely is not the same thing as feeling homesick even though they were often used interchangeably in the context of boarding. Homesickness was linked to a specific desire to be at home, surrounded by '*home comforts*' and family but loneliness was different:

> I would think that homesickness was that urge to want to go home and like see your parents and have all, like your home comforts, whereas loneliness I'd put down to like … feeling isolated.
>
> (Jenny)

In spite of the varied ways of defining loneliness, most expressed a strong dislike of being alone. Only three said they enjoyed solitude and felt totally comfortable in their own company. This theme suggests that loneliness is not only experienced in different contexts, but it feels different – psychologically and physiologically – for different people. Descriptions of loneliness seemed to be intricately bound up with past experiences of loneliness, which may be why some participants referenced times at boarding school when considering their response, and others did not.

6.3 Theme 2: 'I just have to crack on'

Among those we interviewed, it seems loneliness was hardly acknowledged at boarding school and was often stigmatised.

> I think it would be a shame thing. I think there's a pride in popularity at school like not ever looking like you didn't have someone to hang out with.
>
> (Poppy)

Many felt that admitting to loneliness was seen as a weakness which would trigger teasing and bullying. It was not something they could tell anyone about, including friends, staff or even parents, lest they seem ungrateful:

> I remember feeling really upset that I was there and not at a school, say nearer home, where I could go home, there was no one to hang out with, and being really upset about that and not actually … just not saying anything to anyone, I didn't know who to say something to because I guess the person you would naturally speak to should be your parents but I didn't want to come across ungrateful so I just wouldn't say anything.
>
> (Cara)

For those few who could speak to their parents for support, this could be protective:

I did speak to my parents when I was having a bad day – having an outside voice who's not there ... it did help.

(Sam)

Peers and friends could also be supportive for some but all of those interviewed commented that who you shared your boarding house with, and therefore most readily available to befriend, was down to chance and could determine whether you end up lonely or not:

I think it's a lottery, a big part of it is a lottery ... who you end up spending your time with and who happens to be in your boarding house and do you get on ... and I think I didn't win that lottery ... unfortunately hence I spent a lot of my time alone.

(Ben)

For most then, rather than learning to draw on support of others, they developed an attitude of 'just crack on with it' when faced with a distressing situation. This underpinned their adult approaches to managing distress. For example, Rachel spoke about her response to feeling lonely after the breakdown of a serious relationship in her early twenties:

I think, my reaction is, get on with things, keep, keep going, that's probably the attitude of my schooling and my family philosophy I would say.

(Rachel)

In some interviews this approach sounded much like the 'strategic survival personality' and emotional cut-offness described in earlier chapters:

It's that kind of toughness and which I think is quite a good skill to have in some ways, but when it comes to deep emotions or being a grown-up, being an adult, it's all a toughness from the outside, or it's a confidence of knowing how to ... hold yourself and talk and ... be all ... 'oh, all is good', but inside you don't really, you're not that attached to your feelings and that I think feels very, very lonely.

(Rebecca)

This stoicism learned at school seemed to mean that it became hard to reach out for support as an adult, compounding feelings of loneliness.

I'm not the kind of friend that will call you crying on the phone if I've had a bad day. That's just not my thing. If we come back to the whole boarding school thing, if I did that at boarding school, called my parents crying, they can't do anything because they're not there.

(Jenny)

No-one is going to hold you when you cry here [boarding school] so either hold yourself or don't cry and that's still my [modus operandi] now.

(Rebecca)

This gives a picture of a vicious cycle of loneliness for some, in which past experiences in boarding school makes talking about loneliness in adulthood difficult. This perpetuates a further sense of loneliness as attempts are made to manage loneliness and other forms of distress independently.

6.4 Theme 3: Going into the 'big world'

Several people said they felt lonely immediately after leaving boarding school, where they had to adjust to being in a new environment outside of the boarding house. Close attachments to friends and teachers meant that leaving boarding school felt like a lonely time for some.

At my leavers' dinner I was so emotional because they were like my family by the end of it, my friends were like siblings, but then like the teachers were like all parental, in a way ... The holistic care was like unbelievable. You know, people always there and like leaving them felt like leaving because I knew I was never going to be like in touch with them. As, you know, in the way I was back then. I knew I was losing them ... so yeah, I was like, so emotional.

(Simon)

Most went straight to university and while some found the transition '*easy*', others found it more challenging.

I remember my parents dropping me off and I wasn't like in halls, I was in housing and my parents dropped me off and I like chased them down the road and like crying, 'Don't leave me' [laughs]. That transition was hard. I was in a really like very comfortable, secure state in school ... and walking away from that was very scary.

(Poppy)

In spite of some initial distress, there was consensus that university was similar to boarding school; many described university as a continuation of boarding school where they lived with friends and were constantly surrounded by people. There was a shared sense that university had kept them institutionalised. Consequently, participants explained that it was a shock to be alone for the first time in their lives after university ended. Cara moved on her own to a new city to study for a Master's degree after leaving university:

I think it's because, in all seriousness, all my life up until that point, I had been continuously around people; so, from being at home, then junior school [living] with my family, then I was at boarding school, which is continuously with people, then I went to university and I was living in close quarters with friends and then suddenly from that going to a place where I didn't know anyone and I didn't quickly form relationships with people, yeah I'd never felt I, to be honest I'd never felt lonely prior to that.

(Cara)

Some felt the relationships they formed at boarding school enabled them to see that they were able to create strong relationships with non-family members. This has helped them to form relationships throughout adulthood, which have protected them from loneliness. Poppy described how this helped her move abroad after university.

The relationships I formed I'm so grateful for, and I think because we were all at boarding school together it's created those friendships and I think yes, it means that my boundaries are definitely limited – skewed – and it probably sets the mark really high for my friendships now, but it has also taught me like what that bond can feel like and that you can have it with people that aren't your family and I think in a way that's enabled me to travel and live here [Australia] and do all this stuff and not feel lonely during COVID when I haven't seen my family for 18 months is because I have learned that if you can bond like that with people with people you don't – who aren't cut from the same cloth in that sense.

(Poppy)

It seems that for some, attending boarding school therefore instilled a strong sense of independence in adult years which has provided a form of protection from loneliness. For others, behaviours learned at boarding school make them more vulnerable to loneliness as adults:

I would go downstairs as they would keep calling me the same name so it would piss me off – so I would exclude myself even more – I think that's why I'm more excluded now because of all that stuff – maybe that's why I am a bit more lonely [now] from it.

(Sam)

For some, the connections between the past and present seem to be linked to specific times of the day or parts of the body.

I do think there's something, probably in the bed at night-time feeling lonely [experienced now] that did come from boarding school. I didn't think that before, but maybe from this ... I think there's a connection with night-time and feeling lonely [now] from being in that first-year boarding school, maybe.

(Ruby)

... my heartbreak last summer ... I thought I would die, and it was very disarming to have this experience as a 30-year-old woman. Just full stop. The experience of that was so shocking physically in my heart and it reminded me of being homesick at school, and it was like my soul being pulled apart from source, like, I know I'm being dramatic, but it was, that's what it felt like being homesick.

(Rebecca)

This theme paints a picture of how experiences at boarding school can influence feelings and behaviours that can last into adulthood and can continue to perpetuate loneliness or, for some, provide protection from loneliness.

6.5 Theme 4: Keeping busy: Avoidance and resilience

For the majority of ex-boarders we spoke to, acknowledging and addressing loneliness was hard at boarding school and continues to feel difficult now in adulthood. It seemed clear that for many, coping mechanisms used to combat loneliness in boarding school were the same as those used in adulthood. As adults, one way of coping is filling time with activities or people which can be a way of avoiding loneliness as well as a being a protective factor.

The parallel with boarding school seems apparent given that almost all commented on how the number of activities built into their week at boarding school blocked loneliness out.

They kept us so occupied doing stuff all the time, you're never really given a second to think about it, there was so much routine, and structure and it was probably the best thing for everybody you just ... never had that down time.

(Jenny)

Yet for Craig, this busy schedule could serve to amplify feelings of loneliness.

You can feel lonely because there's so much going on that if you're not involved, there is actually a wonder as to why, because there's so much you can be involved with.

(Craig)

As adults, this need for busy-ness was mirrored in terms of activities including sports, choir, painting, parties, watching TV, throwing themselves into work and walking. Some said these activities helped distract them from the feeling of being lonely. Simon described how he coped when he was feeling lonely when sent abroad with the army:

> I volunteered to get sent away on everything I could with the army and ended up going on lots of fun experiences which kind of distracted from what's going on.
>
> (Simon)

This busy-ness could mean that both as children and adults there is no time to acknowledge feelings.

> So what I do to combat loneliness is to book myself up weeks in advance with parties and sports and other activities. I talk to my friends, and I just kept really busy, I play hockey I play netball, I'm in a choir, basically I just get myself so busy, kind of like what I was like in school where – if we are like drawing connections like – I made it where I had no time to just sit and relax. You know, I'm not very good with my own thoughts.
>
> (Scarlet)

> I guess I'll never feel that I'm lonely because I'm always doing something it's not like, I'm not the kind of person who will sit in my room playing PlayStation, as a young adult – that just wasn't my thing – I'd always keep myself occupied – so I've just never been that way.
>
> (Hugh)

Hence, avoiding loneliness through busy-ness and distraction seems to be both a way of avoiding difficult feelings as well as (though perhaps unintended) a way of preventing loneliness. Depending on the context and what sorts of difficult feelings are being avoided, this could sometimes be adaptive and sometimes be problematic but nevertheless the drive to be active or busy all the time seems to stem from the same origin of being constantly busy with activities at school.

6.6 Theme 5: Family closeness versus family remoteness

For some of those we spoke to, loneliness was first experienced in early childhood within the family, where they felt 'different'. This feeling seemed to be carried with them into boarding school and adulthood in some instances. Some spoke about 'tough love' adopted by their parents, conveying a sense of remoteness and lack of emotional attachment. Others seemed to feel close to their family and this offered protection against loneliness.

Those who experienced loneliness early in life talked about feeling lonely being away from their parents for the first time, for example at a sleepover. Others described a more pervasive sense of loneliness at home. They may have been the only girl or the only boy among siblings and cousins; they may have felt left out or been teased and bullied by siblings; parents may have re-married partners they did not get along with; or their parents may have lived in different countries from one another.

> I suppose, maybe I felt sometimes left out as a child. As a sibling because my sister, my other, my other sister and my brother, they got on better than I did and they would like, just leave me and they'd be really mean to me and call me stupid.
>
> (Simon)

For those who felt lonely from early on at home, they continue to feel lonely as adults within their family.

> In my family… I've always felt quite lonely … because I … I don't know just the way I talk about stuff is different to them and they're all quite closed [off] … and strong fronted, I guess … that's not my natural way and I want to talk about stuff and I also feel loads of stuff and want to communicate that but … I understood that that wasn't the way we do it so I've always felt quite unseen in my family in lots of ways and although I'm really, I'm so close with them all … feel very loved by them all … but it's a bit confusing when the people you feel most loved by, you also don't feel truly, truly seen by.
>
> (Rebecca)

We can therefore see how remoteness within the family prior to going to boarding school could lead to feelings of loneliness at school and later on in life; rather than boarding school itself creating a sense of alone-ness. For example, some who felt loneliness at some point during boarding school found this hard to raise with their parents and said they just received and continue to receive 'tough love' from their parents in response to any feelings expressed. Some said they did not have 'motherly mothers' and that at least one of their parents had attended boarding school themselves, which is a pattern also seen in Chapter 4. Similarly, Ben said he feels his parents provided for him and his siblings in a financial sense but not in an emotional sense, highlighting a sense of remoteness in the family:

> I think, being in a big family, and having a lot of space and people doing different things did create a kind of vacuum feeling to some extent, so I think I felt quite distant a lot of the time and not like there was a real connection on an emotional level and I think, growing up, Mum and Dad quite, like, 'provided' more than … taking care of our emotional needs … I think that's fair, there again, I wouldn't have named it that way until recently.
>
> (Ben)

In spite of this, the majority of people we interviewed described having close relationships with their parents and family before going to boarding school and talked about missing their parents when at school. Nobody implied this closeness was in any way damaged or broken by going to boarding school. Some also mentioned having an older sibling at boarding school which sometimes protected them from loneliness and bullying, although this was not universal and some rarely saw their siblings.

> I remember seeing [sibling] and my heart kind of leapt just a little bit, because they were a familiar face and a friendly face there, in a place where, at the time, felt big and scary a lot of the time, so I think it helps to know they were there.
>
> (Ben)

A close relationship with family certainly seemed to provide some protection to some from feeling lonely:

> No matter what happens my family are right there and any one of them would take me in and feed me ... so well that's not always on my mind I don't need that like literally in the back of my mind, as I go out at night, but I guess that gives you an element of security in life.
>
> (Craig)

The pattern seen here in relation to family seems to suggest that loneliness at school and in adulthood may be very much dependent on the degree of remoteness versus closeness within the family and that closeness in the family can both be maintained at school and provide protection from potential difficulties at school.

6.7 Discussion

The study explored experiences of loneliness for eighteen ex-boarders, most of whom were somewhat younger than the average participant in other studies reported in this book with the oldest being 31 at time of interview. We had intended the sample to be within this age bracket partly based on a theory of psychosocial life stages put forward by Erik Erikson which suggests that young adulthood (21–39) is a developmental period during which we tend to experience and reflect on loneliness. This meant it would be possible to tap into young adult thought processes at a relevant developmental stage in life as well as benefit from a fairly recent memory of school and relatively current experiences of important life stages such as going to university or starting a career. Unlike some of the studies in this book, none of the people we spoke to had had any long-term specialist therapy focusing on boarding, although a few had had some brief generic forms of therapy or counselling. The majority of participants were referred into the study by friends. Consequently, the sample is inherently skewed towards people who might be less lonely, in that they had friends. Furthermore, the friendships are likely to have been strong enough to persist into adulthood. It is therefore likely that these close friendships protected individuals from severe loneliness both during boarding school and in adulthood, meaning our findings may be biased towards more positive experiences.

Nevertheless, our analysis sheds light on the role boarding school may play in the development of emotional wellbeing and loneliness among adolescents and potential longer-term impacts. Experiences of loneliness at boarding school were common and were often triggered by bullying. Loneliness at school was short-lived for some, but for others it persisted throughout school and resulted in behaviours that have kept that individual feeling lonely into adulthood. National minimum standards for boarding schools, first issued in 2012 [18], have been updated, strengthening the requirement for an anti-bullying strategy and extended this to include new risks from cyber-bullying. The updated requirement now explicitly recognises the unique risk posed to boarders who cannot escape their bullies. This is an important policy development but it will be critical boarding schools take meaningful steps to implement this requirement.

Separation from parents and higher risk of bullying place boarders at particular risk. However, positive relationships with parents and siblings seem to be important in mitigating these risks. It may therefore be important for boarding schools to be proactive in supporting and maintaining positive relationships with parents and siblings to tap into these protective factors. Indeed, national minimum standards for boarding schools updated in 2022 include a new standard in relation to contact with parents which both encourages contact, making use of new forms of electronic communications, while also noting the importance of preventing new forms of online abuse through the same means (discussed further in Chapter 7).

12.1 Schools [should] facilitate arrangements so boarders can contact their parents/carers and families in private, at a time that is suitable for both parties, considering relevant time zones for international pupils. Schools should operate proportionate systems to monitor and control the use of electronic communications in order to detect abuse, bullying or unsafe practice by boarders. Schools [should be] sensitive and comply with individual children's circumstances such as restricted contact with families. [19]

Many of those we interviewed reported having a network of close and supportive friends at boarding school, which protected them from loneliness at school and continues to protect them from loneliness as an adult. School-based strategies to enhance these protective elements, such as supporting friendships may help to prevent loneliness. New national minimum standards go some way to addressing this, providing schools take action to meet the new standard on 'promoting good relationships':

> 17.1 Boarders are supported to develop good relationships with fellow pupils and staff which are based on mutual trust and respect. Through regulations made under section 34 of the Children and Social Work Act 2017, boarding schools are required to teach relationships education to primary school pupils and relationships and sex education to secondary school pupils.
> 17.2 In schools with both day pupils and boarders, boarders are encouraged and enabled to make and sustain respectful friendships within and outside the boarding community.
> 17.3 Staff understand and help boarders to understand what makes a healthy, nurturing relationship. Staff are trained to think curiously about and recognise the signs of children at risk of or involved in damaging relationships with others, including teenage relationship abuse, criminal exploitation, sexual exploitation and child-on-child abuse, and take appropriate action when they have a concern. [19]

Proactively supporting positive family and peer relationships in these ways is particularly important given the enduring nature of loneliness and how early experiences of loneliness can be pervasive and can trigger later episodes.

Despite recent policy developments, having attended boarding school prior to these requirements may have left many former boarders with a propensity to feel lonely in the presence of others in adulthood. Avoidant coping styles in the form of constant 'busy-ness', developed at boarding school, may have perpetuated into adulthood. This makes it difficult to identify, discuss and address loneliness now. This may be an adaptive coping mechanism for some, where loneliness is effectively ignored. Others may feel a sense of distress and isolation, where they are unsure of how to help themselves manage loneliness. Some participants are currently receiving therapy to address aspects of their emotional wellbeing that they feel have been impacted by boarding school. It seems that for some, discussing experiences at boarding school in therapy now, as an adult, is helping to identify emotionally avoidant strategies that have been used since school. Earlier access to therapy may reduce distress that persists into adulthood. Equally, it may be important for therapists to recognise the importance of early family life and family remoteness in contributing to the development of adult loneliness rather than to focus exclusively on experiences of boarding.

In summary, our interviews with eighteen ex-boarders illustrate how experiences of loneliness at boarding school were common and often triggered by bullying. The findings also indicate that, while for some loneliness was short-lived, for others it persisted both throughout and beyond school.

Furthermore, for many these negative experiences resulted in coping behaviours such as the need to be always busy, becoming stoical, ignoring feelings and not seeking help which may have kept that individual feeling lonely into adulthood. That many ex-boarders still find it hard to seek emotional support likely reflects a continued nationwide propensity to consider discussing loneliness as shameful or embarrassing. There is clearly a stigma around discussing emotions, including loneliness, within boarding school, although this may not be dissimilar to the stigma around these topics in any school or wider society. Changing how society views loneliness will take time and it seems increasingly important to address loneliness in the wake of the pandemic. Strategies for tackling loneliness currently tend to be focused in adult social care alongside community and voluntary initiatives. Tackling loneliness in adults, particularly older adults is critical but it may also be important in terms of future prevention for there to be collaboration across the Department for Education and the Minister for Loneliness to consider ways in which prevention of loneliness through strengthening of positive relationships between schools, children, families peers and communities can be made a priority in state, private and boarding schools.

References

1 Campaign to End Loneliness. The facts on loneliness. 2019. www.campaigntoendlo neliness.org/thefactsonloneliness

2 Victor CR, Yang K. The prevalence of loneliness among adults: A case study of the United Kingdom. *J Psychol* 2012; 146: 85–104. doi:10.1080/00223980.2011.613875.

3 Shovestul B, Han J, Germine L, *et al.* Risk factors for loneliness: The high relative importance of age versus other factors. *PLoS One* 2020; 15:e0229087. doi:10.1371/journal.pone.0229087.

4 Niina J, Topalli PZ, Kainulainen S, *et al.* The portrayal of lonely Finnish people. In: Rokach A, ed. *The correlates of loneliness.* Sharjah: Bentham Science Publishers 2016. 156–183. doi:10.2174/9781681080703116010010.

5 Goodenow C, Grady KE. The relationship of school belonging and friends' values to academic motivation among urban adolescent students. *J Exp Educ* 1993; 62: 60–71. doi:10.1080/00220973.1993.9943831.

6 Arslan G. School belongingness, well-being, and mental health among adolescents: Exploring the role of loneliness. *Aust J Psychol* 2020 [early view]. doi:10.1111/ajpy.12274.

7 Tritt C, Duncan RD. The relationship between childhood bullying and young adult self-esteem and loneliness. *J Humanist Educ Dev* 1997; 36: 35–44. doi:10.1002/j.2164-4683.1997.tb00426.x.

8 Segrin C, Nevarez N, Arroyo A, *et al.* Family of origin environment and adolescent bullying predict young adult loneliness. *J Psychol* 2012; 146: 119–134. doi:10.1080/00223980.2011.555791.

9 Mander DJ, Lester L, Cross D. The social and emotional well-being and mental health implications for adolescents transitioning to secondary boarding school. *Int J Child Adolesc Health* 2015; 8: 131–140. https://search.ebscohost.com/login.aspx?

direct=true&db=psyh&AN=2015-33466-005&site=ehost-live&authtype=sso&custid=s9814295.

10 Pfeiffer JP, Pinquart M. Bullying in German boarding schools: A pilot study. *Sch Psychol Int* 2014; 35: 580–591. doi:10.1177/0143034314525513.

11 Bogaerts S, Vanheule S, Desmet M. Feelings of subjective emotional loneliness: An exploration of attachment. *Soc Behav Pers* 2006; 34: 797–812.

12 Karababa A. Understanding the association between parental attachment and loneliness among adolescents: The mediating role of self-esteem. *Curr Psychol* 2022; 41: 6655–6665. doi:10.1007/s12144-021-01417-z.

13 Stroebe M, Vliet T, Hewstone M, *et al.* Homesickness among students in two cultures: Antecedents and consequences. *Br J Psychol* 2002; 93: 147–168. doi:10.1348/000712602162508.

14 Fisher S, Frazer N, Murray K. Homesickness and health in boarding school children. *J Environ Psychol* 1986; 6: 35–47. doi:10.1016/S0272-4944(86)80033-0.

15 Stroebe M, Schut H, Nauta M. Homesickness: A systematic review of the scientific literature. *Rev Gen Psychol* 2015; 19: 157–171. doi:10.1037/gpr0000037.

16 Sulastri T, Dewi EMP, Nurdin MN. Effectiveness of psychoeducation to reduce homesickness in Islamic boarding school students. In: *Proceedings of the 3rd International Conference on Education, Science, and Technology (ICEST 2019)*. Paris, France: Atlantis Press 2020. doi:10.2991/assehr.k.201027.039.

17 Tang B, Wang Y, Gao Y, *et al.* The effect of boarding on the mental health of primary school students in western rural China. *Int J Environ Res Public Health* 2020; 17: 8200. doi:10.3390/ijerph17218200.

18 Department for Education. Boarding schools: national minimum standards. 2012. www.gov.uk/government/publications/boarding-schools-national-minimum-standards.

19 Department for Education. Boarding schools: national minimum standards. 2022. https://assets.publishing.service.gov.uk/government/uploads/system/uploads/attachment_data/file/1102344/National_minimum_standards_for_boarding_schools.pdf.

Chapter 7

The shadow side of boarding schools

Childhood sexual abuse and its aftermath

Daniel Taggart

In this chapter we draw on the findings of the Independent Inquiry into Child Sexual Abuse (IICSA) undertaken in England and Wales between 2015 and 2021. The Inquiry reported detailed data concerning different forms of abuse in residential schools including boarding schools. We will present some of this data to illustrate the types and scale of historical abuse relating to boarding schools in the UK. One element of the IICSA, the Truth Project, gathered testimonies directly from over 6,000 adult survivors of childhood sexual abuse (CSA). These testimonies will be used to illustrate broad themes around institutional failings; how survivors characterise the impacts of abuse; and what recommendations they point to for future change. The scope of data from the IICSA and the Truth Project in particular, represents relatively large-scale work to identify the scale of abuse in institutional settings and so is a useful contrast to the largely anecdotal nature of more focused clinical theoretical research on the impact of abuse on ex-boarders. The steps taken by boarding schools to address the issues raised by IICSA are also presented and discussed.

7.1 Historical institutional abuse inquiries

Over the past three decades, alongside growing awareness of the impacts of CSA, there has been increased recognition of the scale of public institution involvement in its perpetration and cover up. High-profile international scandals involving but not limited to the Catholic Church, public figures, residential schools, government and other public bodies have led to recognition that institutional abuse is a major social problem [1]. When public outrage at allegations of institutional involvement in child abuse has become politically toxic for government and also in response to long term survivor activism, there has been an inflection point in many high- and medium-income countries which has led to the commissioning of public inquiries. Over the past two decades there have been historical institutional abuse inquiries (HIAs) conducted in all four countries of the UK, Australia, Canada, New Zealand, Ireland, the Netherlands, Sweden, Switzerland, Norway, Jersey and Germany.

DOI: 10.4324/9781003280491-7

One common feature has been the shift in emphasis towards the centring of survivor perspectives in the 1990s; a shift in practice that has been described as a 'turn to testimony' [2]. This shift from privileging expert witness testimony to survivor accounts of abuse is in part due to the influence of the South African Truth and Reconciliation Commission assembled in 1996. The Truth and Reconciliation Commission developed a victim centred model that focused on Inquiries as not only establishing evidence of historical abuse, but creating a 'process that will be therapeutic and promote healing for victims, communities and wider society' [3]. This 'therapeutic turn' led to HIA Inquiries developing new forms of public engagement that augmented the traditional method of providing evidential testimony under oath at a legally driven and open public hearing.

The IICSA for England and Wales was established as a statutory inquiry in 2015 to investigate

> whether public bodies and other non-state institutions have taken seriously their responsibility to protect children from sexual abuse in England and Wales, and to make meaningful recommendations for change, to ensure that children now and in the future are better protected from sexual abuse. [4]

There were three main areas of work: 15 public hearings (including one on residential and boarding schools); primary research and literature reviews; and the Truth Project.

The Truth Project offered survivors of CSA an opportunity to share their experiences as a form of testimonial justice whereby they can have the validation of belief while also contributing to the inquiry's data gathering. The Truth Project was piloted in 2015 and from 2016 to 2021, over 6,000 adult victims and survivors of CSA shared their experiences via face-to-face sessions, telephone and video calls, or in writing. The Truth Project was open to victims and survivors who were sexually abused in England or Wales either within an institution or where there was a link to an institutional failure, and the abuse began when they were aged under 18. The sessions offered were led by what the victim or survivor wished to share with a focus on three main areas: the experience of the abuse itself; the impacts it has had; and their recommendations for institutional change in the future.

In 2019 and 2020, the IICSA conducted public hearing investigations into institutional failings in residential schools including specialist residential schools for children with special educational needs, music schools and boarding schools. Ten boarding schools in England and Wales were included, chosen as a result of allegations of and convictions for CSA at those institutions covering a period from the 1960s to 2017 [5].

Prevalence rates of abuse at residential schools are not routinely collected and so estimates are difficult to establish with any accuracy [6]. However,

Operation Hydrant, the specialist safeguarding police investigations hub established in response to non-recent CSA in 2014, reported that approximately 40% of their referrals are connected to an educational institution with 2,750 schools featuring on their database [5]. This makes schools the most commonly reported location for CSA. A YouGov survey conducted in 2010 found that 21% of all children reported unwanted sexual contact at school, with reporting rates higher for girls (29%) as compared to boys (14%) [7].

The IICSA residential schools investigation found significant institutional failings in boarding school safeguarding practices; their responses to sexual abuse when it was disclosed; and the manner in which survivors were treated both while still at the school and in later life when they came forward as victims [5]. It concluded that failures were present at both an individual institutional level, and that wider regulation was poorly understood and implemented by boarding schools, which, as charities, fall in between different systems of inspection and oversight. There were specific risk factors that children were exposed to at boarding schools which placed them at higher risk of sexual abuse including the distance from family; the school as a surrogate parental system; one to one tutoring in remote locations; and institutions privileging reputational management over child protection [5].

7.2 The research study: the Truth Project as a source of data

The Truth Project represents the largest participation in a public inquiry in UK history and one of the largest datasets on CSA in the world [8]. A sample of around 1,100 Truth Project testimonies were summarised by the IICSA research team, anonymised and made accessible on the IICSA website as 'Experiences Shared'. While this represents only a proportion of all testimonies in a condensed, secondary form, these accessible summaries represent an important source for research and learning in the field of CSA. In this chapter we will focus on the Experiences Shared testimonies available regarding CSA perpetrated in boarding school settings to better understand the particular contextual factors that enabled CSA to occur, and the ways that survivors abused in these settings were impacted as children and across the lifespan. We will also consider survivor priorities for how boarding schools need to change to keep children safe and what they need as survivors of abuse in these settings.

When participants shared their experiences with the Truth Project, they were given the option to consent to their information to be used as Experiences Shared [8]. Further details on how participants were recruited to the Truth Project and what information they were given about the use of the information they shared can be accessed via the Truth Project website (see www.iicsa.org.uk/key-documents/8638/view/truth-project-booklet-english.pdf). All Experiences Shared were given a pseudonym and identifying details were removed by IICSA staff when writing the summaries. For the purposes of this chapter, the summaries were used as a form of publicly available secondary data used for analysis, for which consent had been gained at an earlier stage by IICSA staff.

The entire Experiences Shared database of 1,100 accounts was downloaded from the IICSA website (www.iicsa.org.uk/victims-and-survivors/experiences-shared); transferred into a Word document; and imported into a data management software programme for analysis. The database was searched for any reference to 'boarding school'. A total of 171 accounts had some reference to boarding school. All accounts were read and any that did not concern CSA perpetrated in boarding schools were omitted. These included references to parents who had attended boarding school, the co-occurrence of the words 'boarding' and 'school' in different contexts, or to survivors who were abused in other institutional settings but also happened to attend boarding school at another point in their childhood. When these were excluded, 61 accounts remained, representing 5.5% of the total number of Experiences Shared. The overall Truth Project dataset published in August 2021 found that 15% of all Truth Project sessions concerned CSA perpetrated in any form of school, with no specific information on what proportion of these referred to boarding schools in particular and therefore we cannot be sure how representative this sample is of the wider Truth Project data.

Of the 61 accounts, seven were from women, 52 were from men and two were from transwomen who had been boys at the time of the CSA but had since transitioned in adulthood. In one of these cases the person made clear that their transition was not connected directly to CSA but that their gender fluidity in childhood may have played a part in them being noticed by perpetrators (Muriel), while the other person said she felt more comfortable as a woman and is relieved to 'leave behind the raped boy' (Julianna).

The wider Truth Project research report into sexual abuse in schools [9] found that abuse in schools tended to start later in childhood compared to other contexts with 89% of abuse starting at the age of eight or older in independent schools and 32% starting between the ages of 12 and 15. Age of onset of abuse was not available for all the Experiences Shared summaries, but based on this data it is reasonable to assume the majority started at eight years or older.

A major limitation of the dataset is that it does not systematically include information on when the CSA started, making historical analysis difficult. There are details in some of the Experiences Shared about the survivor having attended boarding school in the 1950s, 1970s, 1980s or later but this is sporadic. However an overall reading of the Truth Project dataset indicates that over half (54%) of the survivors were between the ages of 40 and 60 at the time of participation, with a further 21% over the age of 60 [10]. This means that for 75% of the overall Truth Project population, the abuse will have occurred at least 22 years previously, with a significant proportion of this (51%) having been 32 years or more prior. If we extrapolate from these figures to the boarding school sample analysed in this study, this means that the majority of accounts relate to abuse that occurred in the 1960s up to the 1990s. This historical skew means that the data presented here cannot necessarily speak to the culture of contemporary boarding schools, but it does offer an important insight into how these institutions functioned historically and the impacts CSA in these settings continues to have for survivors today. It should be noted, however, that the residential schools public hearing focused on contemporary practice, as well as historical context, and found that many of the risk factors pertaining to CSA in boarding schools were still present today [5].

The 61 summary accounts were analysed using thematic analysis, an approach described in previous chapters. In keeping with the overall objectives of the Truth Project, experiences have been structured around three central themes: 'the experience of CSA in boarding schools'; 'the impacts on survivors at the time and since'; and 'survivor recommendations for change'. Quotes in italics are verbatim quotes from survivors captured in the summary of the original Truth Project session as recorded by the session facilitator. Pseudonyms are those given in the Experiences Shared summaries.

7.3 Theme 1: Experiences of CSA in boarding schools

'A cap-in-hand role'

Several accounts detailed how those giving their testimony had entered boarding school as somehow different from the other children there and this left them more vulnerable to abuse. Leopold said that he was coerced into a sexual relationship with a teacher with the threat of having his scholarship removed, leaving his proud, working-class mother to pay tuition fees. This state was echoed by Damon who said he was placed in a 'funny, cap-in-hand role; like you were quite beholden'. This was exploited by a senior teacher, who engaged specially selected boys in a series of sexualised rituals and was like a 'god' to them.

Other accounts detailed types of difference that left survivors seeking comfort and protection from their peers, only for this to be exploited by abusive teachers. Danni was bullied and isolated while her family lived overseas. She sought protection from a popular music teacher who moved from offering hugs to more egregious acts of abuse, dressed up as pastoral care. Chase suffered similar bullying, in his case on the basis of his Jewish background, and so he says he spent much of his 'time avoiding them in such a closed environment'. He went to visit one of the live-in teachers to escape the bullies, only to be subjected to sexual abuse at the age of 12 or 13.

Even for children who were there as fee-paying students, and in some senses more typical of the overall boarding school population, the culture of privilege was such that they often felt responsible for making good of their experience on behalf of their parents' financial sacrifices. Austin knew his parents paid a lot of money to send him to a preparatory school at the age of ten, and that he ought to be grateful. This jarred with the reality of his experience when he and other boys were sexually abused by a teacher. When he tried to tell the headmaster what was happening, he was told, 'Children like you end up in prison'. This points to a perverse hierarchy common across the accounts, whereby children were in some senses privileged to be sent to elite institutions, leaving incongruence with their actual experience. When they tried to disclose the abuse or seek protection, their privileged position at the institution was threatened, as if being sent somewhere else could be worse than what they were currently living with.

'Everything was so physical and aggressive'

In some accounts the sexual abuse occurred in the context of a 'special' and initially nurturing relationship that left the survivor feeling confused about the nature of the relationship and ashamed of what they saw as their complicity. As Olivar said, he *'was lonely in a bleak environment, so someone treating you as special giving you cakes and presents, expressing liking for you, then love, was really potent'*.

Olivar believed that his emotional and physical distance from his parents made him *'an obvious person for a child abuser to pick on'*. For other survivors, their experiences of CSA at boarding school were characterised by multiple forms of violence enacted by both teachers and peers, amounting to, as Todd described it *'torture'*. Todd attended boarding school in the 1970s and described *'various forms of sexual, psychological and physical abuse, meted out daily'*.

This was characteristic of other accounts whereby a culture of violence and the fear it induced was an everyday reality to be survived. Erick's sexual abuse went hand in hand with physical violence from the headmaster; it happened every week for four years and was always preceded by a beating for some wrongdoing. To compound this, the school matron was 'complicit' with the abuse, taking him to the headmaster in the middle of the night for talking in the dormitory, providing cover for him to be abused while the rest of the school slept.

James reported that the culture of violence was so pervasive that it was obvious other children and teachers were aware of the systemic abuse. He said that other children 'messed' their beds so they would be left alone and regularly ran away to escape. James felt that the sexual and physical violence were part of the culture there, and 'the physical abuse was just as bad'. Often the bullying perpetrated by older children was tacitly encouraged by teachers, with Horrence being left feeling 'it was pretty nasty ... most of the time I was terrified'. He, similarly to other accounts described above, sought protection in the arms of a teacher, leaving him vulnerable to befriending, grooming and eventually abuse. This cycle of frightened children needing protection in a hostile environment but ending up with this vulnerability being exploited for sexual reasons by teachers, was common across the testimonies.

'I wasn't allowed to write home anymore'

Many of the accounts detail forms of institutional corruption when children did attempt to report sexual abuse, either to the school or their families. Ninette was abused by an older pupil for five years. When she attempted to write her family a long letter detailing how unhappy she was without disclosing the abuse, it was read by her housemaster and she was chastised for upsetting her parents. She noticed that following this she was punished for minor mistakes. Danny suffered similar censorship when writing to his parents and also when he wrote a poem detailing his depression, which he was made to change to something 'bland and generic'.

Even when disclosures were successfully made to school or family, in almost all cases these were badly managed and covered up. Stefan was left feeling angrier with the headmaster he disclosed to who was 'the most powerful person in my world at the time, and because he did nothing. I couldn't even tell my parents.'

Danni successfully reported her abuse to her parents but when it was taken up with the school they were told 'you must not tell the police, we will handle it in house'. Later she found out that the teacher had been moved to another school.

In Kai's account, a school counsellor successfully reported the CSA that he suffered which resulted in a conviction for multiple offences for the teacher against several children. Up until the conviction was secured, many of Kai's peers did not want to believe the teacher was a perpetrator. In another case, Curtis saw a psychiatrist for the emotional disturbances he was exhibiting as a result of the abuse, but he felt unable to disclose anything of what was happening to him. He was told 'children don't have any rights' and said 'you were frightened about what would happen to you if you said anything'.

7.4 Theme 2: Impacts on survivors at the time and since

'A child alcoholic, broken and traumatised'

Many of the accounts detailed a range of physical, psychological and social problems arising from the abuse suffered, and the institutional betrayals that accompanied it. Often these consequences were felt when they were still at the school and the abuse was ongoing. Todd left boarding school in his early teens, 'having suffered the first of countless breakdowns – a child alcoholic, broken and traumatised'. For him these developmental problems that began in his early adolescence have continued throughout his life, with a range of debilitating impacts including relationship difficulties, homelessness and a range of mental health conditions that have manifested in self-harm and suicide attempts.

Difficulties starting while still at boarding school and developing across the lifespan, was a common theme across the testimonies. This highlights the importance of not separating out the impacts in adulthood from what was happening for these children during and in the immediate aftermath of the abuse. Julianna, as a boy at the time of the abuse, began engaging in sexual activity with other boys, leading to a sex addiction, which lasted many years and resulted in risky behaviours that created conditions for further victimisation. This culminated in a diagnosis of borderline personality disorder and several suicide attempts. Suicidality and self-harm were recurrent themes across the testimonies and were often presented alongside information about psychiatric diagnoses and admissions to hospitals.

For many, the disturbances survivors exhibited while still at school were misdiagnosed as problems somehow inherent to them and not connected to what was happening, meaning the labels they gained lacked explanatory power in alerting people to the source of their distress. At the time of her abuse, Seren drank so much alcohol one evening off school grounds that she had to be attended to by paramedics, leading her to be suspended from school and for her head teacher to ask her mother if Seren had an alcohol problem.

Paulie's mother was so concerned about his erratic behaviour that she took him to the doctor several times. When in adulthood Paulie accessed his medical records, he is described there as 'eccentric' with no further action taken in spite of him having extensive bruising on his genitals.

'People might think you're in some way to blame'

Descriptions of stigma and internalised shame were found in almost all of the accounts. Jon-Jay described feeling responsible for the abuse still, even though he can rationalise that it was not his fault. He said 'even when you are an adult and you can analyse it, you still feel it. You don't want to talk about it because people might think you're in some way to blame'. Erick was similarly worried about people finding out about his abuse worrying, 'people will start looking at you differently, judging you differently'. Austin said, 'throughout my adult life I have carried constant shame and guilt … feeling I did something wrong'.

This internalised shame and sense of responsibility, had a silencing impact on many of the survivors, making it more difficult for them to disclose what has happened or form trusting, intimate relationships. Jerome described a familiar pattern of increasing social isolation, withdrawal from positive activities such as sport, which he had previously enjoyed, and dropping out of university.

Relational difficulties were a central feature of what many of these survivors struggled with in the aftermath of the sexual abuse. For Gabriella, the original sexual abuse led on to a number of other violent relationships starting at 14, saying, 'I didn't really think anything of it because of what had happened to me'. The ongoing abuse in other relationships left her in her mid-teens, 'with a terrible alcohol problem ... and terribly depressed'.

These interconnected interpersonal, social and psychological consequences were common across the testimonies and are important to consider together in order to avoid compartmentalising the accounts into different forms of harm for ease of categorisation. For example, Daniel's attempts to deal with his abuse at boarding school included trying to find a social group where he could be accepted, 'I wanted to fit in so I regressed, got in with the wrong people'. This escalated to him drinking, using drugs and committing crimes, 'I didn't care as I was angry with the world'. His drinking led to him passing out and being assaulted by an older man while asleep which, brought the memories of the original abuse, 'flooding back ... you try to bury it'. In cases like Daniel's the internalised shame of the abuse becomes an actual social stigma, as he engages in socially sanctioned behaviours as a way to manage but which further compounds his disconnection from others, placing him at greater risk of re-victimisation.

These types of perverse outcomes were common across the accounts, whereby far from being protected by social systems in the aftermath of the sexual abuse, survivors were punished for their responses to it. Damon ran away from home aged 16 and went into, 'a massive downward spiral, then collapse'. He became involved in drugs and criminal behaviour, and was homeless for a time. Likewise, Simmeon has struggled to maintain employment or any long-term relationships since his experiences at boarding school, meaning the impacts percolate into all aspects of his life.

'I don't think anything good can ever happen to me'

A sense of a foreshortened future is described as one symptom of trauma [11] and there is evidence of similar feelings present in these accounts. Leopold says he feels that sharing his experience with the Truth Project has given him some closure, but he adds 'total closure is something that I regret I may never find. You suffer in your young life, your life gets mucked up and you carry that burden forever'. Narratives of pessimistic determinism were also present in other accounts, for example, Ninette described her mental health problems as meaning, 'I don't think anything good can ever happen to me'.

Other people contrasted their outwardly successful and rewarding lives with intermittent traumatic responses. Muriel said on the surface life was 'all well and good' but then it 'started to unravel ... I was having flashbacks ... if you keep a lid on things, they will erupt'. Gabriella put the experience of contrasting functionality as a result of both the privilege and disadvantage conferred by a boarding school education succinctly, 'I am articulate, I am highly educated, I am all of these things but I am also deeply, deeply broken.'

The minority of accounts that did talk about the future as holding the possibility of healing in the aftermath of sexual abuse tended to emphasise connections with others and public service as key to the recovery of meaning and life purpose. Rick's account suggested ways out of the difficulties of dealing with sexual abuse at boarding schools. He said he had found writing about his experiences helpful, and taking legal action along with some of his peers has allowed him to feel less alone. Several others including Lucas noted that talking about their abuse, either with loved ones or in therapy, has helped them deal with it. For others public service has been key, such as Tommy, who has taken solace in providing support for other disadvantaged children, acting as a foster parent. While Wayne has struggled extensively in the aftermath of disclosing his non-recent sexual abuse to the police, he sees himself as resilient and points to strong family relationships at the core of his recovery.

7.5 Theme 3: Survivor recommendations for change

There were a range of changes survivors wanted to see in boarding school policy, regulation and practice. One common theme across the accounts was the need for well-monitored, developmentally appropriate sexual education in boarding schools. This is in some ways counterintuitive as in some of the experiences of sexual abuse, one mechanism for grooming and normalising sexualised talk and touch was through a pseudo form of sexual education. However, what the accounts recommend is quite distinct from that, in that they suggest that a language is needed for talking about sexuality safely and in the context of an educational environment. An example of this nuanced approach came from Fabian, whose sexual abuse involved his abuser blackmailing him about his sexuality in order to keep him silent. He said that homophobia created the conditions for this blackmail to happen and that a different approach to talking about different expressions of sexuality would have left him less isolated and at risk.

A number of the accounts recommend the need for strengthened links between children and their families while they are at boarding school. This often reflected their isolation from parents. Jonathan felt strongly that as a parent himself he would want to be much more involved and have information shared with him if his children were at boarding school. For Carl and others a surrogate parental figure, such as a key worker might offer a safe person who a child could go to. As Brett said, this would need to be someone who is not part of the 'school hierarchy'.

Some accounts emphasised culture level change, with certain forms of masculinity seen as normalising bullying and dissuading people from expressing vulnerability, which might stifle disclosures of abuse. As Muriel said, 'there is pressure for boys to toughen up, and to have power and control over others'. The Truth Project was seen as evidence of culture change for some. For example, Austin said, 'the fact we're being listened to is a massive change since I was a child'.

7.6 Discussion

Reading about accounts of child sexual abuse can be an emotionally over-whelming experience. It can be tempting to allow the different accounts described to merge into one: a story of institutional negligence, individual malevolence and the tragic destruction of childhood. While this is one important aspect of the accounts presented here, it would be a moral as well as a categorical error to think it is the only one. Many of the pitfalls in reading about CSA in the context of boarding schools have parallels in the institutional responses to allegations of abuse. The reader may distance themselves from the accounts by saying things like, 'That is dreadful but it all happened so long ago, it is different now'. Historical context is an important observation but one which some survivors in these accounts are keen to emphasise does not mean the experiences are distant for them. As Fabian reported, 'labelling of child abuse as "historic" makes victims think that it is abuse that isn't happening now, and allows institutions to excuse it'.

Another risk is that the reader falls into a state of despair, mirroring the hopelessness that pervades some of these accounts. This will be familiar to many who work and live with the aftermath of trauma and can offer some ethical satisfaction that we have been suitably affected by the stories we have read. Despair, however, can be the enemy of action and can lead to a list-lessness that prevents us from acting to change these institutions and the way we treat the people harmed by them. It is therefore important to hold in mind the need for realistic hope for change while engaging with these accounts on their own terms. We will therefore discuss some of the implications of this analysis for policy and practice relating to safeguarding children in boarding schools.

IICSA recommendations for boarding schools

The IICSA made several recommendations for change in the boarding school sector following the public hearing [12]. These included that all residential schools in England and Wales should be inspected against nationally agreed quality standards, including the registration of educational guardians and a standardised system of reporting and responding to concerns and allegations of abuse. They also recommended the amendment of the Independent Schools Standards to develop an effective system of governance based on external scrutiny, transparency and honesty. They recommended nationally accredited, mandatory safeguarding training in schools and a review of the approach to teaching relationships, health and sex education, for children with special educational needs and disabilities. Given the absence of parents from many of these decisions for children at boarding school, we would suggest this was a good approach for all children, regardless of level of need. The final recom-mendations concerned the vetting of all staff and disclosure and barring responsibilities. Many of these recommendations broadly map on to policy level and legal changes that aim to improve the regulatory systems around boarding schools.

In May 2022 the UK government responded to IICSA's recommendations by making three of their own relevant to boarding schools, directed to the Department of Education [13]. These comprised, firstly, requiring that all boarding schools inform the relevant inspectorate of allegations of CSA, with regulatory consequences for any breach of this duty and to make all educational guardians subject to a Disclosure and Barring Service check. Secondly, they required a set of national standards for local authority designated officers and for these to clarify how officers can be contacted for informal advice from teachers and parents. Finally, the government recommended that the Independent School Standards include standards of governance that are open to external scrutiny, transparent and honest.

In IICSA's concluding report published in October 2022, they made further recommendations that are not specifically about, but are relevant to boarding schools [14]. This included Mandatory Reporting: making it a crime for some professionals to fail to report evidence or allegations of CSA. This would include teaching and educational staff at boarding schools. This recommendation is intended to address the reluctance, bias and anxiety many professionals have about reporting CSA, in some cases due to the institutional protectiveness and normalisation described by survivors in this chapter. It means that there are organisational and individual responsibilities, with the threat of criminal sanctions for negligence.

The recommendations made by survivors who attended the Truth Project were taken into account when the Chair and Panel were making recommendations but the high-level nature of IICSA recommendations are to some extent disconnected from what Truth Project participants actually said. In this final section therefore, the aim is to critically engage with the findings of the Truth Project data analysis in order to draw out further focused implications for boarding schools, both in safeguarding children, and also in responding to survivors.

Comparison of findings with other literature and implications

An initial observation is the lack of balance in the survivor accounts analysed here, in terms of boarding school culture more broadly. This is a necessarily skewed sample reflecting the perspectives of people who were abused when attending school and is not generalisable to all boarding school experiences. A recent review, conducted as part of the Scottish Child Abuse Inquiry, found that for boarding schools between 1970–2000, students were 'generally quite satisfied with their experience' [15]. There was no evidence that teachers at boarding schools were less helpful, or behaved any less appropriately than their counterparts in non-residential schools. We also have some information from other chapters in this book that only a minority of our participants report that they were sexually abused at boarding school. Therefore the findings described here likely correspond to a subset of overall boarding school experience.

The next consideration is how these accounts correspond to accounts of CSA in general, both based on the Truth Project testimonies and the broader literature. Many aspects of the experience of abuse and the impacts are similar to abuse in other settings. In the Truth Project research report on CSA within all schools [9], there are a number of notable similarities with the findings of this analysis but also some differences. The experience of the abuse itself was similar to the overall school data in that the grooming process often involved the teacher seeking out particular forms of intimacy with certain pupils and this then being exploited over time.

What was distinct was that in the boarding school testimonies, there was a much stronger sense that the teachers had become alternative attachment figures in the absence of parents, and therefore had more opportunity to exploit 'special' relationships. The level of protection the boarding school sample needed to seek out for protection from bullies meant that once they had latched on to a teacher, it was much harder to escape. This links to 'betrayal trauma' theory [16], which suggests that abuse perpetrated within close relationships is more harmful than abuse from a stranger because of the violation of trust involved. There is evidence that betrayal trauma is associated with higher levels of trauma and other mental health problems [17], making it more complex to successfully treat. The residential nature of boarding schools also makes escape more difficult, and chronic abuse in childhood from which there is limited opportunity to get away from the abuser is associated with increased propensity to develop complex post-traumatic stress disorder [18].

A further impact of abuse distinctive to boarding schools relates to 'institutional betrayal' [19], a concept that describes institutions responding poorly to allegations of harm. It can include silencing and delegitimising victims, and covering up wrongdoing to protect the institution's interests which leads to a more severe traumatic reaction [20]. There was a wealth of evidence of institutional betrayal in this analysis which clearly added to the harm caused to survivors over the long term. This has important implications for how people disclosing abuse at the time and afterwards are treated as it may compound their traumatic responses and set up boarding schools as an ongoing accomplice abuser who denies, minimises and obfuscates people seeking justice.

A final observation of the distinctive impacts of CSA in boarding schools concerns the complex role that privilege played in this data. In the wider literature, children from socially disadvantaged backgrounds are more likely to be victims of most forms of abuse, but not sexual abuse [21]. There is a relationship between socioeconomic status and health related trauma outcomes, suggesting that social disadvantage is linked to worse outcomes for childhood abuse [22]. From that perspective, one would expect that children who enjoyed the relative educational and social advantages of a British boarding school education, to be relatively protected across the lifespan from the long-term health and social impacts of trauma. However, in this analysis, the privileges afforded by a British boarding school education were undermined by the sense people had that this relative advantage meant they should tolerate abuse and remain grateful for their education. This risks creating a form of psychological double bind whereby their response to the abuse is minimised by both the boarding school itself and the assumptions of wider society. This is a theme explored in more detail in Chapter 8 about ex-boarder experiences of psychotherapy.

Linked to the above is the perverse outcome described in some accounts where people responded to their abuse in such a way as to invite social stigma and marginalisation, through engaging in coping strategies that were socially sanctioned such as substance abuse, homelessness and associated criminal activities. In some sense this leaves many of the survivors in these accounts as not belonging either in the privileged position of their boarding school peers, or the social marginalisation more typically associated with people who experience childhood adversity from already disadvantaged backgrounds. It seems ironic, that in claiming to provide these children with a new form of home, they were left feeling like they belonged nowhere at all.

The future of safeguarding in boarding schools

In this chapter, we analysed the experiences of 61 boarding school attendees who participated in the Truth Project. While not representative of boarding school pupils in general, there was important information about the role that institutions played in enabling abuse to occur and neglecting safeguarding responsibilities. There was an emphasis on protection of the institution over child-centred care, and while this was often non-recent, it still has relevance for contemporary boarding schools who manage their brand carefully in the independent school marketplace. The impacts of abuse were varied, but there was a consistent pattern of ex-boarders feeling betrayed by the institution and many described life-long debilitating health and social difficulties that began while they were still at school. The institutional negligence at the time was compounded by some accounts describing negative impacts of attempting to re-engage the school in adulthood.

In the wake of IICSA and other investigations into boarding school regulation, boarding schools have improved from the abuse described in this study. While IICSA were clear that CSA in institutional settings is not a historical relic, but a contemporary problem, there have been changes in regulation that have improved safeguarding practice. For example, the National Minimum Standards for Boarding Schools [23] highlight the changing nature of CSA, with an emphasis on peer-on-peer abuse, child sexual exploitation and online abuse. They make it clear that all boarding schools should be subject to inspections requiring quality standards that regulate children's homes. They also require staff to receive safeguarding and child protection training at induction with regular updates. This is connected to the requirement that all boarding schools have a duty to provide relationship and sexual education at developmentally appropriate stages, again something raised by survivors in this chapter who warned of how this type of education is exploited. It is reassuring to note that boarding schools are already subject to much of the regulatory and governance processes that IICSA are recommending, and that they align with survivor priorities.

In summary, our analysis of 61 accounts from the Truth Project provide unique insights into the experience of CSA in boarding schools, the impact of CSA at boarding school on survivors at the time and since and the survivors' own recommendations for change. We want to conclude this chapter by making a broader point about the legacy of CSA in boarding schools and the need for humility in addressing survivor accounts of harm, while avoiding the repetition of past mistakes. There is a risk of historisation in focusing on CSA as something in the past. This can lead to complacency about contemporary abuse. The residential music schools investigation at IICSA addressed CSA at Chetham's and Purcell's in the 1990s after all. However it can also lead to oblique harm to survivors of non-recent abuse. One of the consistent findings in the Truth Project was the extent to which CSA survivors feel abandoned by institutions, not only as children but as adults seeking justice. It is difficult to convey how much harm is caused in these secondary interactions, which compound the original abuse by reinforcing the lack of status of the survivor by denial, minimisation, lack of responsibility taking, and resorting to bureaucratic processes to avoid human to human communication. We therefore conclude this chapter by quoting an apology from the headmaster of Chetham's music school to IICSA [24]. We think this apology gets the tone right in terms of past and present practice, and taking responsibility for the harms caused. It offers some ideas for apology to other schools in similar positions, and, we hope, solace to survivors of all abuse in boarding schools:

> I am deeply sorry that teachers at our school abused their position of trust to hurt young people. Current parents and students would not recognise what was said at the Inquiry … but this is of no consolation to victims and survivors. I am deeply sorry the school did not do more to provide emotional support to the victims and survivors of abuse and their families. I would welcome any … getting in touch with me if they feel it can help to rectify some of the appalling mistakes of the past.

References

1 Wright K, Swain S, Skold J. *The age of inquiry: A global mapping of institutional abuse inquiries.* 2nd edition. Melbourne: La Trobe University 2020. doi:10.4225/22/591e1e3a36139

2 Swain S, Wright K, Sköld J. Conceptualising and categorising child abuse inquiries: From damage control to foregrounding survivor testimony. *J Hist Sociol* 2018; 31: 282–296. doi:10.1111/johs.12176.

3 Wright K. Challenging institutional denial: Psychological discourse, therapeutic culture and public inquiries. *J Aust Stud* 2018; 42: 177–190. doi:10.1080/14443058.2018.1462237.

4 Fisher C, Goldsmith A, Hurcombe R, *et al*. The impacts of child sexual abuse: a rapid evidence assessment. 2017. www.iicsa.org.uk/reports-recommendations/p ublications/research/impacts-csa.

5 Jay A, Evans M, Frank I, *et al*. The residential schools investigation. 2022. www. iicsa.org.uk/reports-recommendations/publications/investigation/residential-schools.

6 Ward M, Rodger H. Child sexual abuse in residential schools: A literature review. 2018. www.iicsa.org.uk/key-documents/7747/view/child-sexual-abuse-residential-schools% 3A-a-literature-review-november-2018.pdf.

7 End Violence Against Women. YouGov poll exposes high levels sexual harassment in schools. 2010. www.endviolenceagainstwomen.org.uk/yougov-poll-exposes-high-levels-sexual-harassment-in-schools.

8 King S, Brähler V. Truth project research: Methods. 2019. www.iicsa.org.uk/docum ent/truth-project-research-methods.

9 Brown S, Redmond T, Rees D, *et al*. Truth Project thematic report: Child sexual abuse in the context of schools. 2020. www.iicsa.org.uk/key-documents/24715/view/ truth-project-thematic-report-child-sexual-abuse-context-schools-.pdf.

10 Independent Inquiry into Child Sexual Abuse. Truth Project dashboard June 2016-June 2021. 2021. www.iicsa.org.uk/document/truth-project-dashboard-august-2021.

11 Ratcliffe M, Ruddell M, Smith B. What is a 'sense of foreshortened future?' A phe-nomenological study of trauma, trust, and time. *Front Psychol* 2014; 5. doi:10.3389/ fpsyg.2014.01026.

12 Independent Inquiry into Child Sexual Abuse. Recommendations – residential schools. www.iicsa.org.uk/recommendations/recommendations-residential-schools-investigation-report#873536697.

13 UK Government. Response to IICSA residential school report recommendations. 2022. www.iicsa.org.uk/key-documents/31119/view/2022-06-government-legal-depa rtment-response-to-recommendations-1-6-residential-schools-investigation.docx_.pdf.

14 Independent Inquiry into Child Sexual Abuse. The report of the Independent Inquiry Into Child Sexual Abuse – October 2022. www.iicsa.org.uk/document/report-independent-inquiry-child-sexual-abuse-october-2022-0.

15 Patterson L. Student experience of Scottish boarding schools, 1970s–1990s: Report for the Scottish Child Abuse Inquiry. 2020. www.childabuseinquiry.scot/resource-centre/student-experience-of-scottish-boarding-schools-1970s-1990s/.

16 Freyd J. *Betrayal trauma*. Cambridge, MA: Harvard University Press 1998. doi:10.2307/ j.ctv1c3pd18.

17 Freyd J, Birrell P. *Blind to betrayal: Why we fool ourselves we aren't being fooled*. Hoboken, NJ: John Wiley & Sons 2013.

18 Hyland P, Shevlin M, Elklit A, *et al*. An assessment of the construct validity of the ICD-11 proposal for complex posttraumatic stress disorder. *Psychol Trauma Theory, Res Pract Policy* 2017; 9: 1–9. doi:10.1037/tra0000114.

19 Smith CP, Freyd JJ. Institutional betrayal. *Am Psychol* 2014; 69: 575–587. doi:10.1037/a0037564.

20 Smith CP, Freyd JJ. Dangerous safe havens: Institutional betrayal exacerbates sexual trauma. *J Trauma Stress* 2013; 26: 119–124. doi:10.1002/jts.21778.

21 Olafson E. Child sexual abuse: Demography, impact, and interventions. *J Child Adolesc Trauma* 2011; 4: 8–21. doi:10.1080/19361521.2011.545811.

22 Mock SE, Arai SM. Childhood trauma and chronic illness in adulthood: Mental health and socioeconomic status as explanatory factors and buffers. *Front Psychol* 2011; 1. doi:10.3389/fpsyg.2010.00246.

23 Department for Education. Boarding schools: national minimum standards. 2022. https://assets.publishing.service.gov.uk/government/uploads/system/uploads/attachm ent_data/file/1102344/National_minimum_standards_for_boarding_schools.pdf.

24 Chetham's School of Music. IICSA statement (01.10.19). 2019. https://chetham sschoolofmusic.com/about/safeguarding-2/iicsa-statement-01-10-19/.

Chapter 8

Having psychotherapy to help with boarding school experiences

The role of denial, shame and privilege

Mairi Emerson-Smith, Susan McPherson and Penny Cavenagh

> What they always tell you at boarding school is, 'You are so lucky to be here. Your parents are making sacrifices for you to be here, and you're very privileged you're at such a good school.' And yet you do not feel like that; you feel as though you have been ... rubbished and put in this kind of ghastly place.
>
> (Study participant)

Psychotherapeutic work with ex-boarders has generated considerable case material and data to support theories about the long-term psychological impacts of British boarding schools discussed in earlier chapters. Client case material has been used by psychotherapist authors who weave those client experiences into broader theoretical tapestries. The material (life stories, memories, feelings and so on) offered by clients to their therapists is given in the context of a therapeutic conversation rather than directly for the purposes of research; the psychotherapist who writes books and papers using this material creates a second purpose for the material to support theories and ideas about the field in general. The present chapter also has psychotherapy as its context. Yet the data drawn on here have come about in a different way and may therefore shed a different sort of light on the issues. This chapter presents an analysis of data generated by the authors specifically for the purpose of research.

8.1 The research study

Our research participants were adult ex-boarders who had received psychotherapy to address psychological distress which they attributed to having attended boarding school. They found out about the study through adverts and flyers sent to UK organisations which support people with distress linked to attendance at boarding school (such as Boarding Concern). On finding out about the study, participants contacted the lead researcher for more information. If they wanted to go ahead, they then completed a consent form and arranged a time to be interviewed by the researcher. Interviews lasted about an hour and

DOI: 10.4324/9781003280491-8

covered topics such as expectations of therapy; how psychotherapy related to their boarding school experience; their relationship with their therapist; and the impact of therapy on their distress. Interviews were designed to be fluid such that participants were asked broad questions in each area followed by prompts to explore each individual's experience but not following any rigid interview script. Interviews were not intended to be therapeutic or to serve a wider therapeutic aim but were designed specifically to find out about each individual's experience of psychotherapy and how it may have impacted on the psychological distress they felt had come about because of having attended boarding school.

There were twelve participants altogether, aged between 44 and 82. Eight were women and four were men. They had received different types of psychotherapy, the most common being group therapy, psychoanalytic psychotherapy and counselling. Therapy had usually been once weekly and had lasted a minimum of 18 months; although some had up to 30 years of therapy with an average of 11 years. Ages of starting boarding school ranged from age 4 to 13 and they had attended for between 4 and 12 years. The types of psychological difficulties participants reported included relationship difficulties, anxiety, depression, low self-esteem, dissociation, physical health issues, separation anxiety and trauma symptoms.

Each interview was audio-recorded and transcribed and then subject to a systematic process of textual analysis known as thematic analysis [1]. This is a way of generating a set of themes which seem to the researcher to be prominent features across the whole set of interviews. The themes are presented and discussed in the rest of this chapter using quotes from participants to illustrate each theme.

To some extent, because all the participants had been to boarding school as a child and felt some of their distress experienced as an adult related to this, a lot of what they talked about in their interviews was about their difficult experiences at boarding school. This overlapped a great deal with the British psychotherapy literature already presented in earlier chapters. There were therefore several familiar themes in the data mirroring existing descriptions of the impact of boarding school on children such as the shutting down of emotions; a loss of self and the construction of a mask or false self; loss of childhood relationships; sense of abandonment; and the trauma of separation from parents. It is important to acknowledge that these themes were clearly present in our data and fully support all the ideas presented in existing psychotherapy literature. However, to provide a novel focus for the present chapter we will not describe these themes in detail and will focus on themes specifically relating to experiences of psychotherapy. The five themes are: 'Discovering an emotional language through therapy'; 'Rebuilding the self through therapy'; 'Transforming relationships after loss of intimacy'; 'Overcoming the triple bind of shame, denial and privilege through therapy'; and 'Trauma focused therapy and therapist expertise'.

8.2 Theme 1: Discovering an emotional language through therapy

Having talked about the ways they felt their emotions were shut down while at boarding school, participants described a lack of emotional literacy in adulthood. This seemed to be a key difficulty which could be improved for ex-boarders through the process of psychotherapy. Participants described an emotional block linked to the distress of the boarding school experience and an important part of therapy was processing these emotions.

> Learning to reconnect with my own emotions, which I completely blocked off, because they were just too horrifying as a young man to encounter ... But of course, when you isolate yourself from your own emotions, you isolate your ability to be able to be in emotional relationships with others. So that has been a huge part of the therapeutic work from my early twenties – it's kind of reconnected to that part of me.

Participants spoke about how different it felt to have their emotions validated in therapy compared to the boarding school experience where emotions were not expressed.

> I think one of the troubles with boarding school is that you learn not to make a fuss. You learn here that your unhappiness is not worth mentioning, that you just have got to get on with it. And I think one of the things that therapy helped me to do was to say this – I am allowed to make a fuss about this ... It gave me confidence really to recognise that my feelings are sort of ... valid.

However, one participant noted that as their emotions were so blocked off due to the boarding school experience, they felt they were unable to express emotion in therapy.

> But I could never cry about something because crying was not something you did at school. So that is something I very, very rarely do. So I never cried in therapy. I just felt emotional. But I have never been able to let my emotions go and spill out and that probably still is the case. I always feel like they've got to be kept in mostly.

Nevertheless, the discovery of some kind of emotional language through therapy appeared for some participants to be a component of the change enabled by therapy.

> Yes, I think I am far better able to distinguish different aspects of how I'm feeling and to be able to put words to it or to put images to it; so I can define what I'm feeling much better.

Allowing the expression of emotions linked to boarding school experience seemed to be critical and could lead to improvements in psychological wellbeing.

> I am now, after many years, more able to speak about my feelings, and speak about what happened in the past. It took me a long time. Quite often, I just could not get the words out, as though they were sort of stuck in my throat and would not go any further. I think I am leading a freer, happier life because I am less anxious. I'm certainly not so depressed.

Other participants noted improved expression of their emotions or a more remarkable ability to manage emotional expression in others and, as a result, enhanced relationships. Considering the emotional shut down and language deficit in childhood described by participants, a therapist skilled in boarding school distress seems potentially helpful. Since distress related to boarding school is so well hidden, armoured against and denied, it can be challenging for a therapist to observe and understand. Therefore, for this client group, a vital part of the therapy process is for the therapist to name, understand and validate the emotional distress connected to the boarding school experience. This resonates with the psychoanalytic idea that voicing painful emotions from the past in therapy aids in the understanding of distress and trauma, which leads to a greater sense of self-coherence [2]. Similarly, in counselling practice it is thought that the therapist's validation of clients' emotions can lead to clients developing a greater sense of self-worth, empowerment and self-acceptance [3].

8.3 Theme 2: Rebuilding the self through therapy

The 'false self' described in the boarding school psychotherapy literature refers to a lack of authentic and genuine identity characteristic of ex-boarders [4, 5, 6]. The 'false self' is thought to be learned by some child boarders in order to present as successful, happy and confident when masking desperate feelings below the surface. A helpful process in therapy described by many of our participants was the building of the self. This was depicted in stark contrast to boarding school, which had left participants feeling they did not have a true identity; that they had little voice or control over their experience and where they had created the mask to hide their true self.

> I think the process of therapy was a unique gift to me; it was time spent just entirely on me, which I never had. As opposed to just being at school and just being a number, or a problem or … not being allowed to be an individual.

Therapy enabled participants to build genuine self-confidence, as opposed to faking it.

> So outwardly I probably might have looked the same and been out-going … whereas I would be shrinking inside. But now I could be out-going and it's genuine.

A crucial part of change within the therapy process, therefore, was the process of self-development. Participants had explained how the lack of voice, self-individuation and control in boarding school had led to a lack of self-knowledge and low self-esteem in adulthood. A valuable part of therapy was the building of the self as well as developing genuine self-confidence.

8.4 Theme 3: Transforming relationships after loss of intimacy

Mirroring previous psychotherapy literature, some of our participants spoke of the range of ways that boarding school damaged their relationships and ability to form new ones.

This included the loss of childhood relationships, loss of connection to the family and home, early separation from caregivers, feelings of abandonment and psychological trauma. For many, this carried through to difficult adult relationships with siblings, parents, partners and children. Some described long-term difficulties with trust and abandonment in all relationships includ-ing partners, work colleagues, professionals and friends.

> I think difficulty [about attending boarding school] with intimate rela-tionships; one has to build a kind of protective layer which is often called a strategic survival personality. So that nobody actually can get very near you. You put up those defence systems when you are small because you dare not trust or believe or give yourself to somebody fully in case you are hurt or abandoned or let down again.

Therapy appeared to be able to positively impact this damaging cycle for all types of relationship.

> I would say that my therapy, as a result of the impacts of boarding school, has been nothing short of transformative upon my relation-ships to my family of choice – with my wife and my children; but also, my family of birth – with my brother and my sister and my mum and dad.

Some described the impact of therapy on relationships with children and parenting style.

I think it did help me alter how I parented. She did an exercise with me when we talked about the conditional love that I had received as a child. And she made me write on little stick-its all the things; there were a lot of 'don't be's' in childhood, which were more to do with going to boarding school – like do not be upset, do not be selfish, do not be … and so I wrote them all down and we put it on this big bit of paper. And I looked at it and she said 'well, there wasn't a lot of room, what were you meant to do? There's so many 'don't do's'. And that really struck me as such an important thing in parenting. So, I think allowing my daughters to be what they needed to be and to be in a bad mood, to be demanding, to be all the negative things, was really helpful.

Therapy can potentially break the trauma element of parenting for families who have generations of attending boarding school.

What happened to me is you grow up without parental role models … an enormous amount of the therapeutic work I have been involved in … which is actually helping to build … memories of what it would have been like to have parents … my parents … both of them went to boarding school and both of them were raised within a certain privileged class in the UK. So, they were already, even the day I was born, were not able to build proper or healthy relationships with their children. So, I have had … a massive, steep learning curve about how to be in relationships with my kids. That has been a huge part of my therapy.

According to the adult attachment literature, experiences of early relationships create internal working models and attachment orientations and the attachment orientation of the parent impacts the attachment bond their children have with them [7]. The lack of availability of primary caregivers for children attending boarding school could have similar damaging effects on parent-child attachment patterns and consequences for social and emotional development. Yet adult attachment patterns are not fixed, can be developed, and are changeable within a process of personal therapy and personal growth [8]. The types of therapies received by participants in this study appear to have the potential to help adults develop healthier ways of forming and maintaining relationships with children, siblings and partners. The therapy process may break the trauma element of non-parenting for families who have successive generations attending boarding school. For example, some participants described the impact of therapy on their relationships with their own children and how they learned to allow their children to express emotions rather than shut them down. An integral part of the therapeutic process is aiding the client in transforming their relationships.

8.5 Theme 4: Overcoming the triple bind of shame, denial and privilege through therapy

As previous psychotherapy authors have indicated, attending boarding school teaches children to deny their feelings, deny that there has been any trauma, or that being sent away from key attachment figures and the safe space of home to strangers, can indeed be an awful thing for a child. This denial carries through to adulthood. Our data suggest this culminates in a triple bind in which the privilege attained from attending boarding school prevents anything negative being said about it. Many participants felt their parents had strongly emphasised the privilege of going to boarding using words such as 'special', 'lucky', 'parental sacrifice', and 'be thankful'. This so-called privilege was felt to be a juxtaposition to their real feelings.

> There was a lot of hypocrisy at my school and that summed it up for me ... you are privileged to be here but you are ... actually ... really unhappy. You're very lucky girls but this is the worst time of your life.

How then is it possible to enter therapy to address all the psychological consequences of a traumatic childhood if one is not allowed to describe boarding school as anything other than a privilege? What therapist could feel sympathy for someone who has been so lucky, whose parents made such sacrifices for them, who should be nothing but thankful? This was a significant barrier to therapy for many of our participants and was a central feature of therapy once it had begun. A critical element of the therapy process was to overcome the barrier of denying boarding school distress, by voicing the impact of boarding school and to be believed about its implications.

> And it [therapy] has validated me, but also given me an ability to explain to mates of mine ... why it's important not to invalidate abuse when it happens ... in [the] context of privilege.
> And what did that acceptance look like in therapy? Well, it is a physical thing in terms of a look of the body and expression of the body. But it is also the content of the words... also the way that the words are expressed. And the complete belief that my experience was what I said it was ... So it was everything – verbal and non-verbal in the way that the therapist heard and never questioned ... never doubted what I said. It was important to me.

Participants underwent a slow process of realisation; of coming to see themselves as trauma survivors and that this kind of trauma was a thing worthy of therapy.

> In my very early experiences of therapy, I never even realised that the issue was boarding school. And it is only after years of therapy that I

realised that everything begins and ends with my experience of boarding school and being subjected to boarding school. Especially as you are very, very small – at a young age. When I first started therapy I had no idea that anything was anything to do with boarding school. It never even crossed my mind. Whilst now I'm at a place where I absolutely realise.

The privileged element of attending boarding school seems to be instilled in children from every angle including parents and society. This overemphasis on the privilege of boarding school can create a disconnect between the painful feelings and the actual experience, enhancing the sense of being emotionally cut-off. In some cases children were even accused of being selfish by their parents if they brought up difficulties they were having at boarding school. Denial would then be coupled with shame – the shame of having negative feelings toward something so magnificent. This shame is compounded as an adult when going to university or starting a job and meeting new groups of people having to face the widely held assumption that having attended boarding school must have been a great privilege. Consequently, boarders are left with a form of trauma that is not recognised or acknowledged by themselves, family, friends or society.

Societal denial of any type of psychological trauma has been found to have a damaging impact on therapy processes and can act as a barrier in therapy [9],[10]. Similarly, shame is known to have debilitating effects, both for the client and in the therapy process as it can silence the client and mask distress [11]. These were both in play for our participants, compounded by the idea of privilege. The triple bind of denial of trauma in the guise of privilege leading to shame appears to follow ex-boarders into adult life and can be an ongoing barrier to receiving any support or help for the psychological traumas endured and their impact on adult mental health and relationships.

Once in therapy the triple bind can persist. Some participants said they felt their therapist assumed because they were privileged by attending boarding school, they cannot possibly feel any negative emotion toward it. They must be overreacting, easily irritable, seen as over excessive. This generated more shame and fear of irritating others with their frivolous complaints. This context of privilege, shame, and trauma makes therapy a unique, complex, and challenging process for the client and therapist since the client and therapist may both avoid talking about experiences of boarding school. Therefore, a critical element of therapy when boarding school trauma is spoken of is to have acceptance from the therapist – to be believed.

8.6 Theme 5: Trauma focused therapy and therapist expertise

Considering the role of trauma in ex-boarder psychological distress, it may be helpful to consider the need for a trauma focus to psychotherapy. Trauma-focused interventions had felt helpful to some of our participants including breath work, body work, trauma healing work and trauma-sensitive mindfulness.

> I began to see that what could help me at this point is trauma healing work, which involves a focus much more on body work instead of psychological discussion. Somatic experiencing is one of the phrases they talk about ... and I really see for myself how the experience – the damaging experiences – literally become locked up in the body ... And they can be released ... And I can see now it is equally important alongside of having conscious awareness of the whole thing [boarding school trauma].

Another consideration is the expertise of the therapist with some participants suggesting that it was critical to have someone with specialist understanding of boarding school distress due to the protective nature of the 'defences' and 'hard shell' developed by ex-boarders.

> So many therapists who are not trained or aware of this syndrome ... they are not going to be able to be of a huge amount of help. Because we are so defective, we are so ... we have such thick skin and a hard shell.
>
> I could see that I was almost too slippery for that person to be able to help get underneath my defences and my shiny survivalist like ... the person just did not have the skill. I was too resistant or there was a resistant energy in me that did not want to be seen – did not want to reveal itself – did not want to enter the process. And... that is boarding school syndrome in a nutshell.

There was also a sense from participants that being part of a network of fellow survivors could help normalise distress and enhance therapeutic impact. Group therapy could for example help with validation, normalisation, acceptance and reducing the hold of the triple bind.

> I was actually in a group with three boarding school survivors on that first weekend – on a year's course – and I was with other people who were as fucked up and had such a shitty time as a child as I had. So, I think the most helpful thing ... has been just being totally accepted for who I was. And again, it is the listening – not giving any advice – and total, total acceptance ... That started me being more specific and realising that boarding school had played such a magnanimous part in my health and my life and my relationships.

We know from trauma research that memories of traumatic events can be fragmented and sometimes held within sensory processes [12]. Therefore, an important part of therapy is to help past trauma be more fully processed and laid down more accurately in memory while the survivor or client is in a grounded state and feeling safe. Considering boarding school as a form of trauma means that trauma-based therapeutic and specialist interventions do seem a potentially useful tool for supporting ex-boarders with psychological distress. However, there is limited data from our study to be able to conclude empirically, which type of therapy or therapist is most effective.

8.7 Discussion

This study involved interviewing twelve adults who relate their psychological distress to attending boarding school about their experiences of psychotherapy. Much of the data (not presented in detail) mirrored concepts found in British psychotherapy case study research concerning the damaging impacts of boarding school on children and subsequently on adult ex-boarders including the trauma of abandonment and the creation of a false self. These are the two key features which played out in therapy for our participants and appear to be amenable to a skilled and empathetic therapist. Yet fundamental to therapy success was the ability of the therapist to enable the client to overcome the triple bind of privilege, shame and denial. Working therapeutically with this particular client group may be complex and challenging owing to this triple bind which may yet keep many potential clients from even reaching therapy in spite of high need. It would seem critical for therapeutic intervention to be attuned to these complexities in order to be beneficial.

Before considering more definitive clinical recommendations it is important to remind ourselves of the scope of our data and any limits to what sort of conclusions we can draw as a result. Our sample was twelve adults all of whom were of the view (at the point of volunteering for the research) that the distress they experienced as adults was in some part a result of having attended boarding school. Many people attend boarding school and also experience psychological distress as adults but may factor in other reasons for their distress (such as family history, biology or other separate traumatic or distressing events). People who attribute their distress primarily to other factors may have different experiences of therapy. It is conceivable that the focus or special interest of the therapists could potentially have influenced the way the participants came to locate some of their difficulties in boarding school as opposed to, say, family or other influences. Other people who went to boarding school may consider boarding school as only a minor part of a bigger puzzle and may therefore choose, want or need therapy with a wider focus. The type of therapy someone ends up in (or the specific interests and focus of therapist they encounter) may in various ways influence the way they think about and frame the causes of their distress. It is therefore not possible to draw firm conclusions about what sort of therapy or therapist might be most beneficial for all those who feel they may have been psychologically harmed by attendance at boarding school nor that the cause of participants' distress was necessarily solely derived from attending boarding school.

With this in mind we should consider the idea that therapy for ex-boarders should necessarily be trauma focused. We know from trauma research that the experience of not being believed or avoiding talking about a traumatic event can be re-traumatising [13]. It can create feelings that the individual is to blame for the trauma; that nobody cares; that therapy would be pointless. This therapeutic understanding would clearly be useful for ex-boarders, but it may of course depend on the nature of the trauma. For some ex-boarders, boarding school was the enabling environment for emotional, physical and/ or sexual abuse in addition to the trauma of abandonment. For others the principal trauma was the abandonment itself and therefore different in terms of therapeutic need. Inevitably, in either scenario (and all the shades in between), openly discussing and recognising boarding school distress as a form of trauma, having acceptance from the therapist and being believed seems vital – especially in order to help overcome the denial, shame and privilege triple bind. Yet there should also be scope for thinking about each client's need on a case-by-case basis in terms of the degree and nature of trauma focus required.

Beyond therapy, the study also raises wider questions about how to support ex-boarders who have experienced psychological trauma from attending boarding school. Clearly there are many ways that boarding schools themselves could adapt and respond to the various research findings in his book which we will discuss in a later chapter. Some may go further to argue that British boarding schools should be abolished, resolving the issue altogether. The abolitionist stance may derive from a view about intrinsic child abuse or other views about private education. Either way, there is likely to be, for the time being, cohorts of ex-boarders experiencing distress in adulthood and perhaps only gradually coming to terms with the idea that attending boarding school may have contributed to their current distress.

In summary, interviews with these 12 adults illustrate the ways in which psychotherapy can help with negative experiences at boarding school. In particular, the findings indicate that psychotherapy can help its recipients find an emotional language to express their feelings, can contribute to rebuilding their sense of self, can support their ability to build relationships and can offer trauma-focused therapy where necessary using techniques such as breath work, body work, trauma healing work and trauma-sensitive mindfulness. Furthermore, the findings highlighted the complex triple bind of feelings of shame and denial coupled with an assumption of privilege which can be helped if the client feels believed and accepted by their therapist. Therapy is therefore key to supporting ex-boarders who need additional support for their distress following boarding. In addition, the present study indicates that societal attitudes about privilege can clearly fuel the triple bind of shame, denial and privilege and add to this distress. It would therefore be helpful to increase public awareness of boarding school trauma in order to reduce prejudice and shaming.

References

1 Braun V, Clarke V. Using thematic analysis in psychology. *Qual Res Psychol* 2006; 3: 77–101. doi:10.1191/1478088706qp063oa.

2 Lilliengren P, Werbart A. A model of therapeutic action grounded in the patients' view of curative and hindering factors in psychoanalytic psychotherapy. *Psychother Theory, Res Pract Train* 2005; 42: 324–339. doi:10.1037/0033-3204.42.3.324.

3 Knox R. Clients' experiences of relational depth in person-centred counselling. *Couns Psychother Res* 2008; 8: 182–188. doi:10.1080/14733140802035005.

4 Duffell N. *Wounded leaders: British elitism and the entitlement illusion – a psychohistory.* London: Lone Arrow Press 2014.

5 Schaverien J. Boarding school syndrome: Broken attachments a hidden trauma. *Br J Psychother* 2011; 27. doi:10.1111/j.1752-0118.2011.01229.x.

6 Simpson N, editor. *Finding our way home.* Abingdon: Routledge 2018. doi:10.4324/9781351065542.

7 Rholes WS, Simpson JA. Attachment theory: Basic concepts and contemporary questions. In: *Adult attachment: Theory, research, and clinical implications.* New York: Guilford Publications 2004. 3–14.

8 Levy KN, Meehan KB, Kelly KM, *et al.* Change in attachment patterns and reflective function in a randomized control trial of transference-focused psychotherapy for borderline personality disorder. *J Consult Clin Psychol* 2006; 74: 1027–1040. doi:10.1037/0022-006X.74.6.1027.

9 Siegel DJ. Memory, trauma, and psychotherapy: A cognitive science view. *J Psychother Pract Res* 1995; 4: 93–122.

10 Solomon Z. Oscillating between denial and recognition of PTSD: Why are lessons learned and forgotten? *J Trauma Stress* 1995; 8: 271–282. doi:10.1002/jts.2490080208.

11 Gilbert P. Shame in psychotherapy and the role of compassion focused therapy. In: *Shame in the therapy hour.* Washington, DC: American Psychological Association 2011. 325–354. doi:10.1037/12326-014.

12 Rothschild B. *The body remembers: The psychophysiology of trauma and trauma treatment.* New York: WW Norton & Company 2000.

13 Ehlers A, Clark DM. A cognitive model of posttraumatic stress disorder. *Behav Res Ther* 2000; 38: 319–345. doi:10.1016/S0005-7967(99)00123-0.

Chapter 9

Escape, autonomy, friendship and resilience

Positive experiences of British boarding school

Remy Hayes, Frances Blumenfeld, Susan McPherson, Penny Cavenagh and Caitlin Phillips

Throughout this book we have reviewed clinical theories and case studies of trauma and attachment difficulties resulting from attending British boarding schools. We have also reviewed survey research examining psychological impacts of attending boarding schools, such as (but not limited to) depression, anxiety, alcohol use, suicidality and homesickness. Very little research to date has looked at the potential role of boarding school in building resilience and positive mental wellbeing in boarders. In Chapter 1 we briefly considered findings from research showing benefits of attending boarding school, including a large survey of 1477 Australian boarders which identified positive parent-child relationships and positive life satisfaction among boarders [1]. However, we noted some methodological problems with this study, including that the study may have been biased as a result of having been funded by the Australian Boarding Schools Association. It was also only able to examine immediate impacts on children who were boarding at the time of the study rather than long term impacts on adult ex-boarders.

In Chapter 1 we also mentioned that some of the case studies from British psychotherapy literature identified benefits of boarding school, such as taking part in team sports giving a sense of belonging and identity. Supporting this idea, we quoted findings of an alumni survey run by Gordonstoun in which ex-boarders reported that they gained 'confidence, self-belief, leadership skills, the ability to remain calm and determination through adversity from these experiences' [2]. Again, we noted the potential bias in these findings given the project was funded by Gordonstoun. Yet taken together these pieces of evidence may indicate that resilience, confidence, interpersonal skills and independence are potential benefits of boarding school. In this chapter we return to this question, namely of the potential benefits of boarding school, and describe a study in which we aimed to identify ex-boarders who felt they had an overall positive experience of boarding school and feel they benefitted psychologically in some way.

DOI: 10.4324/9781003280491-9

9.1 The research study

In Chapter 2, we described an online survey study of UK ex-boarders which collected information about past experiences of boarding along with questionnaires about current depression, anxiety, trauma symptoms, adult relationships, resilience and experiences of early family life. We used the same survey for this study with the same ethical and consent process described previously, including the invitation at the end of the survey to take part in an interview. However, for this study we specified that we were 'particularly interested in hearing from ex-boarders who feel the experience was on the whole mainly positive'. Information about the study was circulated through social networks using a 'snowballing' technique, which means that we ask members of our own networks to pass on the information to people in their social networks and for them to do the same. This technique enables us to reach more potential networks of eligible participants. The survey was also advertised on social media such as Facebook to enhance access to social networks.

In total, 26 ex-boarders responded to the survey questions and 14 of these took part in an interview. Table 9.1 provides information about how the 26 boarders scored on average on our questionnaires. We calculated the mean score for each of the adult mental health and relationship scales in order to find out whether, on average, our respondents appear to be scoring higher or lower than the previous sample of respondents described in Chapter 2. On

Table 9.1 Average scores on mental health, relationship and parenting scales.

Adult wellbeing and relation- ship styles	Number	Mini- mum	Max- imum	Mean	Stan- dard devia- tion	Higher or lower than our sample from Chapter 2
Depression	25	0	10	2.6	2.6	Lower
Anxiety	26	0	14	6.1	3.5	Lower
Trauma symptoms	25	0	43	13.9	13.2	Lower
Resilience	25	2.3	3.3	3.0	0.3	Same
Anxious attachment	25	1	4.8	2.4	1.1	Lower
Avoidant attachment	24	1	4.2	2.4	1.0	Lower
Parental rejection	24	7	16	9.4	2.7	Lower
Parental warmth	24	9	24	17.2	4.3	Higher
Parental overprotection	24	11	28	16.9	4.4	Lower

average, it seems the group of people who responded to this survey have broadly better wellbeing as adults than the previous sample, although two individuals have elevated trauma symptoms (in the clinical range). One of these also scores in the 'moderate' anxiety range. Another two individuals score in the 'mild' and 'moderate' range for anxiety. On average, the group report lower levels of parental rejection and parental overprotection and higher levels of parental warmth in their early family life. They report similar levels of resilience. This suggests that we broadly succeeded in identifying a group of people who currently have overall good mental wellbeing, have reasonably good adult relationships and who seem to have had slightly more positive experiences of their early relationships with their parents than our previous sample.

Table 9.2 provides more detailed information about the 14 people we interviewed. We interviewed eight men and six women. At the time of

Table 9.2 Participant characteristics.

Pseudonym	Gender	Age	Marital status	Children	Age started boarding	Highest qualification	Ethnicity
David	Male	29	Married	0	8	Degree	White British
Jay	Male	28	Co-habiting	0	8	Degree	White British
Richard	Male	58	Married	3	11	A Levels	White British
Suzanna	Female	60	Married	1	11	Degree	White British
Georgia	Female	57	Married	3	11	Degree	White
Michael	Male	85	Married	4	6	A levels	White
Rupert	Male	59	Married	6	Unknown	Degree	Anglo Saxon
Rachel	Female	54	Married	3	8	Masters	White British
Jenny	Female	69	Married	5	13	A levels	White
Elizabeth	Female	45	Co-habiting	0	11	PhD	Other
Robert	Male	28	Married	0	10	Degree	White British
Daniel	Male	53	Married	3	Unknown	Masters	White
Penelope	Female	65	Married	4	5	Masters	English
Andrew	Male	78	Married	3	13	Masters	White British

interview, they were aged between 28 and 85 and so would have boarded from the 1940s to the 2000s. The youngest age any of them started boarding was five years old; less than half were 11 or older when they started boarding. Two females had experienced a traumatic sexual experience such as rape or molestation before the age of 18. All participants were married or co-habiting at the time of interview. All but one of the participants were White, though described this in different ways when asked about their ethnicity (see Table 9.2). Six of the participants said that either one or both of their parents had attended boarding school. Academic achievements were varied ranging from A-levels up to PhD. Some of the people we interviewed were currently retired but all were, or had been, in some form of work before retiring. Two were currently employed in professions relating to mental health such as psychotherapy or counselling.

The 14 interviews were transcribed and analysed using thematic analysis in the same way as described in previous chapters. Below we present in detail four main themes identified: 'Family relationships: contrasting perspectives'; 'Having autonomy, control and choice'; 'Development of interpersonal skills and individual strengths'; 'Developing a sense of responsibility, resilience and independence'.

9.2 Theme 1: Family relationships: Contrasting perspectives

In this theme we see that some of our participants appeared to have valued their boarding school experience, at least in part, because it felt preferable to being at home. Others had a very different perspective on their family and having been able to maintain regular contact with their loved ones at home enabled them to enjoy boarding.

Escape from the family

Many described growing up in families characterised by difficult relational dynamics. Although the dynamics within each family differed, it seems that the interaction of this with the temperament of the individual child is what helps us understand the relief that boarding school sometimes offered. For Rachel, her strict and stiff family context where feelings could not be spoken about conflicted with her natural curiosity and desire to express herself.

> It was also quite old fashioned in the stiff-upper-lippy type sense, you didn't talk about your feelings much and as long as you did what you were supposed to do, everything was fine but if you stepped out of line there was my mother's wrath on you.
>
> (Rachel)

For Georgia, her ability to experience and express 'negative' feelings was compromised in her family home.

For my parents the idea of ... being depressed or upset or under the weather ... was not something they could really tolerate for very long.

(Georgia)

It was palpable in many respondents' narratives how desperate they were to escape from the scenarios they faced at home, perhaps because of chronic relational conflict or a parent managing their own distress.

My parents were dysfunctional, they argued all the time. Psychologists would have a great ball with my parents ... there was shouting matches every single day. I mean just, just nothing enjoyable about that.

(Rupert)

My father worked away. My mother was depressed for quite a lot of the time, and I think an alcoholic, looking back on it.

(Michael)

I mean I loved my mother, absolutely adored her but I think because we had quite an intense relationship and I confided so much in her ... I think she perhaps became too interfering in my life.

(Georgia)

It was boarding school that gave these individuals the opportunity to escape from the elements of their individual family lives that were making them unhappy.

In my case, it gave me an opportunity to opt out. It was fine, it gave me that choice and I took it.

(Rupert)

Boarding school could provide stability missing from home life, could allow participants to be a more authentic self, or follow their aspirations.

At least when I was at school I could be more myself ... and be silly and whatever it was. I had more freedom from her judgement whereas if I'd been at home ... It allowed me to escape from it and go off and do things that my parents sort of wouldn't have approved of. She wanted me to marry a doctor or live just down the road.

(Rachel)

There was going to be stability [at boarding school]. My life had been totally unstable. I'd been, on one or two occasions, in care. So it had been a completely chaotic life ... my mother basically would pick the best person she thought she knew who could look after me for school holidays or whatever, and that's where I would be. So this offered an opportunity of much more consistency in my life and I was aware of that even at that age. It gave everything that was missing.

(Penelope)

Valuing contact and support from family

In contrast, some participants described having experienced what they considered to be normal childhoods. They defined this as having home lives where they generally felt happy and where they enjoyed warm and supportive relationships with their parents and other family members.

We had fun as a family, I'd say. My mum used to take us down to the beach in the summer and stay on the beach with us. It was good. We had lots of open, noisy discussions around the dinner table.

(Andrew)

Although the initial separation was hard, being at boarding school could be an opportunity for parents to show how much they cared for their children, with the effort they were willing to put in to support them.

I think there were two days at the beginning when I was crying non-stop, well I say nonstop, every opportunity I got. I think my mum came back to visit two weeks after I started. She stayed in the UK to make sure I was okay.

(Robert)

Many participants kept up regular contact through writing and receiving letters. This allowed participants to continue to feel connected with their family while they were away.

A letter was a big thing ... they'd be handed out every morning and you'd just be absolutely hanging out for your name to be called out when the letters were handed out.

(Georgia)

Many respondents' parents made considerable efforts to stay in contact which participants appear to have appreciated. They talked about their parents travelling long distances, taking them out for trips out or doing their best to visit each weekend.

My mother wrote me a letter every day, but we also actually went home every weekend, so my mother learnt to drive just from home to school and back, and she clutched the steering wheel and ... just did that.

(Elizabeth)

My parents always came to pick me up you know for all those holidays. So even though it's a long trek back up to [the school] they'd come and get me after congregation practice on Saturday and then poor Dad would have to drive me all the way back on Sunday evening.

(Georgia)

Doing without family

School restrictions on family visits brought into sharp focus how much each parent visited their child when the opportunity arose. For those who felt they had come from loving families this provided an opportunity for parents to demonstrate how much they cared by the effort they put into visiting. For those who felt they had escaped from unhappy family situations, they reported not being particularly impacted by the times their family members failed to visit. This was something they had come to expect and learned to cope with.

I did start playing in the first eleven when I was quite young and I scored the most goals in the first season. My mother could have come to watch. It would have only taken her an hour and a half to get to [the school], but it never happened. It didn't bother me, funnily enough. I never thought about it.

(Andrew)

Indeed, for some participants having very little family contact became their way of being, their norm which continued into adult life. They valued the independence they had developed and saw it as a major strength. They no longer went to their parents as a source of support and instead relied on their own abilities.

I don't think I ever spent more than the summer holidays, two months at home, from the age of seven, and I probably never spent more than two months at home again for the rest of my life.

(Daniel)

Some found that even when they were offered the opportunity to resume the role of child, cared for by a parent, they resisted it. Their independence and freedom had become more deeply valued than parental connection.

Having that perception of freedom at such a young age made it very hard to then go back to home where you are suddenly treated more like a child ... When it came to phoning my parents, oftentimes I didn't want to. Oftentimes it came back to that feeling a restriction, of the sense of freedom I had by going to boarding school.

(Robert)

9.3 Theme 2: Having autonomy, control and choice

In previous chapters we have seen some participants feeling they had no choice about going to boarding school and this contributing to their overall unhappiness about being at boarding school. In this study, we see a contrast with many participants describing wanting to attend boarding school and having made the choice to go themselves. There was often a social element to this such as wanting the same privilege as siblings or staying connected to friends.

> I said to my parents, 'I don't see why I should be staying here when my brothers are going to England with double-decker buses and chocolates and sweets and I'm stuck here!' [laughs]. So, in the end, they said, 'Well, if that's what you want to do and go overseas, to boarding school, we will do that.'
>
> (Jenny)

> Yeah, it was my decision really. I was really keen on doing it because the school that I was at originally you could do either day or board, and a lot of my friends were boarding so I wanted to be with them.
>
> (Jay)

Others wanted to attend boarding school due to holding slightly romanticised fantasies about what boarding school would be like. These were often based on depictions in contemporary popular media.

> I was very influenced by Enid Blyton, the books on boarding schools, and I really wanted to go.
>
> (Georgia)

Others wanted to attend boarding school to escape the instability they had experienced in their early lives.

> Apparently I asked to go away to boarding school but I wouldn't be surprised if I did because I knew we were going to be moving again. So when I was eight I went to a boarding school. Yes, so I kind of went with the sense that this is what I wanted to do because at least school wouldn't change.
>
> (Rachel)

Some even had a choice of which school to attend after visiting potential options. This seemed important in terms of offering autonomy and control.

> I did a trial weekend and loved it and then said basically that I want to do that. We looked around. It was my decision. But we looked around I think three or four different schools. And I just really loved the one at

[place], I thought it was fantastic, I could really see myself there. I just remember absolutely loving it, just saying that's definitely where I want to go.

(Jay)

However, as seen in previous chapters, some participants felt that the decision for them to attend boarding school was made more for their parents' benefit than their own, either to facilitate the parents' work or social life, and this did leave some sense of resentment.

He was an entrepreneurial man, so while he was flying, he was also running businesses and I think perhaps he felt he would have more time for his businesses while we were away at school.

(Andrew)

About a third of the sample were under 10 when they went to boarding school and this may impact on the extent to which they could genuinely participate in making the choice. Those who were 11 or older tended to feel that they had sufficient maturity to be able to handle the transition and that their wishes were respected.

When I was just turning 11 my father decided to go back to [overseas workplace] for a year to practice and my mother worked in London and doesn't really drive, so it became logistically impractical for us to stay in day school. Plus, we both played the piano and the violin, and our piano and violin teachers both taught at [school], and we'd met a lot of their [School] pupils already, and we were very impressed with them. It was very important to me to keep having the same piano teacher, so that was the only school that we would consider boarding at, and because it was near enough home, it wasn't too big a deal.

(Elizabeth)

9.4 Theme 3: Development of interpersonal skills and individual strengths

In Chapter 1 we commented on how boarding schools often market themselves on the grounds of children's access to extracurricular activities and the potential to develop confidence and social skills. Some of the participants in this study appear to echo this idea in the way they talk about the interpersonal skills and strengths they believe they developed through being at boarding school.

Extra-curricular activities build confidence and individual strengths

Participants spoke of how their experiences at school helped them to identify what they enjoyed and were good at and to develop in those areas and gain confidence.

The focus on the individual students and finding their passions and their interests and helping them explore those, whatever they were was excellent. This focus on the whole person was excellent.

(Daniel)

Jay describes the sense of freedom this provided to explore who you are, what matters to you and where you excel.

Loads of opportunities to do the things that you're interested in. I was in a band at the time, which was encouraged, and you could do that, concerts put on all the time. Yeah, it was just a really broad spectrum of opportunity and things that you could do.

(Jay)

I did everything, I was an academic scholar and a music scholar, and I also was a prefect, and I did all of the Duke of Edinburgh awards. I did everything except sport, I didn't do any sport. I ran house events, I wrote music ... I did all of the things.

(Elizabeth)

Many spoke of the importance of sports not just for their own interests but for achieving peer acceptance, social status and avoiding persecution from other boarders.

Games and sports were everything, even back in those days. I was quite good at them. So, that meant I never experienced any bullying or pressure really. Now I look back, I sailed through it.

(Michael)

Many described enjoying being in positions of social power and status at boarding school. These included being captain of athletics teams, being a Head of House or Head Boy. It is possible that holding these positions was one of the factors that made boarding school more rewarding for these individuals, especially if they contributed to doing well socially at boarding school. Being given these positions of responsibility and power allowed boarders to have a taste of these roles and was one of the factors that prepared them for taking up similar positions in adult life.

I quite enjoyed playing lacrosse and hockey and tennis and I was in fact quite good at swimming. Obviously, living [overseas], I ended up being swimming captain.

(Jenny)

I wanted to be head boy at school of course, and naturally was; then I wanted to be head boy when I came out of school.

(Michael)

Another type of extracurricular activity was the completion of chores which was felt to help build character, keep boarders grounded and contribute to a sense of camaraderie. Participants expressed pride in themselves for having got involved in these.

Everyone had to take turns cleaning the common room or filling up hot water bottles or whatever. They always gave us kind of chores, tasks, at the weekend. I think that was quite good for us all. So, nobody felt they were above doing anything menial because they were rotated around. So, I think that was a good thing.

(Richard)

Boarders spoke of the physical grounds of the boarding school being set up in a manner that allowed them to pursue the interests that had meaning for them and allowed them to develop as well-rounded confident individuals able to pursue deeply valued personal interests. This contributed to the formation of relationships and social bonding.

There was lots of countryside around and actually I did used to go running on my own off into the countryside. I was a long-distance runner and I remember loving that. And actually when we first joined ... when you're essentially still a little girl, I used to go with friends at the weekend. We'd walk out into the fields and ... go roaming and exploring but as we got older ... with my boyfriend, we did, we used to go and meet at [Name] reservoir and go on long walks together. And ... we'd go off on our bikes and have ... lovely days out together.

(Georgia)

School values, culture and environment

Experiences of adult support at boarding school were variable and seemed to depend on individual staff attitudes or school culture. However, whether staff were experienced as supportive or not, participants seemed to think of themselves as having become self-reliant, something they had to develop due to living away from their parents. Becoming more resilient was intimately linked with the sense of becoming more independent and seemed to be valued.

We would just be figuring it out for ourselves, you don't have to rely on other people, so it's really taking responsibility for your day-to-day life without having to then get some parent to come and pick you up or figure out how you're going to get from A to B. It was really important I think for becoming a responsible adult contributing to a community.

(Elizabeth)

Where schools offered some forms of freedom, this seemed to have an enhanced impact on independence and resilience. There was a sense of an environment that created the space for boarders to develop in their own way towards their full potential. Jay describes how boarders being given the freedom to curate their personal spaces facilitated this.

> The bedrooms were really nice, they said you can make it your own, bring your own stuff, whatever you want to bring with you. I'm quite a homemaker, I like to have my things with me. I'm a bit of a techy and all that sort of stuff, so I was like I can bring a stereo, I can bring this, this just sounds brilliant.
>
> (Jay)

Many participants described having set bedtimes and curfews and only particular days when they could leave the school to visit other places. This focus on safety could limit socialising outside of boarding school. However, the relative freedom while within school bounds in terms of not having parents to monitor homework, for example, meant some found it difficult to be motivated academically with consequences for career choices.

> I didn't study and there was nobody to make you study. There's that lack of framework that you would get in a home environment with the parents peering over your shoulder ... you were just an unguided missile. I just ended up in an interview.
>
> (Rupert)

> I didn't do great academically. I didn't do terribly but I didn't do certainly as good as I would have if I'd had a more focused structure in place to revise for exams. That's certainly somewhere where boarding school is a lot more regimented suffers a little bit. You're given a lot of freedom, particularly on study leave where you're revising for exams and things like that. But if you're not a particularly motivated or regimented person, which at that age I wasn't because of too many distractions, you might not be revising as much or be taking homework as seriously you should.
>
> (Robert)

Nevertheless, some school values did seem to be internalised by some participants, such as expectations about achievement.

> The school that I was at, you were expected to achieve, you were expected to do well at the things you do. And I definitely think that has rubbed

off on me. I'm not somebody who thinks I'll just do this half-hearted and get it done ... So, I think I've definitely taken that forward into my work life and the life I live now.

(Jay)

Many of the female boarders who attended single-sex schools deeply valued having grown up with their female peers. This often meant they were not exposed to, and so had not internalised, the kind of gender stereotypes that their non-boarder peers had often been exposed to.

The thing that was really important was that being at a girls' school meant that I never was subject to gender stereotypes when I was growing up. So, I don't think I was really aware of the stereotype about boys being better at maths, and girls not, I just wasn't aware. But then, because I had good teachers, they made me aware of it before I went to university so that I would be prepared.

(Elizabeth)

Single-sex girls schools were also appreciated because they created a context where the girls could develop at their own pace, outside of the often more boisterous, distracting and attention-grabbing mannerisms of some boys. This allowed the girls' individual talents to be more easily recognised and developed by their teachers.

I'm glad to have been to a single-sex school as well, I have to say. A lot of people don't like it or disapprove of it, but I personally am glad that I did at that time. I think it gave more chance for some of the girls to flower and get attention in some classes where I think boys would be more domineering.

(Suzanna)

These boarders also deeply valued being exposed to an environment where female leadership was modelled by staff and older peers and boarders had the opportunity to practice these roles themselves through the day-to-day running of social activities at school.

Living with others strengthens social skills

Most of the participants spoke of having made close friends at boarding school. These were connections they deeply valued, that they had often made fairly quickly after starting and which impacted on how they viewed the school environment overall.

The school was great, amazing facility, amazing opportunities. But as with most things, experiences come down to the people you're with. It could be a complete shithole, excuse my French, but you could have amazing people around you, in which case you'd probably have a great time. Or you could live in the Shangri-La and the Shard, and be surrounded by unpleasant people, and you'd probably have quite a dull time.

(Jay)

Participants talked about the benefits of being with friends all through the day, having midnight feasts and talking together at night extending opportunities for exploration and connection.

We were embedded in a way that I just don't think could happen at a day school, even if you stayed there until 10 p.m. We would carry on talking about stuff until 11 or midnight, and so you work on your house play, and then you'd keep discussing it in whispers after the lights were out until midnight.

(Elizabeth)

I think probably simply the sheer amount of time that you spend together, because you never spend time like that together with anyone else really, unless university maybe. It's intense amounts of time. Because it seemed to me at the time quite an intense experience, perhaps you fast-forwarded to a level of intimacy that you might not have had if it was playing for an hour at their home every so often.

(Suzanna)

Friends seemed to replace previous family relationships and would be missed during holidays.

I never felt alone at boarding school. I never felt bored. There was always someone there and like I say, it didn't take very long into my time there to get really excited at the end of school holidays to fly back and see all my friends.

(Robert)

Boarders described fond memories of the camaraderie, fun and closeness that they experienced with enormous value placed on these social experiences which included friends of the same age as well as support from older boarders.

There was a very big, strong atmosphere of older girls take younger girls under their wing because everyone is away from their family, and that was one of the wonderful things about it.

(Elizabeth)

This highly sociable environment seemed to create a necessity to adapt and quickly develop social skills which were a foundation for adult life.

I think definitely people skills and not managing people but being able to deal with different types of people and all that sort of thing helped being at boarding school, because you didn't have a choice, that was the life you lived. When you're at boarding school and you're living with ... I lived with 60 other boys day in, day out. I think you learn quite a lot about how to deal with people and how to interpret what people say, how to get along with people, how to manage tricky situations. And I definitely think that personable side of things has helped work situations.

(Jay)

I think I found it quite easy to make friends through my life after that time, know how to be sociable. I think I learnt how to fit in with people and I'm quite adaptable.

(Suzanna)

One of the most fundamentally valuable things boarders spoke of learning at school was how to be in a community. How to get on with others, work together and manage conflict. Social skills were learned through living together as a community from morning to night.

You're having to get on with people, you're constantly in touch with them 24 hours a day. So you've got to learn to almost be team players the whole time. I think they all learn to interact well with people having come through that system. And so, I think you learn to deal with lots of people around you the whole time.

(Richard)

It was a lot of learning for me about what a family looked like. You know, what stability meant. How families operated, because I didn't have any of that knowledge. I was trying to pick the positives out of relationships and model them, if that makes sense. Because I'd got no model. There was no kind of lexicon for me to hang anything on so I was trying to find my own learning in terms of relationships.

(Penelope)

Most participants had remained in touch with the friends they made at boarding school and valued these adult friendships highly. They spoke of having a strong and special bond that helped them to stay connected.

My best friends to this day are people I met in the boarding-house. In a way I have much closer relationships I boarded with and lived with in those dorms with for six/seven years than I do my brother.

(Robert)

We're all now knocking 60 and I would say, apart from two deaths ... the entire year is in communication ... we have a bond.

(Rupert)

Importance of personality fit

Crucially, what may determine why these particular ex-boarders seemed to have thrived overall at boarding school, is that it seemed important for there to be a good fit between the personality of the child and the boarding school.

The right boarding school for the right child is a better option. But my sister... it didn't suit her and she might have done better at home, so I think it really depends on the character of the child primarily and then it's like, what's the school like? What's the culture of the school? Is that going to suit them?

(Rachel)

Having a confident temperament and feeling that boarding school was something that could be managed was helpful for allowing the participants to adapt to their new environment but was thought to have negative social consequences for those who did not fit this personality type.

I think maybe to have a good time there, you have to have an element of resilience when you turn up ... just being quite confident in yourself and I suppose popular. This is the sad thing, I think if you're anything other than quite confident, and I don't want to use the term normal but I'm trying to think ... If you have a lot of friends at school and you get on with a good group of people, you'll probably be okay. But if there's any quirks of your personalities or if you're a bit different or you like doing something that's a bit left field, then I think you get shoehorned at boarding school.

(Jay)

To be able to make the most of the many opportunities offered by the school boarders spoke of having to arrive 'pre-packaged' with a drive to achieve and self-discipline. Without these attributes, the relative freedom and independence given to boarders might lead to some falling through the gaps academically or socially.

9.5 Theme 4: Developing responsibility, independence and emotional strength

It's your responsibility

An attribute that many participants spoke of having internalised from their boarding school experience was an increased sense of responsibility. This included taking responsibility for one's own actions and the consequences of these, working in a group and developing a moralistic understanding of the difference between right and wrong and one's responsibility for decisions based on this.

> I had a bigger sense of independence and ability to just deal with life, because I think you're taught that through boarding school. You don't have a mum and dad... Not waiting on you hand and foot, but taking care of things in the background. It's your responsibility to get your homework done, it's your responsibility to pack the right things when you go to school, it's your responsibility to change your bed sheets, it's your responsibility to fold your clothes. And that had just been the norm for me since I was 13.
>
> (Jay)

> We would just be figuring it out for ourselves, you don't have to rely on other people ... It taught me about how to be a responsible human to help others who are less privileged. I really attribute that sense of contributing to society to that education.
>
> (Elizabeth)

Learning 'mental toughness'

Many linked responsibility and independence to resilience, emotional strength or 'mental toughness'. Some spoke of how they valued the resilience they had developed through boarding school. There was a sense of no matter what life throws at you, having the strength to keep going: 'you've got to knuckle down and crack on'; 'you had to sink or swim and get on with it'.

> I would call that having deep inner strength or something, but the kind of strength that's like the roots of a tree so that the tree can bend and sway, but its roots are still there. Sometimes I do think back to the core essence of me that I think I found when I was at boarding school, to remember that that's still there.
>
> (Elizabeth)

> I think it helped develop a mental toughness of ability to think this is rotten, but it will get better, and I will get through it. And you can get through it in your own time.
>
> (Suzanna)

> I do think I'm a very resilient person. I'd definitely say I would be a survivor. I'd like to make the best of things really.
>
> (Georgia)

This emotional strength or toughness was often pitched in a positive light as in the quotes above. Yet sometimes this emotional strength seemed to veer towards a suppression or silencing of emotions, a defence mechanism borne of necessity in order to overcome obstacles and approach difficulties with determination.

> The school itself wasn't negative ... what was negative was leaving home ... feeling homesick ... it was like it wasn't the done thing to be homesick ... I felt really homesick and people were trying to comfort me and instead of saying I felt homesick, I made up this big lie, I made up a story about a pony I had at home which I didn't have at all, that it had died ... then I had to keep up this story ... because I didn't want to say, 'I'm missing my mummy and daddy' ... I guess I needed to be strong.
>
> (Rachel)

> I do not get so close to people. I'm close to all of them up to a limit, but nobody realises it doesn't go past a certain ... as a defence mechanism. And it worked fine, so it's how I am I think.
>
> (Rupert)

> I do have this capacity to block things out ... I mean the obvious example is being in the blast ... I have a crisis a week later even though I had my head bandaged up ... I'm not gonna sit here and moan about it for the rest of my days. Just water off a duck's back.
>
> (Rupert)

> The reason he was with the school matron was because he'd heard that day that his father had died in a prisoner of war camp in Japan ... he re-joined the rest of us and none of us said anything to him about it, nor did he say anything to us about it. So, you were expected to withhold your emotions really.
>
> (Michael)

Despite the apparent strength of determination and resilience among participants, there were examples where it appeared to have come at a very high emotional cost and indeed risk to life.

> So my second year there, I made a suicide attempt in the boarding house, and it was a hanging. Now, I have regretted that hugely since then. I don't at this point even remember why I did it ... I am so thankful that I am still alive ... I don't just tend to dwell on it ... I just know it was a huge mistake ... when I tell people about it, I think one of the things they must think is, that wouldn't have happened if you had that support or if you were with parents at home. In fact, if anything being a boarder

probably saved my life because there were more than just my four other family members around to walk in, see what was happening, and run and get help ... I never self-harmed, I don't think I was particularly depressed at any point.

(Robert)

Similarly, Georgia developed anorexia while at school and suggests she was not actually unhappy, she just wanted to be thin. This seems to reflect a survival mechanism akin to the protective mask or shield of 'boarding school survivors' referred to by Nick Duffell described in previous chapters [3]. Yet these participants seem to have turned this into a relatively successful defence mechanism, however extreme, to get them through adult life. Others, however, found that emotional compartmentalisation honed during their formative years at boarding school affected their capacity for intimacy as adults.

When I tried to build a relationship with my first wife I realised how emotionally locked up I'd become due to boarding school.

(Michael)

Transition to adult life

Many spoke of having found the transition from boarding school to university a smooth one and tended to do well academically.

Together with having no trouble with the transition, because so many people have trouble just making that transition from school to university, I felt like it was completely normal, it felt very smooth, it was really the same.

(Elizabeth)

Many also spoke of having little difficulty finding work after graduation, making their way into workplaces they found stimulating, interesting and exciting, moving up through the occupational hierarchy quickly. Some managed large numbers of people. Others ran major international companies. Still others formed their own companies. This gives some indication of how social advantage may operate in practice as an effect of the sorts of social skills and confidence acquired in a boarding setting.

I think my super skill at work that enabled me to be as successful as I was, was the ability to be able to read what was being said in a room when there were no words. I could read body language. And I think part of that is walking into a room in boarding school full of testosterone leaded men, what's the dynamic in this room? What's going on right now?

(Daniel)

[I] built my own career that had no blueprint, nobody does what I do, plenty of people said it wouldn't be possible. I just thought I might be able to do it, and so I did it.

(Elizabeth)

There was an awareness of coming from a privileged cohort, and that many of their peers that joined them at top tier universities also had a boarding school background and this being a major contributor to later occupational success.

I know I have benefitted from unconscious bias. I know I've probably benefitted from conscious bias, I can't think of any instances, but I might not have been aware of that. And I know I benefitted from this kind of class structure or whatever you want to call it that meant I could go to a boarding school to begin with. But I did benefit so the outcome wasn't bad. I was aware at the time that the opportunity I was being given was that it was an opportunity. I was aware that this was an investment where the return could be meaningful.

(Daniel)

A good number of participants spoke of having strong relationships with their families of origin following boarding school. Having ongoing strong relationships with their parents and siblings, sometimes still going on family holidays together, although there was some tendency towards greater emotional distance in family relationships. Participants seemed very satisfied in their relationships with partners and it is notable that all participants were married or co-habiting at the time of the interview, whereas groups in earlier chapters were more often divorced, separated or single at the time of interview.

The participants had taken contrasting stances towards whether they had sent their own children to boarding school and their rationales for their decision varied widely. There seemed to be a tendency to think of the child's welfare and individual needs above other factors. For those who chose not to send their children to boarding school there were a multitude of reasons, such as not wanting to risk fracturing family relationships. Some wanted their children to experience a more 'normal' upbringing, to have friends and be able to spend time alone. Some found contemporary boarding schools too expensive. For others it was important for them to feel that they were a part of their children's childhood and that their child was embedded in a family.

We liked our kids, we still like our kids. They're all back from university at the moment. We wanted to spend time with our kids.

(Daniel)

Despite the seemingly positive reflections on their own experiences on boarding school described above, this comment seems to imply that on some level at least, participants may assume that their own parents did not like them enough to keep them at home.

9.6 Discussion

In this chapter, we interviewed men and women with a wide range of ages who came forward because they considered they had had a generally positive experience of boarding school. This overall positivity does come through in our findings across both the questionnaire data and the themes that have emerged. Questionnaire data indicated that, on average, the ex-boarders who came forward for the study were not experiencing any particular psychological distress with the exception of four individuals who have elevated scores for anxiety and/or trauma. Notably, these four individuals were not the same two people who reported traumatic sexual experiences in childhood.

Our sample is necessarily small compared to the survey research that was carried out, as it was designed to explore individual experiences in some depth. We therefore cannot infer any statistical relationships between abuse and trauma based on this. In other words, we are not suggesting that traumatic sexual experiences in childhood do not lead to adult psychological distress, since that would contradict quite a large body of research that already exists. What our findings may be pointing to is that there are a range of complex individual factors that may determine adult psychological wellbeing for ex-boarders which are not solely dependent on whether or not the child experienced particular types of trauma or more general trauma from attending boarding school.

There appears to be a common thread in our themes suggesting that early family relationships and psychological resources developed by the child before they go to boarding school have an important role to play in how the child adapts to boarding school. Further, while some children arrive from families with strong positive parenting, for others, going to boarding school and 'escaping' their family, facilitates the development of psychosocial resources that may not have occurred if they had remained in the family home.

Strong family relationships prior to attending boarding school seem to influence whether or not the child is able to benefit from the developmental advantages boarding school can offer. The people we interviewed appear to have drawn a range of benefits from their experiences including social, financial and psychological success in life. They appear on the whole to have developed strong healthy relationships with their partners; a strong network of friends; satisfaction with life and work; and a resilience and determination to face life's challenges. Many appear to relate these advantages to their experience at boarding school in keeping with the promotional material offered by boarding schools (extracurricular activities, freedom from commuting, opportunities to develop independence and social skills). Yet it may not have been these opportunities *per se* that enabled these individuals to succeed. Rather, it seems possible that the nature of early family life prior to attending boarding school may have enabled them to benefit from these opportunities. In many ways, the boarding school experience may not have differed much in a material sense between participants in this study and participants in earlier studies seen in this book; yet participants in this study seem to have framed their experiences in a very different way.

For example, in earlier chapters we saw children feeling abandoned by their parents and missing them terribly with lasting damage; here we see the same scenario but with examples of how this was mitigated by a mum checking in often and visiting until the child felt reassured and settled. In earlier chapters we heard about cruelty and bullying from peers and staff; here we have heard of the same issues but from children who were lucky enough to be witnesses rather than victims, perhaps because they had the social skills or sporting reputations to protect themselves effectively. Maybe they were just lucky. In earlier chapters we heard about children emotionally shutting down to such a degree that adult relationships were very difficult, unhappy and often broke down. Here we hear of what we might call robust emotion management where emotions are very highly controlled but in a way which appears to enhance emotional regulation and enable strong attachments to partners. In Chapter 6 we saw a theme around the idea that children at boarding school 'just have to crack on'. This reflected an emotional shutting down to avoid being stigmatised for expressing or revealing distress or loneliness boarders felt. Here we see a similar sentiment, 'you've got to knuckle down and crack on', entirely reframed to express a process for developing resilience, emotional strength and a determination to crack life's problems.

It is important not to reinforce any stigmatisation here by suggesting that participants in our earlier chapters may have been somehow weaker than participants in the current chapter. Rather, it is important to notice that the participants in the current study appear to have arrived in boarding school with different combinations of advantages which enabled them to protect themselves and grow in strength. These included positive parenting and strong family relationships or a strong motivation to 'escape from the family'; choice and autonomy in the decision to board; pre-existing social skills; a combination of interests which fitted the school's non-academic offers; a personality that happened to fit the culture and ethos of the school. Some also may have just been lucky in finding friends they connected with quickly, helping them to be buffered from feelings of abandonment followed by victimisation than we have seen can occur at the very start of the transition to boarding and cause lasting damage.

These findings would suggest the possibility that much of the promotional material used by boarding schools along with some of the more positive findings from survey research contains a degree of accuracy. Nevertheless, the accuracy may only apply for certain children with certain family contexts and certain characteristics matched carefully with certain schools. This may further suggest that there can be no particular generalisation made about whether sending a child to boarding school is inherently abusive or traumatic. Rather, where boarding is being considered for any child, it seems critical for parents and schools to consider each child as an individual including their needs, preferences, interests, emotional capacities, degree of independence and the strength of existing family relationships.

Findings also point some way towards the idea that family relationships need to be strong as a pre-requisite for boarding and that family relationships should be nurtured as far as possible while the child is away. National minimum standards for boarding schools have, since 2012, made provision for parent-child contact to be maintained [4]. New standards issued in 2022 [5] have strengthened this requirement by noting the need for contact provisions to accommodate time zone differences and individual family circumstances. However, this remains a fairly limited requirement which could be strengthened further, perhaps through a more proactive stance towards encouraging contact rather than facilitating it. Standards could also go further to require schools to create many and varied ways for parents to take a more active role in school life which is now made more possible through new remote communication options.

In summary, our findings from both the survey and interviews indicate some people can benefit from boarding school and that not all ex-boarders report psychological harm. In particular, such benefits included either being able to escape from a problematic home life or using the distance from home as a means to develop perspective and improved family relationships; finding pleasure in the newly derived sense of autonomy, control and choice; enjoying the social connections at boarding school and developing interpersonal skills and individual strengths and thriving away from home to develop a sense of responsibility, resilience and independence. Further, the findings indicated that the ability to find benefit at boarding school was not automatic and was often facilitated through strong family relationships either formed before the onset of boarding or nurtured and maintained while away at school. Fundamentally, therefore, our findings suggest that if children are to make the most of their time at boarding school and maximise its potential benefit, families whose children are accepted into a boarding school should be assessed to explore that they have already demonstrated a commitment and motivation to maintain strong positive family relationships while their child is away from home.

References

1 Martin AJ, Papworth B, Ginns P, *et al.* Boarding school, academic motivation and engagement, and psychological well-being: A large-scale investigation. *Am Educ Res J* 2014; 51. doi:10.3102/0002831214532164.

2 Beames S, Mackie C, Scrutton R. Alumni perspectives on a boarding school outdoor education programme. *J Adventure Educ Outdoor Learn* 2020; 20: 123–137. doi:10.1080/14729679.2018.1557059.

3 Duffell N. Boarding school survivors. *Self Soc* 1995; 23. doi:10.1080/03060497.1995.11085543.

4 Department for Education. Boarding schools: national minimum standards. 2012. https://www.gov.uk/government/publications/boarding-schools-national-minimum-standards.

5 Department for Education. Boarding schools: national minimum standards. 2022. https://assets.publishing.service.gov.uk/government/uploads/system/uploads/attachment_data/file/1102344/National_minimum_standards_for_boarding_schools.pdf.

Chapter 10

British boarding schools on trial

Making the case for 'boarding family syndrome'

Penny Cavenagh and Susan McPherson

Establishing causality (whether one thing is caused by another) is a major challenge for researchers in all fields in both modern and ancient times, exemplified by Virgil:

> *Felix qui potuit rerum cognoscere causas* [Lucky is he who has been able to identify the causes of things]. [1]

Nevertheless, research practice is often predicated on the discovery and confirmation of causal relationships. Causal relationships – where one factor is shown to have a direct effect on another – can be very difficult to prove, particularly without large samples, randomised groups and appropriately designed trials or experiments. Neither of these crucial elements (random sampling and large numbers of participants) have been present in UK research into the effects of boarding school to date. In the case of previous clinical case study research on ex-boarders [2],[3], the inference has been that the 'cause' (boarding school) has a negative 'effect' on its graduates (ex-boarders). A key component of our rationale for researching the psychological impact of boarding school has been to further understand and clarify the validity of these claims. Can the experience of boarding school alone be the cause of later problems with relationships, depression, long-term emotional or behavioural difficulties and other issues captured within the concept of boarding school syndrome? As set out in Chapter 1, the inspiration for the research presented in this book came from the publication in recent years of several books about the impact of boarding school. These have been widely referenced in preceding chapters and are either collections of personal narratives or based on observations from clinical practice and analysis of case histories. Although case history analysis is an established form of research in the field of psychoanalytic psychotherapy, it is doubtful whether it can establish cause and effect convincingly.

The adverse psychological impacts of boarding school have also been well rehearsed in the popular press. *The Times* recently published a series of articles under the banner of 'Readers' Boarding School Stories' exposing a vault

DOI: 10.4324/9781003280491-10

of suffering and a torrent of harrowing personal accounts [4]. These individual and collective experiences mirror the literature written by academics, researchers and psychotherapists in the field which have focused on the negative effects of boarding school.

Our research aimed to build on previous approaches and move the investigation into the effects of boarding school from a predominantly therapeutic, theoretical lens to include the use of empirical methods. We recruited participants from a wider range of non-therapy settings including community sampling. As far as possible we wanted our research design to move closer to the criteria for establishing cause and effect. The most challenging of these criteria is 'nonspuriousness' [5] which refers to a relationship between two factors (such as attendance at boarding school and ensuing psychological issues) that cannot be explained by a third variable. Quite simply, we were unable to establish a direct cause and effect between these factors but uncovered several other mediating factors that could be part of the explanation for the unhappy experiences of some ex-boarders and the subsequent effects on their adult lives.

The collection of research studies presented in this book has involved the participation of 186 ex-boarders. In the UK, there are more single-sex girls' schools than single-sex boys' schools, but co-educational schools tend to have slightly more boys than girls [6]. Across the research studies we have presented, we have roughly equal proportions of men and women, which is generally representative of UK boarders. The age range across all participants ranged from 19 to 85. Over 50% were aged 30–60, approximately 30% were over 60 and approximately 10% were under 30. In addition, Chapter 7 examines the testimonies of 61 ex-boarders (the vast majority of whom were men) who had experienced sexual abuse at boarding school.

The majority of ex-boarders represented in this book are likely to have boarded between the 1950s and 1980s, while a smaller proportion will have boarded even earlier than this as well as some more recently in the 1990s and 2000s. The data collected thus reflects several decades of boarding experience. Interpretation of our data needs to be sensitive to the changing contexts of boarding schools and in particular to the legislation set out by the Department of Education in 2012 [7] (updated in September 2022 [8]) which set out the minimum standards that boarding schools must meet to safeguard and protect children in their care. These standards would have come into play for less than a fifth of ex-boarders (those under the age of thirty) when they participated in our research.

10.1 The first quantitative research survey in the UK

Richard Beard, an ex-boarder and author, comments in his book *Sad Little Men* that 'as yet there is no formal quantitative research into psychological outcomes for ex-boarders' [9]. Although most of the new research presented in this book is qualitative (based on analysis of interviews), in Chapter 2, we present findings from the first independent survey of ex-boarders in the UK. Our survey research reflects the experiences of a more diverse and representative sample than used in UK psychotherapy case study research in that we used an online survey platform and recruited participants via social media. This method of recruitment is fundamental to improving the generalisability of our findings to the wider population of UK ex-boarders. That said, it is quite possible that ex-boarders identified in this way were drawn to participate because they had particularly strong views about boarding school and that those who have more neutral views are not well represented in our findings. Variation in the ages of participants also means that participants were exposed to varying conditions of boarding and pastoral care. In particular, the younger generation may have been exposed to better provision of care. Participants also spent different lengths of time at boarding school, introducing more variation to the data.

To balance the possibility that participants may have been more drawn to the research because of negative experiences, we proactively recruited a further 26 participants who had positive experiences of boarding school, described in Chapter 9. Taking into account ex-boarders surveyed in Chapters 2 and 9 using the same set of questionnaires, our survey research represents the experiences of 128 ex-boarders in total.

In common with previous research on boarding school, our findings are limited by the lack of comparison with non-boarders. Notably, we also attempted to recruit independent school day pupils as a control group for our survey research, but very little interest was shown. Perhaps the lack of response tells its own story. Nevertheless, through focused analysis of the data from this survey we are able to challenge the orthodoxy of assuming adverse psychological effects of boarding school. Firstly, we found across the board the mean scores for depression, trauma and anxiety were in the normal range on our standardised scales with resilience medium to high and scores for anxious and avoidant attachment moderate.

However, as with all sample means they are derived from a diverse range of scores and so we looked more closely at the minority of participants who did score within the clinical range on some of the measures. The clinically anxious outliers had boarded slightly younger, had felt more rejected by parents as children and experienced less parental warmth and more overprotection. They also reported more traumas in early life. The clinically depressed outliers again felt more rejected by their parents and less parental warmth in their early life. The extent of early experiences of trauma are a novel finding from our survey research, with over 40% of our ex-boarders in Chapter 1 experiencing clinical levels of trauma. These reported levels were associated with earlier boarding, problematic parenting and other early life traumas. The nature of early life traumas experienced ranged from loss, parental separation, sexual assault, physical assault, serious illness or major upheavals and were not necessarily directly related to separation from caregivers. As noted however, beyond highlighting these associations in the data, cause and effect are difficult to establish as there is no control group, there are several variables associated with distress and our sample size is too small to carry out more detailed modelling of the data.

10.2 Interviews with ex-boarders

Most of our studies involved semi-structured interviews using thematic analysis to explore the impact of attending boarding school. Thematic analysis is a distinct analytic approach [10] which allows for identification, analysis and generation of patterns across data sets [11]; it allows for synthesis of large amounts of qualitative data through the construction of codes which are developed into themes. The advantage of this method is flexibility which enables the interviewer to adapt and reorganise topics across transcripts to obtain a rich narrative. Researchers keep reflective diaries throughout the process [12], with the aim of reducing the risks of bias and predilections which may influence interpretation of the findings [13]. Thematic analysis ultimately enhances the validity of findings relative to seeking out confirmation of therapeutic theories with unspecified clients as a data source.

In all, 88 semi-structured interviews were analysed using thematic analysis along with 61 Truth Project testimonies. Recruitment of participants for these interviews relied on people opting in, hence, they were not randomly selected. While some of the samples were recruited via ex-boarder support organisations (in particular Chapters 3 and 8), others were recruited via a range of social media and snowballing techniques. While participants in Chapter 8 had by definition received psychotherapy, the majority of participants across the other studies were not receiving therapy (although some may have done in the past). Inevitably there is some bias across these samples in that those who engaged in the research could have experienced more challenges for whatever reason at boarding school which they attribute to their current disquiet. We believe, however, that the research methodologies and diverse recruitment strategies used in our research enable us to draw conclusions which build on and enrich findings from earlier psychotherapy case study research. We have embraced the challenge of establishing causal relationships and recognised the difficulty of demonstrating 'non-spuriousness', given there are so many factors at play.

In this chapter, we summarise some of the key themes that emerged from this set of research studies and consider what conclusions can be drawn. We will use data from all chapters and first address the question: what is the psychological impact of boarding school? We will then argue for a more nuanced approach to this question and highlight the role of a number of factors such as the age a child starts boarding; the role of friendships; and the key role of parenting and family dynamics. We will argue that it may be helpful to begin to shift the lens from thinking of boarding school syndrome, to a lens concerned with boarding families. We will then conclude with a consideration of why children go to boarding school and the lessons for life they may learn.

10.3 The psychological impact of boarding school: Summing up the evidence

This book started in Chapter 1 with an analysis of the case for and against boarding schools and described the existing evidence from surveys, interviews and case studies. The findings across the different studies in this book add to this debate and here we sum up this new evidence both for and against boarding schools.

Much of the data points to some of the problems boarders face while at school and the longer-term negative consequences of being a boarder. For example, the survey of 102 ex-boarders in Chapter 2 illustrated that subgroups of those sampled reported high levels of anxiety and trauma and moderate levels of anxious and avoidant attachment which may well be linked to problems with forming relationships in later life. Qualitative interviews with men in Chapter 3 suggested that their time at boarding school created a sense of powerlessness, challenged their ability to form intimate relationships and seemed to have had a fundamental impact upon their sense of self and their notion of masculinity. Interviews with women with disordered eating in Chapter 5 indicate that while boarding school may not be a singular cause of problematic eating it clearly plays a contributory role and may well exacerbate any existing issues with body shape or food. Chapter 6 found that loneliness could be triggered by bullying at boarding school and that these experiences often resulted in coping behaviours such as the need to be always busy, becoming stoical, ignoring feelings and not seeking help which may have sustained a sense of loneliness into adulthood. Analysis of the testimonies from the Truth Project in Chapter 7 provides insights into the experiences of child sexual abuse while at boarding school and how these can have repercussions through life. Finally, interviews with those having psychotherapy in Chapter 8 highlighted how being at boarding school can generate a complex triple bind of feelings of shame and denial coupled with an assumption of privilege if they have been told they are fortunate to have been sent away to school.

In contrast, however, findings from the studies in this book suggest that not all boarders have negative experiences at school. For example, both survey data and interviews in Chapter 9 indicated that boarders can be relieved to be able to leave home for their education to escape from a problematic home life. This is reflected to an extent in Chapter 4 which found that the emotional unavailability of parents could be more problematic than school itself and tended to precede boarding school. In Chapter 9, some found that being at boarding school helped them to gain perspective and improve family relationships while our interviewees also reported a number of benefits such as a sense of autonomy, control and choice, enjoying the social connections at boarding school and the opportunity to develop a sense of responsibility, resilience and independence. In addition, findings from the UK survey in Chapter 2 indicated that the majority of those sampled did not show levels of depression or anxiety comparable with needing treatment and many also reported moderate to high levels of resilience.

Attending boarding school therefore seems to have a negative impact on some but not all boarders, which indicates a more nuanced approach is needed rather than just a dichotomous characterisation of boarding as either good or bad. The findings from the studies in this book highlights the role of factors which may either protect or facilitate the impact of boarding school. The particular factors that we will address in turn below are the age that children start boarding; the role of friends and peers; and the role of parents and parenting both before and while children are at boarding school.

10.4 The role of age: The psychological impact of junior boarding

The age at which children start boarding school has been mooted as a relevant factor in determining the psychological impact boarding will have. This idea is grounded in attachment theory, discussed in earlier chapters, taking into account that separation from parents can be more damaging the younger the child is. Across the studies presented in this book, 88 ex-boarders were interviewed of whom half started boarding below the age of ten. In the last two decades there has been a significant reduction in the number of children boarding below the age of ten: 6,273 in 2000 compared to less than 4,500 in 2022 [14].

Our interview research findings are therefore skewed because of the ages of the participants and the higher incidence of junior boarding in their eras and is not representative of patterns of boarding today. Again, these findings were not differentiated on the age at which our participants started boarding and so we cannot draw any conclusions about younger versus older boarding from these interviews. The incidence of junior boarding in our interview samples is, however, very high and perhaps significant. We must surmise whether this was a factor in our ex-boarders being drawn to take part in this research as they wanted to share their experiences.

Our survey research specifically examined whether the age at which boarders first boarded is linked to their adult wellbeing. Our findings show that those children who started boarding at a younger age were more anxiously attached in adult relationships. Those who boarded younger also experienced more trauma symptoms and more anxiety symptoms.

Can we draw any conclusions from this in terms of the 'effects' of going to boarding school at a young age? Is boarding school the cause of ex-boarders' anxious attachment, anxiety and trauma? Not necessarily, but the data point towards a relationship between these factors and attachment theory would support the idea that early separation from parents can have a negative impact on psychological development. Attachment theory research suggests that developing a healthy attachment in early life with an accessible and consistent attachment figure is crucial for a child's sense of safety and security [15], and that anxiety in adulthood is related to attachment styles developed as a child. A range of attachment styles formed in childhood tend to last across an individual's lifespan [16], and inconsistent or unavailable attachment in a child's early life can result in a range of mental health issues [17]. Attachment strategies developed within an individual's childhood environment also have major implications for how individuals learn to act in close interpersonal relationships [18].

Even very young boarders who go to boarding school at the age of four will have formed an attachment style with their primary caregiver, most likely their mother. There is an argument that ex-boarders with an anxious attachment style may have formed this prior to going to boarding school with perhaps the more traumatic separation compounding the issue and accounting for some of the traumatic experiences recounted by our ex-boarders. In other words, it is possible that early relationships for many of our ex-boarders who boarded before the age of eleven, may have been impaired prior to attending boarding school and this may have been relevant to the decision to send them to boarding school at a younger age.

10.5 The psychological impact of peers and friendships: The friendship lottery

Enid Blyton perhaps has a lot to answer for with the promise of nirvana in her stories of boarding school where midnight feasts, fun, escapades and above all tremendous camaraderie define the territory: 'I was very influenced by Enid Blyton, the books on boarding school, and I really wanted to go.' Today, families may be similarly influenced by more recent depictions of boarding such as those implied in Harry Potter novels and films.

Strong camaraderie and friendship at boarding school are perhaps the steady sails that can navigate the passage of boarding school life, but they can equally capsize a vulnerable boarder. It is potluck who a boarder ends up being in a year group with and sharing a dormitory or room with at the beginning of every year or even term: 'it's luck of the draw because you don't meet anybody you are going to live with for five years until you arrive'. Whoever you were in a dormitory with could dictate the course of the whole year. Most of the ex-boarders who had positive experiences described very strong and lasting friendships made at boarding school which is likely to have been a key reason for their enjoyment, but they appreciate that this could have been a different scenario: 'If I hadn't liked the people I was rooming with it would have been different ... I imagine that would impact your outlook – it is a driving force of the whole experience.' These boarders mainly describe a strong sense of camaraderie ('it was just great companionship'), enabling them to develop deep enduring friendships and excitement at returning to school after the holidays.

However, rather than being entirely down to luck, the ability to form close relationships with peers at boarding school may be related to the early family environment and attachment to parents. For some boarders with attachment issues from childhood, friendships may feel threatening and dangerous with the risk of rejection running high if they show too much emotion and vulnerability. Some boarders therefore prefer to go it alone and rely on themselves for fear of being let down. Some boarders talked about pride in popularity at school and the shame of admitting being lonely, having no one to hang out with, or being unable to conform to the social needs and norms of their peers. To survive, it seems boarders needed to fit in with the needs of their social group or 'tribes' or face being bullied or ostracised. Jungle hierarchies operated where those who loved boarding school tended to be alpha males, the 'silverback gorillas' of the tribe. The silverbacks' moods were closely observed by those lower in the pecking order to maintain membership of the tribe. There was always the chance of being ejected at any time if they contravened the social norms of the group or upset the boss. These modes of social interaction may well have been learned from or modelled by parents at home.

By sending children to boarding school without a tailored set of social skills, parents may therefore run the risk of their child being ejected from the very group or tribe that they so coveted for them and themselves in the first place. A strange irony. The careful monitoring and observation of the leader in particular and fellow members of the group at boarding school is perhaps why some ex-boarders felt they had learned to be adaptable, to get on with people, to be sensitive to their moods and to be able to 'read a room'. They have learned as a matter of survival to fit in with group norms.

Involvement in extracurricular activities and in particular sports could provide protection from bullying and could secure a place in a group: 'I played games and sports – I was quite good at them – that meant I never experienced any bullying or pressure – I sailed through boarding school'. Partaking in sports, drama, and musical activities facilitated friendships and a sense of belonging and provided a sense of enjoyment for boarders. Some boarders in Chapter 9 talked about the 'amazing' theatres, the 'fantastic' sports facilities and 'loads' of opportunities. They derived pleasure from the beautiful grounds, games fields, athletic tracks and countryside, and seemed to grab all these opportunities with open arms, make use of what was on offer, while at the same time appreciating how lucky they were to have it all on their doorstep.

In contrast, other ex-boarders in Chapter 6 talked about feeling lonely because there was so much going on and they did not feel part of it.

Popularity at boarding school seems to have been earned or achieved from having something to offer or admire, be it sports, music, drama, academic or leadership prowess. Even food could be used as a status symbol, with the giving and receiving of food linked to popularity and pecking order within the group. Never has the position of a slice of cake held such significance!

10.6 The psychological impact of parents

Parents attitudes and behaviours towards their children in terms of emotional warmth, rejection or closeness, appear to be a constant variable in our ex-boarders' reports of anxiety, depression, trauma and the development of anxious attachment styles. A pattern has emerged from our quantitative data in terms of a perceived lack of parental warmth and the reporting of anxiety, depression and trauma symptoms. Conversely the survey data from our ex-boarders with positive experiences in Chapter 9 revealed higher scores for parental warmth, lower scores for parental rejection and parental overprotection and showed no elevated depression, anxiety or trauma symptoms overall. There were inevitably outliers in this sample in that two individuals scored in the clinical range for trauma symptoms. Nevertheless, the sample in Chapter 9 reported more positive experiences of early relationships with their parents than our other generic sample in Chapter 2. The psychological impact of parenting styles is also evidenced in our interview findings. Many ex-boarders in Chapter 9 reported happy family homes and good relationships with their parents: 'home life was very nice before boarding school – my parents were lovely parents – we had a dog and lots of family – it was a jolly normal home life'. Others were relieved to have escaped unhappy homes with 'dysfunctional parents', and it was 'a relief to be away in the school world and not dealing with difficult issues'. These boarders were perhaps doing relatively well psychologically as adults because 'boarding school was better than the home environment'.

Attachment theory has underpinned and been a dominant axis of discussion for the collective research in this book. Disrupted attachment and the development of unhealthy attachment styles have been central to the concept of boarding school syndrome [2] involving a withdrawal of intimacy and suppression of feelings and emotions that may have major implications for future close interpersonal relationships. So strong is this primeval need for emotional warmth that research in the 1950s showed that comfort and affection from the primary caregiver were valued more highly by monkeys than the survival need for food [19]. Early childhood is a crucial time for children to develop secure attachments and to learn emotional regulation from a responsive and loving caregiver. If they do not acquire the capacity for emotional expression, they may dismiss or repress their emotions to protect themselves [20].

Considering the range of findings presented in this book, we propose that boarding school syndrome could be reframed along the lines of a 'boarding family syndrome', reflecting the intergenerational factors that seem to contribute to both psychological distress as well as decisions to board. Some of our findings appear to depict parents of ex-boarders as a cohort who were emotionally illiterate, cold and unable to create a nurturing environment for their children. Such parents may well have been recipients of a transgenerational effect of emotional abstinence and cold parental styles which are transmitted down the generations in a never-ending cycle. Indeed, some ex-boarders reported that home was not always the warm, loving, and secure environment they longed for, and they never felt at home. There were rarely demonstrations of affection – physical or verbal – and parents were 'emotionally unavailable', encouraging the suppression of emotions in their children. Some ex-boarders described feeling unwanted by their parents, not being made to feel special and not being parented with the kindness they needed. In some cases, boarding school was better than their 'cold, hard, emotionless' home. Some ex-boarders were in a double bind – they were not happy at home or boarding school, although each environment was an escape from the other. It could be argued that they were fortunate to have an alternative environment to home. Children at day school who have cold, unloving homes and parents have no option to escape in this way.

How might this legacy of cold or unemotional parenting play out at boarding school? Children deprived of love and affection may seek to fulfil this need by finding alternative attachment figures in the form of teachers, matrons and peers. Attachment issues from early childhood may be ameliorated by the formation of such bonds. Indeed, as discussed in Chapter 8, research has pointed to the possibility of children at boarding school being able to develop secure attachments with an adult other than their parent, but that such attempts at bonding are likely to be rebuffed due to staff being strict and unmaternal, confirming further for the child the need to be self-reliant [21]. A possibly devastating prognosis for children in this situation is their susceptibility to bullying, grooming or both and subsequent sexual abuse. We were shown in the testimonies from the Truth Project in Chapter 7 how emotional and physical distance from parents led to vulnerable and frightened children, who rather than receiving warmth and affection from their teachers were sexually abused by them. Perhaps even worse, some were groomed with the very comfort they needed only to be subsequently sexually exploited.

Through the introduction of safeguarding policies and national standards, the threat of sexual perpetrators has been significantly reduced in boarding schools, although it cannot be guaranteed in any setting that sexual abuse will never happen. Vulnerable children with dysfunctional attachments to their parents are still lurking in the corridors of these schools and present easy prey for potential abusers. Boarding schools have worked hard in the last decade to protect the children in their care, but none of these policies directly address the impact parenting styles can have on children sent to boarding school. An unhealthy dynamic between children and their parents reported by ex-boarders is the mutual but unacknowledged silence in the sharing of painful emotions and experiences at boarding school. Many ex-boarders seem to have shielded their parents from their misery and felt that they could not be honest with them. Boarders 'never tell their parents' and female boarders in particular felt the need to protect their parents, rather than their parents protecting them.

This attempt to protect the parents may be a survival strategy built on subconscious collusion by both parents and children. Perhaps it is driven by the biggest threat of all to the parents – the ignominy of downward social mobility, loss of status and success: 'in return for abandonment and institutionalization of their child, the parents gained status' [9]. The cost is borne by the child who subconsciously or not recognises the significance of survival of the family and its values. The child will not want to be seen as damaged goods or indeed damaging the family's reputation, and certainly would not want to risk losing the conditional love of their parents. Perhaps a child senses the fragility of their own family, any factions and fault lines within it and thus becomes complicit to ensure their survival and place in the family. In addition, as we saw in Chapter 5, children are often in a double bind of privilege and shame. They have been made to feel lucky and privileged, benefitting from significant financial sacrifices made by their parents. They should feel grateful for the opportunity, despite the pain that they may be feeling. These children learn to hide genuine feelings even from themselves. As we talked about in Chapter 1, some high-profile ex-boarders such as Louis de Bernières have only spoken out about their abusive boarding school experiences since the death of their parents. They have held on to their feelings until the coast is clear and the unleashing of emotion can no longer harm their parents.

One might assume that children could have communicated their unhappiness to their parents by letter even if they couldn't see them. Indeed, the main method of communication between children at boarding school and their parents was via the written word: 'A letter was a big thing at boarding school.' However, evidence suggests that in past decades, most letters were designed to please the parents with emotional deprivation expressed in terms of material need. Published accounts of boarding experiences explain that letters tended to start with 'reassurance through boasting' (academic grades or sports prowess), followed by 'neediness' (asking to be sent things) and then 'thanks' and 'gratitude' [9]. Where children shared their real feelings in their letters, letters were read and doctored by staff to protect the parents and ultimately the school. It seems that a *'folie à deux'* existed between the school and parents, a tight collusion that ignored, suppressed, and excluded the child's needs and feelings.

Technological advances in the form of mobile phones have significantly changed communication patterns between boarders and their parents: 'circumstances have changed – there's all this communication – you're not as remote – in those days I was physically remote – things have changed'. The instantaneous contact has almost caused a shift of power in the staff-parent-pupil triad with housemasters noting that it is difficult to reprimand pupils as they are immediately in contact with their parents. Technology may have caused a revolution in modernising boarding school culture and ethos and has enabled pupils to maintain a relationship or at least contact with their parents on a very regular basis. Ofsted standards for boarding schools have also expedited this process with children actively encouraged to communicate with their parents. Evidence from the sample of boarders who had positive experiences showed how important maintaining contact with their parents was and how this contributed to their positive experience. These boarders enjoyed and appreciated their frequent parental visits. In contrast, those boarders who enjoyed boarding school for the very opposite reason of escaping from the family home, had no expectation of parental visits and valued the independence and freedom that this arrangement offered.

10.7 Why do children still go to boarding school?

In Chapter 1 we considered the case for and against boarding schools. New evidence presented in this book suggests that many ex-boarders have negative experiences of boarding school which can result in feelings of loneliness, the exacerbation of eating related problems, problems forming relationships in later life and raised anxiety or trauma symptoms. In contrast, however, many also see benefits in their time away from home and report becoming resilient, valuing their friendships and feeling that they were able to become more responsible and have more autonomy and choice from an earlier age. Our findings also point to three key factors that can protect a child from or exacerbate negative psychological impacts of boarding: the age children start boarding; peers and friendships; early parenting and parent-child relationship. The latter seems particularly fundamental, and we therefore propose the notion of 'boarding family syndrome' as an alternative way of conceptualising boarding school syndrome as a more useful way to understand how and why a child experiences going to boarding school in the way that they do. With this in mind, we now ask why children go to boarding school?

The gathering momentum of negative press surrounding boarding school does not seem to be a deterrent to families determined to send their children there. Indeed, a comment from the Independent Schools Council Annual Census 2022 indicates a recent growth in boarding school numbers: 'If we consider pupils registered to board at any point during the academic year 2021–2022 there were 69,937 boarders – an increase of 4,592 from last year' [14]. There is also a trend for more weekly and flexi boarding. In 2016 15.7% of boarders were flexi or weekly boarders. In 2022 the figure has risen to 22.8%.

There is perhaps recognition that many personalised accounts of boarding school in the UK press are out of date. Although these experiences are very real and the impacts current for the authors who are often older generation and eloquent writers such as Louis de Bernières [22], Richard Beard [9], Alex Renton [23] and Anthony Horowitz [24], parents with children currently at boarding school may not relate to these experiences. We are now familiar with the modern rhetoric on the advantages of boarding school, which suggests that they provide greater academic opportunities and the chance to engage regularly with a broad range of extracurricular activities. They create opportunities for access to other elite educational systems and facilitate connections with high-powered institutions [25]. In short when parents send their children to boarding school they are 'investing money in making [us] future-proof' [9]. Therefore, horrific as they are, accounts from times past may be disregarded by families currently looking to purchase an elite education.

During our research, we consulted with an ex-headmaster of a prep school which was a feeder school for certain elite boarding schools. He considered the opportunities provided by boarding schools to be the driving force for many parents who 'really felt that they were doing the best for their children'. The quality and availability of local schools was also considered another key reason for parents sending their children to boarding school. This idea was supported in our survey research in Chapter 2 which found that 10.8% went to boarding school due to a lack of comparable academic institutions locally. Other reasons identified in our survey included family circumstances, parents working long hours or abroad, divorce, separation and parental mental health issues. Armed services families featured in 13% of cases, which is understandable as many families with a parent in the armed forces are highly mobile and boarding school provides stability in their children's lives. The Ministry of Defence offers help towards the cost of boarding in these circumstances [26]. For some parents there seems to be no explicit rationale and about a fifth of our ex-boarders did not know why their parents had sent them to boarding school. Some participants remember having been included in a discussion about the decision, others remembered just being told with no opportunity to object.

About a third of participants reported family tradition as the main reason for going to boarding school and over half had at least one parent who had boarded: 'I was the thirteenth member of my family to go to that boarding school'. This accords with our headmaster's experience who said that 'because Dad went' was a common reason for going, particularly to elite schools like Eton, Rugby and Harrow. He referred to this as 'continuity of dynasty'. Unpicking the facets of family tradition is akin to opening Pandora's box with deep seated and unquestioned values and belief systems passed from one generation to the next. It could be conceived of as a type of 'family pathology' that 'rolls from generation to generation like a fire in the woods, taking down everything in its path until one person in one generation has the courage to turn and face the flames' [27]. Attendance at boarding school was the never-spoken-about norm of these families where the supreme value placed on education was non-negotiable and any challenge or negativity ignored or repressed. In Chapter 4, an ex-boarder described how his mother was aware of the effect boarding school was having on her eldest son since he 'went away a bright cheerful little kid but came back much more subdued'. Regardless, she sent the younger one to board at the age of seven.

Richard Beard in his book *Sad Little Men* depicts these families and the larger social groups that they are part of as having developed some sort of 'herd immunity' [9]. This sentiment is echoed by an actor interviewed for a national newspaper about the effects of his boarding school experience from the age of seven, even though his father had experienced a 'terrible time' at Harrow. He talks about parents still sending their children away at a young age who 'know what they're doing' and 'doing it willingly'. [28]. James Purefoy concedes in reference to his own therapy, 'you come to the realisation that they [the parents] were just doing what thousands of other parents were doing. There was no malignant side to it' [28].

Families where the tradition of boarding school is the norm could be conceived of as re-affirming their social and personal identity through the membership of this elite group of parents. In terms of the theory of group behaviour they may 'categorize themselves with a high degree of consensus in the appropriate manner and are consequently categorized in the same manner by others' [29]. Thus, within 'a small but influential tribe an odd and unnatural idea had been normalized' [9].

Along with social standing and identity there may be a more basic survival instinct that perpetuates the boarding school tradition in these elite groups – the prevention of downward social mobility [30]. Unhappiness at boarding school may be accepted in these families and the larger societal group to which they belong as a fair opportunity cost for a first-class education and to keep the dynasty where it belongs in the upper echelons of society. 'Groupthink' may perpetuate this attitude down the generations. Groupthink is defined as 'a psychological drive for consensus at any cost that suppresses dissent and appraisal of alternatives in cohesive decision-making groups' [31]. Although this concept has traditionally been applied to foreign policy fiascos, the essence of it can be seen operating in societal groups where the paramount importance of belonging and membership necessitates collective suppression of doubt.

Our ex-headmaster witnessed a similar phenomenon at his prep school. In one academic year, eleven pupils went to the same public school (with high social standing), which was unprecedented. He attributed this to a combination of circumstances initiated by the synergy and herd response of both pupils and parents. No doubt groupthink was at work in this scenario for the better or worse for each child.

Our research has shown that there are many reasons for going to boarding school and at face value many of these seem to be eminently practical and will advantage a child in terms of opportunities and academic success. For others the rationale may appear to be more subconscious and historically driven, as an acceptance of how things are within these family dynasties. What has become apparent is the relevance of how the decision is communicated to the child and whether they have any leverage in the decision-making process: 'I'm not sure I'd have been happy if my parents had just said you're going there – off you go – I think that would have had a different effect on me.' The context and way the decision is made could be a factor in determining how children experience boarding school and its subsequent impact on them.

Empowerment and involvement in the decision to go to boarding school features more often than not in boarders' dialogues in Chapter 9: 'I got to choose boarding school; it was my decision'. These ex-boarders felt that they had agency and power and control and that their feelings and desires were considered. This is in contrast to other ex-boarders where decisions were made for them and not with them. They spoke of feelings of sadness, anger and impotent rage at having been rendered powerless in this key decision. There are examples of ex-boarders who wanted to go to boarding school to remove themselves from unhappy homes, and they felt relieved to be in the school environment, but it was still ultimately their decision which they were empowered to make. Choice of school was part of the decision-making process for those children consulted, with parents taking their children around several boarding schools to find the right fit. For others there was no such consultation, 'some of the people I know, their family always went to the same boarding school, the choice was pretty much taken away from them – they had to go to the school whether they wanted to or not or whether they felt it was right'. We mentioned earlier how groupthink may operate in parents' and children's decisions to go to a particular school. Perhaps not a recipe for a positive experience if the popular choice is not the right fit for the individual child.

It is also important to consider that the reason children still go to boarding school is that the marketing materials and the claimed benefits of boarding are real for many boarders as suggested by some of our findings; and that these benefits may be appealing to parents and children alike. It is impossible to extrapolate from our research the proportions of ex-boarders who lie along the spectrum from loathing to loving boarding school or indeed from feeling severely damaged to having greatly benefitted from the experience. We have noted some limitations with our research methods which must continue to be borne in mind, but nevertheless, our findings provide some insight into what factors may determine an enjoyable experience at boarding school and what sorts of benefits can be derived that will endure into adult life.

'Boarding school encourages you to be resilient'

The concept of resilience, or toughness and an ability to bounce back from difficulties has stimulated varied interpretations in research on ex-boarders. Previous research by UK psychotherapists has framed resilience negatively as a 'false self', appearing as a successful, happy and confident person when masking desperate feelings below the surface. Ex-boarders in our research talk about learning not to make a fuss, getting on with it, not to be emotional, not to cry and to fit in at all costs. Both of our survey samples in Chapters 2 and 9 reported moderate levels of resilience, which was not connected to any early life factors, and so there may be an association between attendance at boarding school and the acquisition of resilience. Because we cannot claim cause and effect with any certainty, however, it is equally possible that children who board are resilient before they go to boarding school, for example as a result of family financial security. Some ex-boarders certainly seemed to suggest this: 'I was born with a friendly, positive minded and gregarious outlook'; 'I think to have a good time at boarding school you have to have an element of resilience when you arrive'. Other ex-boarders talk of having been encouraged by their parents to have a stiff upper lip at home, to get on with life, not complain, don't cry – all the same messages they receive at boarding school: 'keep going, keep going, is the attitude of schooling and family philosophy'.

Boarders who had good experiences tended to speak about the building of resilience in a very positive way and felt it had been a tremendous advantage in their lives. They felt that whatever life had thrown at them they had the confidence to cope, and this coping mechanism contributed to a feeling of positive mental wellbeing. Becoming resilient was also linked with a growing independence. Whether this is a defence mechanism or not, as suggested by the concept of the 'false self', the building and feeling of resilience appears to have equipped them well for the trials and tribulations of life. In other words, we might see it as a defence mechanism that is, to all intents and purposes, working very well, at least at the time of taking part in the research.

'Boarding school gave a sense of independence'

Some ex-boarders were grateful for the strong sense of independence instilled within them at boarding school and felt that this had set them up well for life and acted as protection from loneliness. Those who were able to function independently described themselves as happy. Independence was fostered by boarders learning to take responsibility for themselves, their actions and the consequences thereof in everyday life, having self-discipline, time management skills, and building self-reliance. For some ex-boarders independence was fostered out of necessity before going to boarding school as a result of not being looked after properly at home. Mental health issues in parents and an inability to provide nurture and support resulted in self-reliant children doing everything for themselves. Finding it hard to ask for help in difficult situations is a hallmark of many boarders but this may be the effect of the home environment, boarding school or the synergy of both. Overall, the gaining of independence seems to be highly valued as a life skill but taken to its extreme, over-independence could also have damaging consequences.

'I learned to get on with people, to be very adaptable, to communicate with people'

Learning to get on with others is a valuable life lesson acquired by some of our ex-boarders. Boarding school was described as all about people and being around people all the time. Boarders had to learn diplomacy, how to fit in, communicate and manage differences. They talk of having developed the ability to read a room, to become highly attuned to others' feelings. They felt they gained confidence from these constant interactions which had served them well socially and professionally throughout their lives. These social skills and confidence also came from building strong relationships with peers at school, deep, solid and enduring friendships. Alongside this acquisition of social skills, they felt they had also developed a sense of responsibility for the community they lived in and a desire to contribute to it.

Taken together, these potentially positive life skills and benefits may be a large part of the reason children continue to be sent to boarding school together with improvements in safeguarding and in the physical environment.

10.8 Conclusion: Summarising the case for 'boarding family syndrome'

This book has focused on the psychological impacts of boarding school to the neglect of wider social, cultural, economic and political impacts which would require a different sort of analysis and would need to drill more deeply into issues around privilege, class, society, values and the rights of *all* children to a good education. Without wanting to deny the relevance of social and political arguments for and against boarding schools in the UK, we have deliberately taken a relatively narrow lens specifically examining the issue from a psychological perspective in order in part to provide an empirical perspective on the idea that boarding schools should not exist on the grounds that they are psychologically harmful to children. Within this lens, it is clearly important to acknowledge the hideous reality of some ex-boarders' experiences of boarding school and the profound impact it has had on the rest of their lives. The trauma and misery suffered for their supposed academic and extracurricular privileges appears not to be worth the opportunity cost their parents perceived it would be.

However, as we have shown, the causes of deep unhappiness and difficulty with adult relationships are multifactorial. Sexual abuse aside, there are many variables that mediate between a miserable and positively enjoyable experience of boarding school as well as between experiences at boarding school and adult wellbeing. Research presented in this book indicates that parenting styles, the home environment, friendships, involvement in decision making, age of boarding, pursuit of rewarding extra-curricular activities, full or weekly boarding, personality 'fit', and quite frankly sheer luck as to who a boarder ends up with in their house and year group may all impact on children's experiences and later adult wellbeing. The latter point is perhaps under-estimated in the massive effect room sharing decisions can have and may alone determine the trajectory of happiness for a boarder. Of all these factors, family context, home environment and parenting seem to be particularly dominant across several of the studies, leading us to question whether boarding school is the primary 'cause' of adult distress. Hence, we propose the concept of 'boarding family syndrome' as an alternative way of conceptualising boarding school syndrome.

We have described the improvements made in safeguarding in schools in the last couple of decades to minimise risks, and the introduction of minimum national standards, reviewed at regular intervals by the Department of Education. Boarding schools are well policed in this respect and there are also good practice and guidance policies to promote and maintain wellbeing. The physical environment of boarding schools has also vastly improved with sparseness, wash bowls and iron beds of the past replaced with comfort and luxury. Boarding schools have certainly moved on in many ways; but some boarding families probably continue to be troubled in different ways such that advocates of reform may do well to widen their gaze from a narrow lens on safeguarding and standards to a wider lens which takes in family functioning and emotional literacy within families.

References

1 Knowles E, editor. Virgil (Publius Vergilius Maro) 70–19 BC. In: *Oxford dictionary of quotations*. New York: Oxford University Press 2009. doi:10.1093/acref/9780199237173.001.0001.
2 Schaverien J. *Boarding school syndrome: The psychological trauma of the 'privileged' child*. Abingdon: Routledge 2015. doi:10.4324/9781315716305.
3 Duffell N, Basset T. *Trauma, abandonment and privilege: A guide to therapeutic work with boarding school survivors*. Abingdon: Routledge 2016.
4 de Bernières L. Readers' boarding school stories: 'The cruelty scarred me for life. At 75, I am still hurting'. *The Times*. 2021. www.thetimes.co.uk/article/readers-boarding-school-stories-the-cruelty-scarred-me-for-life-at-75-I-am-still-hurting-2jgbw69zx.
5 Frankfort-Nachmias C, Nachmias D, editors. *Research methods in the social sciences*. 5th edition. London: St Martin's Press 1996.
6 Independent Schools Council. *ISC census and annual report 2021*. Kent: Independent Schools Council 2021.
7 Department for Education. *Boarding schools: national minimum standards*. London: Department for Education 2012. www.gov.uk/government/publications/boarding-schools-national-minimum-standards.
8 Department for Education. *Boarding schools: national minimum standards*. London: Department for Education 2022. https://assets.publishing.service.gov.uk/government/uploads/system/uploads/attachment_data/file/1102344/National_minimum_standards_for_boarding_schools.pdf.
9 Beard R. *Sad little men: Private schools and the ruin of England*. London: Vintage 2022.
10 Braun V, Clarke V. *Thematic analysis: A practical guide*. London: Sage 2022.
11 Boyatzis RE. *Transforming qualitative information: Thematic analysis and code development*. London: Sage 1998.

12 Braun V, Clarke V. Using thematic analysis in psychology. *Qual Res Psychol* 2006; 3: 77–101. doi:10.1191/1478088706qp063oa.

13 Finlay L. The reflexive journey: Mapping multiple routes. In: Finlay F, Gough B, eds. *Reflexivity*. Oxford: Blackwell Science 2003. doi:10.1002/9780470776094.ch1. 3–20.

14 Independent Schools Council. *ICS census and annual report 2022*. Kent: Independent Schools Council 2022.

15 Bowlby J. Attachment and loss: Retrospect and prospect. *Am J Orthopsych* 1982; 52: 664–678. doi:10.1111/j.1939-0025.1982.tb01456.x.

16 Kobak R, Madsen S. Disruptions in attachment bonds: Implications for theory, research, and clinical intervention. In: *Handbook of attachment: Theory, research, and clinical applications, 2nd ed*. New York: Guilford Press 2008. 23–47.

17 Crawford TN, John Livesley W, Jang KL, *et al*. Insecure attachment and personality disorder: a twin study of adults. *Eur J Pers* 2007; 21: 191–208. doi:10.1002/per.602.

18 Stein H, Koontz AD, Fonagy P, *et al*. Adult attachment: What are the underlying dimensions? *Psychol Psychother Theory, Res Pract* 2002; 75: 77–91. doi:10.1348/147608302169562.

19 Harlow HF, Zimmermann RR. The development of affectional responses in infant monkeys. *Proc Am Philos Soc* 1958; 102: 501–509.

20 Palmer J. Boarding School: a place of privilege or sanctioned persecution? *Self Soc* 2006; 33. doi:10.1080/03060497.2006.11086268.

21 Schaverien J. Boarding school syndrome: Broken attachments a hidden trauma. *Br J Psychother* 2011; 27. doi:10.1111/j.1752-0118.2011.01229.x.

22 de Bernières L. Louis de Bernières: 'Aged 8, I was sent to hell'. *The Times*. 2021. www.thetimes.co.uk/article/louis-de-bernières-aged-8-i-was-sent-to-hell-q9xg63nm6.

23 Hill A. Alex Renton: The abuse survivor still shining light on 'vicious' elite schools. *The Guardian*. 2022. www.theguardian.com/education/2022/jul/27/alex-renton-private-school-abuse-radio-series-in-dark-corners.

24 Danziger D. Anthony Horowitz: 'As I've got older, I've come to question the value of public schools'. *The Telegraph*. 2022. www.thetelegraph.co.uk/education-and-careers/2022/11/09/anthony-horowitz-got-older-come-question-value-public-schools/.

25 Ministerial Council on Education Employment Training and Youth Affairs. Melbourne declaration on educational goals for young Australians. 2008. www.curriculum.edu.au/verve/_resources/national_declaration_on_the_educational_goals_for_young_australians.pdf.

26 Army Families Federation. Boarding. https://aff.org.uk/advice/education-childcare/boarding/ (accessed 15 December 2022).

27 Andrew Billon: 'Have you got marital hatred? Probably. Terry Real talks to Andrew Billon'. The Times. 2022. www.thetimes.co.uk/article/have-you-got-marital-hatred-probably-jjc59zs3s.

28 Gordon B. James Purefoy: 'I was finding it difficult to have proper, intimate relationships with women'. *The Telegraph*. 2022. www.telegraph.co.uk/health-fitness/mind/james-purefoy-finding-difficult-have-proper-intimate-relationships/.

29 Tajfel H. *Human groups and social categories: Studies in social psychology*. Cambridge: Cambridge University Press 2010.

30 Turner, David, The Old Boys: The Decline and Rise of the Public School (2015) in Beard, R Sad Little Men: Private Schools and the Ruin of England. London: Vintage 2022.

31 Janis I. *A psychological study of foreign-policy decisions and fiascos*. Boston, MA: Houghton Mifflin 1973.

Index

Printed in Great Britain
by Amazon

27146603R00110